PAUL'S EPISTLE TO THE GALATIANS

Bible study by
Dr. Ian A Fair

Commentary on Paul's
Epistle to the Galatians

HCU MEDIA Heritage Series Study Guides

GALATIANS
A Commentary on Paul's Epistle to the Galatians
Dr. Ian A. Fair

HCU Media LLC
Accra, Ghana ◊ Frisco, TX

GALATIANS
A COMMENTARY AND STUDY GUIDE ON PAUL'S ESPISTLE TO THE GALATIANS

HCU Media LLC
www.HCUMedia.com

Published and Copyright © 2019
By Dr. Ian A. Fair & HCU Media LLC

ISBN-13: 978-1-939468-10-9 (Paperback Edition)

Also available in Kindle form

Printed in the USA

ALL RIGHTS RESERVED
No part of this publication may be reproduced, stored in a retrieval system, or transmitted in any form by any means – electronic, mechanical, photocopying, recording or otherwise – without prior written consent.

Scripture quotations, unless otherwise noted, are from The Holy Bible, Revised Standard Version, copyright 1971, Zondervan Bible Publishers.

Cover Design by Dale Henry – www.dalehenrydesign.com

First Edition September 2019
10 9 8 7 6 5 4 3 2 1

CONTENTS

Bibliography 1

Key Thoughts to Galatians 2

Preface 4

Chapter 1: Overview of Galatians 6

Chapter 2: Gal 1:1-9 – Praescript/Salutations and the Occasion for the Letter 16

Chapter 3: Gal 1:10-24 – Paul's Apostolic Authority 42

Chapter 4: Gal 2:1-10 – Paul was Accepted by the Leaders of the Jerusalem Church 58

Chapter 5: Gal 2:11-21 – Confrontation with Peter 66

Chapter 6: Gal 3:1-14 – Paul's Doctrine of Justification 78

Chapter 7: Gal 3:15-18 – The Abrahamic Covenant.................. 96

Chapter 8: Gal 3:19-4:7 – The Proper Function of the Law..... 106

Chapter 9: Gal 4:8-31 – The Danger of the Galatians' Impending Return to Bondage 128

Chapter 10: Gal 5:1-15 – Christian Freedom and the Law 140

Chapter 11: Gal 5:16-26 – Responsible Freedom in Practice .. 158

Chapter 12: Gal 6:1-10 – Exhortations and Warnings 170

Chapter 13: Gal 6:11-18 – Conclusion: Liberty and the Cross 180

Addendum 1: Paul's Doctrine of Righteousness...................... 194

Bibliography

Commentaries and Resource Books

Bruce, F. F. *Commentary on Galatians*, Grand Rapids: Wm. B. Eerdmans, 1982.

Cole, R. Alan, *Galatians*: Tyndale New Testament Commentaries, Grand Rapids: Inter-Varsity Press, 1965/88.

Fitzmyer, Joseph A., *Romans*, The Anchor Bible, New York: Doubleday, 1992.

Longenecker, Richard N., *Galatians*, Dallas: Word Books,1990.

Morris, Leon, *The Epistle to the Romans*, Grand Rapids: Wm. B. Eerdmans, 1988.

Schneider, Thomas R., *Romans*, Grand Rapids: Baker Books, 1988.

Soulen, Richard N., *Handbook of Biblical Criticism*, Atlanta: John Knox Press, 1976.

Wright, Norman Tom, *Justification*, Downers Grove: IVP, 2009.

Lexicons

Kittel, Gerhard, *Theological Dictionary of the New Testament*, Grand Rapids: Wm. B. Eerdmans, 1964.

Balz, Horst and Gerhard Schneider, *Exegetical Dictionary of the New Testament*, Edinburgh: T. & T. Clark, 1990.

Friberg, Timothy, Barbara Friberg, Neva F. Miller, *Analytical Lexicon of the Greek New Testament*, Grand Rapids: Baker Books, 2000.

Zodhiates, Spiros, *The Complete Word Study Dictionary: New Testament*, Chattanooga: AMG, 1993.

Bauer, Walter, William F. Arndt, Wilber F. Gingrich, Frederick W. Danker, *A Greek-English Lexicon of the New Testament*, Chicago: University of Chicago Press, 1958.

Dictionaries

Freedman, David Noel, Ed. *The Anchor Dictionary of the Bible*, New York: Doubleday, 1992.

Elwell, Walter, *Baker Encyclopedia of the Bible*, Grand Rapids: Baker Books House, 1988.

Richardson, Alan, *A Dictionary of Christian Theology*, London: SCM Press, 1969.

Key Thoughts to Galatians

Jews and Gentiles are saved, reconciled, justified with God by grace through faith in the death, burial, and resurrection of Jesus Christ, and by being united with Christ in baptism.

Gal 3:23-29
Now before faith came, we were confined under the law, kept under restraint until faith should be revealed. [24] So that the law was our custodian until Christ came, that we might be justified by faith. [25] But now that faith has come, we are no longer under a custodian; [26] for in Christ Jesus you are all sons of God, through faith. [27] For as many of you as were baptized into Christ have put on Christ. [28] There is neither Jew nor Greek, there is neither slave nor free, there is neither male nor female; for you are all one in Christ Jesus. [29] And if you are Christ's, then you are Abraham's offspring, heirs according to promise.

Col 2:12
... you were buried with him in baptism, in which you were also raised with him through faith in the working of God, who raised him from the dead.

Rom 6:3-5
Do you not know that all of us who have been baptized into Christ Jesus were baptized into his death? [4] We were buried therefore with him by baptism into death, so that as Christ was raised from the dead by the glory of the Father, we too might walk in newness of life.
[5] For if we have been united with him in a death like his, we shall certainly be united with him in a resurrection like his.

The Law of Moses, and keeping the Law, cannot save or justify anyone, neither Jew nor Gentle!

Rom 3:20-24

For no human being will be justified in his sight by works of the law, since through the law comes knowledge of sin. ^{21} But now the righteousness of God has been manifested apart from law, although the law and the prophets bear witness to it, ^{22} the righteousness of God through faith in Jesus Christ for all who believe. For there is no distinction; ^{23} since all have sinned and fall short of the glory of God, ^{24} they are justified by his grace as a gift, through the redemption which is in Christ Jesus.

Gal 2:16

We ourselves, who are Jews by birth and not Gentile sinners, ^{16} yet who know that a man is not justified by works of the law but through faith in Jesus Christ, even we have believed in Christ Jesus, in order to be justified by faith in Christ, and not by works of the law, because by works of the law shall no one be justified ... ^{19} For I through the law died to the law, that I might live to God. ^{20} I have been crucified with Christ; it is no longer I who live, but Christ who lives in me; and the life I now live in the flesh I live by faith in the Son of God, who loved me and gave himself for me. ^{21} I do not nullify the grace of God; for if justification were through the law, then Christ died to no purpose.

Preface

This brief commentary is intended to be a resource for teachers of Bible classes. Where possible, I have refrained from making too many references to technical terms, or to the Greek text. However, in a study of such depth as justification by grace through faith in Jesus Christ it is necessary to make some reference to the original language in which Paul thought and wrote as he defined the definitive theological topic of justification. Where it has been necessary to refer to Greek words I have spelled the words out in the English alphabet for ease of reading by the non-specialist.

Regarding preparation for teaching Bible text courses we recommend beginning with Fee, Gordon D. and Douglas Stuart, "Galatians," *How to Read the Bible Book by Book*, Grand Rapids: Zondervan, 2002. The other resources in the bibliography are intended for advanced preparation.

The problem experienced by the Gentile Christians in Galatia regarding the role of the Law of Moses, also reflected in Paul's epistle to the Romans, and in passing in the other Pauline epistles, primarily had to do with Jewish and Gentile Christians struggling over the role of the Law of Moses and such issues as the circumcision as the mark of identification, and of a covenant relationship with God. Furthermore, since Jewish Christians from Jerusalem were challenging Paul's ministry, it became necessary for Paul early in his ministry to confront the traditional Jewish understanding of the role of the Law in God's plan of redemption, and stress faith in Jesus' death and resurrection over the Law in this process.

Since the theme of justification by grace through faith in Jesus Christ, as developed by Paul in both Galatians/Romans, has made a significant impact on Christian theology, some additional attention will be given in an addendum on the topic of justification and righteousness.

All students of Galatians, notably regarding the dating of Galatians, experience difficulty harmonizing Paul's account of his conversion and journeys to Jerusalem in Galatians with the record of his conversion in Luke's Book of Acts. On the surface the accounts do not align! However, neither Paul nor Luke attempted to record everything that Paul did in his remarkable ministry. The fact that Paul was constantly on the move over a vast area of the Mediterranean world would make it difficult to harmonize his extensive travels and ministry in any one book such as the Book of Acts. Both Paul and Luke chose to document those aspects of Paul's ministry that were germane to their literary and theological purpose.

For this study, we will adopt the early dating of Galatians, ca. 48/49 CE, locating Paul's ministry reflected in Galatians in the Southern Roman Provincial region of Galatia.[1] This would tentatively place the writing of Galatians somewhere between Acts 14 and the large meeting of Paul with the leaders of the Jerusalem church reflected in Acts 15.

---

[1] We will discuss this further in Chapter 1, the Recipients of the Epistle.

Chapter 1: Overview of Galatians
Orienting Data for Galatians[2]

The Message of Galatians

Galatians is a heated argument against Jewish false teachers in the churches in the Southern Galatian region, namely certain Jewish Christian "missionaries" arriving from Jerusalem who insisted that Gentiles be circumcised if they were to be *justified*[3] and included among the people of God. *Paul argued that faith in Christ, not Law keeping, was the only valid avenue to justification and righteousness before God.*

Author: The Apostle Paul

The epistle claims to be written by the apostle Paul, joined by *"all the brothers and sisters"* with him (Gal 1:2). Paul intended to demonstrate that he was not alone in his conclusions regarding the Gospel of Christ. There were others who agreed with him. He was careful, however, in this letter to mention that his Gospel strength was not simply that others agreed with him or that he received his Gospel from them. *His Gospel came by a personal revelation of Christ.*

Date

The epistle was probably written ca. CE 47-48, although some think it was written a little later ca. CE 55, with no indication of place of writing.

---

[2] Fee, Gordon D. & Douglas Stuart, *How to Read the Bible Book by Book: A Guided Tour*, 2009, pp. 340ff, Kindle Edition.

[3] We will note as the study develops that justification is a legal term that Paul has adapted to refer to those who have been saved by faith in Jesus Christ, and thus brought into a right relationship with God.

Recipients: The Galatians

The Galatian people were descendants of Celtic tribes that migrated east over centuries from Western Europe, more specifically Gaul/France, into the Greek speaking world of Asia Minor, today's Turkey. Thus, the Galatians originated as a part of the great Celtic migration from Europe (see maps below). They invaded Bulgaria and Macedon just north of Greece. These early Celts settled in Thrace (Greece) ca. 278/277 BCE, with some settling in the south-east region of Phrygia and Bithynia.

The following two maps indicate the region of the Celtic peoples in Galatia ca. 46-48 CE.

Permission to use this map granted by Hamish Burgess, MauiCeltic.com

Permission to use map granted by Bible History Online

A minor problem relating to the dating of Galatia arises when determining whether Paul was referencing churches in the Southern Roman Province of Galatia, or the ethnic or geographic Northern region of Galatia (see map below). We have reference in Acts 13, 14 to Paul establishing churches on his first missionary journey in the Southern Roman Provincial region of Galatia (Pisidian Antioch, Iconium, Lystra), but no mention in Acts of any Pauline mission activity in the Northern geographic or ethnic region of Galatia.

For a detailed discussion of the Northern and Southern theories of dating Galatians, refer to Bruce, *Commentary on Galatians*, New International Greek Testament Commentary.[4] Bruce and others support the Southern Galatian Roman Provincial theory. We recognize that good scholars can be cited

---

[4] Bruce, F. F., *Commentary on Galatians*, New International Greek Testament Commentary, Wm. B. Eerdmans, 1982, pp, 3ff; R. Alan Cole, *Galatians*, Tyndale New Testament Commentaries, Grand Rapids: Wm. B. Eerdmans, InterVarsity Press, 1965/88, pp.16ff; Cf Richard N. Longenecker *Galatians*, Word Biblical Commentaries, Dallas: Word Publishers, 1990, for a detailed discussion on this issue. Longenecker favors the Southern Theory, cf. p. lxx, "So on the basis of historical and exegetical considerations, I conclude in favor of a South Galatian understanding of the letter's addressees."

in support of both theories. R. H. Cole, and Richard N. Longenecker, in similar fashion to Bruce, set out the arguments of each view, but favor the Southern Roman Provincial theory over the Northern ethnic or geographic theory.

In the end, the only difference relates to the dating of Galatians and the absence of a missionary activity for Paul in the Northern region of Galatia.

As stated above we will adopt the Southern Roman Provincial Galatian theory in this commentary.

The recipients, therefore, were Jewish and Gentile Christian believers in the Southern Provincial region of Galatia in central Asia Minor (the Southern theory). These churches would be churches established on Paul's first missionary journey (Acts 13:1-14:28, ca. CE 46-48).

If we accept the later date ca. CE 55, this would place the Christians in churches living in the larger ethnic geographic region of Galatia (the Northern theory), which would also include peoples of Pisidia, Lycaonia, and Phrygia (Acts 13-14; 16).

Note the map of Paul's first missionary journey.

Permission to use map granted by Bible History Online

Occasion

The churches of Galatia had been infiltrated by some Jewish Christian agitators (Gal 5:12) who had questioned Paul's gospel and his apostleship; apparently, some Galatians were on the verge of capitulating to them. This sparked a vigorous defense by Paul of his gospel message, and of his apostolic calling.

Paul aggressively defended both the authority and divine origin of his apostleship and gospel (Gal 1:1-2:10). The major portion of Galatians is devoted to Paul's argument that although the Law of Moses had served a valid purpose of leading people to faith (Gal 3:19ff), now that faith in Jesus Christ had become a reality, the Law had served its purpose and was no longer needed. Christians are not defined in their relationship with God by circumcision and keeping the Law (Gal 6:11ff), but through faith in Jesus Christ. In Christ, but not under the Law, there is no division of Jew and Gentile, slave or free, male or female, for all are heirs of the promises to Abraham (Gal 3:26-29).

Emphases

Paul stressed that his apostleship and gospel came directly from God and Christ, not through human mediation. He had not learned his gospel from any human source but had received it by a revelation of Jesus Christ. For Paul, the death and resurrection of Jesus had brought an end to ethnic religious observances based on the Law of Moses. Faith in the atoning sacrifice of Jesus on the cross, and his resurrection from the dead, were all that was necessary to restore a righteous relationship with God. Furthermore, Paul argued that the Galatians had not received the Holy Spirit by keeping the Law of Moses. They had received the Spirit through an obedient faith in Jesus Christ. The Law had served the purpose of instructing the Jews regarding sin, leading them in their walk with God. It had not been intended to atone for sin. The purpose of the Law was to instruct the Jew regarding the nature of sin, and to lead the people to a faith in Jesus Christ as the only atonement for sin, and path to a right relationship with God.

Now in Christ, the Holy Spirit, not the Law, enables believers to withstand sinful desires and to seek and experience the working of the Spirit in their lives. The Holy Spirit working in harmony with faith produces the fruits of the Spirit such as love, joy, peace, etc.

The Narrative Flow of Galatians

As elsewhere in his epistles, namely 2 Corinthians 10-12, Galatians contains three major themes: 1. Paul's concerns for the gospel of Christ and his apostolic authority; 2. the spiritual challenges faced by the Galatians; and 3. instruction against the false Judaizing teachers.

Paul was obviously greatly agitated, and angry with those who were denigrating the Gospel of Christ. He opened his epistle without the prayers and praise that became standard in his epistles to the churches of his ministry. He was abrupt and went straight to his concerns:

> *I am astonished that you are so quickly deserting him who called you in the grace of Christ and turning to a different gospel—* [7] *not that there is another gospel, but there are some who trouble you and want to pervert the gospel of Christ.* [8] *But even if we, or an angel from heaven, should preach to you a gospel contrary to that which we preached to you, let him be accursed.* [9] *As we have said before, so now I say again, If any one is preaching to you a gospel contrary to that which you received, let him be accursed.*
>
> [10] *Am I now seeking the favor of men, or of God? Or am I trying to please men? If I were still pleasing men, I should not be a servant of Christ.* [5]

Paul was concerned for the genuineness of the Gospel of Christ he proclaimed. Note Paul's comment at 1 Cor 1:17ff regarding the heart of his gospel:

> *For Christ did not send me to baptize but to preach the gospel, and not with eloquent wisdom, lest the cross of Christ be emptied of its power.* [18] *For the word of the cross is folly to those who are perishing, but to us who are being saved it is the power of God ... When I came to you, brethren, I did not come proclaiming to you the testimony*

---
[5] Gal 1:6-10.

of God in lofty words or wisdom. ² For I decided to know nothing among you except Jesus Christ and him crucified.

The message of both Corinthians and Galatians was full of Paul's concern for protecting faith in Jesus as the heart of the doctrine of justification, and the role of the Holy Spirit as opposed to the working of Law-keeping. Paul's argument was that one does not receive the life-giving power of the Holy Spirit by Law-keeping. The gifts of the indwelling Holy Spirit come only through faith in Jesus Christ.

Thus, in keeping with the serious nature of the issue under consideration Paul wrote with passion and vigor.

The high point in Paul's Christ-centered theology in Galatians is found in Gal 3:23-29:

Now before faith came, we were confined under the law, kept under restraint until faith should be revealed. ²⁴ So that the law was our custodian until Christ came, that we might be justified by faith. ²⁵ But now that faith has come, we are no longer under a custodian; ²⁶ for in Christ Jesus you are all sons of God, through faith. ²⁷ For as many of you as were baptized into Christ have put on Christ. ²⁸ There is neither Jew nor Greek, there is neither slave nor free, there is neither male nor female; for you are all one in Christ Jesus. ²⁹ And if you are Christ's, then you are Abraham's offspring, heirs according to promise.

Thus, in Galatians one encounters caustic and biting jibes at the agitators as well as fervent, sometimes cajoling, pleas to the Galatians to not give in to them.

It is only when we understand the imminent danger of the subverted gospel being proclaimed by the Jewish agitators from Jerusalem that we can understand Paul's brazen claims that those who proclaim their false gospel are *accursed*! The meaning of being *accursed* is being cursed by God and *doomed to hell*! Spiros Zodhiates has this interesting definition and explanation of the term *accursed*. It means being *"given up to the curse and destruction, being given over to divine condemnation!"*[6]

---

[6] Spiros Zodhiates, *The Complete Word Study Dictionary: New Testament*, ἀνάθεμα, *anáthema*, … A gift given by vow or in fulfillment … and given up

Consequently, one could say that being accursed is serious, solemn, and sobering. Paul's condemnation was consequently, and appropriately, direct!

Paul's primary concern was that the pure gospel of Jesus Christ was at stake, especially as it refers to and includes the Gentiles. Furthermore, in view of what the Jews would claim regarding Paul's seemingly disrespectful attitude toward the Law, it was essential that Paul explain in clear terms the correct purpose and use of the Law of Moses. In keeping with this, Paul consequently clarified the definition of "the people or Israel of God" (Gal 6:16). They are those who come to God through faith in the death and resurrection of Christ, and not through Law-keeping.

Consequently, in Galatians it was necessary for Paul to be at pains to argue for his *divine calling as an apostle of Christ* which was the foundation of his authority, *and the truth of his gospel of Jesus Christ*.

Fee emphasizes the seriousness of the situation by declaring that "Paul comes out with guns blazing."

> First, he takes on the agitators who slander of his apostleship. In a series of three narratives, he starts by distancing himself from Jerusalem (Gal 1:13-24; his apostleship and gospel do not have human origins in any form), then he points out the leaders of the Jerusalem church agree with him (Gal 2:1-10), and finally he notes that any failure to keep the accord originated solely with the Jerusalem Jews (Gal 2:11-14).[7]

Discussion Questions and Thoughts
1. What are the key issues in the Galatian letter?

---

or devoted to destruction for God's sake (Sept.: Num. 21:1-3; Deut. 13:16-18); therefore, given up to the curse and destruction, accursed (1 Cor. 12:3; 16:22; Gal. 1:8, 9). In Rom. 9:3, estrangement from Christ and His salvation. The word does not denote punishment intended as discipline but being given over or devoted to divine condemnation. It denotes an indissoluble vow. See also Acts 23:14; Gal. 1:9.

[7] Fee and Stuart, *op. cit*, p. 341.

2. Why was Paul concerned to spend so much time defending his apostleship?
3. On which missionary trip did Paul visit Galatia and establish the churches in Pisidian Antioch, Iconium, and Lystra?

Chapter 2: Gal 1:1-9 – Praescript/Salutations and the Occasion for the Letter

Paul's Epistolary Style

We learn from the vast amount of manuscripts from the ancient near-east that a recognizable epistolary form existed on a broad front, notably among literary scholars, but not exclusively so.[1] Paul adapted this well-established epistolary form into what we recognize in our New Testament and other early Christian writings as a distinct literary form. This form consisted of:

A *Praescript* or *Salutation*.

A *Prayer* section sometimes identified as a *Laudatio* (praise section). In the *Laudatio* one can normally identify the theology or chief concern of the letter.

The *Body* of the letter consisting of two basic sections:

A doctrinal section containing mostly theological principles, and

A *parenetic* section of practical material (a practical, ethical, or moral application of the doctrine) explaining the implications of the doctrine.

A *Conclusion* which would often repeat the central concern or theology of the letter.

This form can clearly be identified in all the Pauline Epistles with one variation in Galatians. Paul modifies the *Prayer/Laudation* section of *praise* into one of severe reprimand and condemnation. Nevertheless, in this quasi-Laudation section, Gal 1:6-9, we find a direct indication of his primary concern, the denigration and challenge to the true gospel message by a *substitute* gospel.

In his conclusion to the Epistle, Paul remains true to his form, identifying the primary issue again: the Law-keeping and demanding the practice of circumcision as a mark of identification for a relationship with God.

---

[1] Cf. Adolf Deissmann, *Light from the Ancient East*, Grand Rapids: Baker Book House, 1965; Hans-Josef Klaus, *Ancient Letters and the New Testament: A Guide to Context and Exegesis*, Waco: Baylor University Press, 2006.

The Text of the Praescript and Salutations – Gal 1:1-5

> *¹ Paul an apostle—not from men nor through man, but through Jesus Christ and God the Father, who raised him from the dead— ² and all the brethren who are with me, To the churches of Galatia:*
>
> *³ Grace to you and peace from God the Father and our Lord Jesus Christ, ⁴ who gave himself for our sins to deliver us from the present evil age, according to the will of our God and Father; ⁵ to whom be the glory for ever and ever. Amen.*

Gal 1:1, 2. *Paul, an apostle …*

Too often we pass over lightly on who Paul was other than that he was an apostle! This is unfortunate since he was one of the most significant persons of early Christianity, and even today stands out as one of the most profound thinkers and theologians of the Bible, standing alongside Elijah, Moses, and Isaiah, as one of the pillars of both Judaism and Christianity. The following extract from the *Baker Encyclopedia of the Bible* provides an excellent introduction to Paul, the Jew, the Roman Citizen, and the Apostle:

> Known as Saul of Tarsus before his conversion to Christianity and the most influential leader in the early days of the Christian church. Through his missionary journeys to Asia Minor and Europe, Paul was the primary instrument in the expansion of the gospel to the Gentiles. Moreover, his letters to various churches and individuals contain the most thorough and deliberate theological formulations of the NT.
>
> Most of the biographical material available comes from the Book of Acts. Though modern critics question the reliability of this narrative, there is every good reason to use it as the basis for outlining Paul's life. Moreover, the teachings of Paul, as set forth in his letters, are best summarized within the historical framework provided by the Acts narrative.
>
> *Date of Birth.* Little is known of Paul's life prior to the events discussed in Acts. He is first mentioned in

chapter 7 in connection with the execution of Stephen. According to verse 58, "the witnesses laid their clothes at the feet of a young man named Saul." The term "young man" probably indicates someone in his 20s, though this is uncertain.

The events mentioned in Acts 7 may have occurred as early as A.D. 31 if Jesus' death took place during the Passover of A.D. 30. On the other hand, if Jesus' death is dated in the year 33 then those events could have taken place no earlier than 34, but no later than 37. (Second Cor 11:32, 33 states that when Paul escaped from Damascus that city was being ruled by the Nabataean king Aretas, who died in the year 40. Since, according to Gal 1:17, 18, Paul left Damascus three years after his conversion, the year 37 must be regarded as the latest possible date for Stephen's death.)

Using the year 34 as an approximate date for the time when Saul is described as a "young man," and assuming that Saul was no older than 30 years at that time, then it can be concluded his birth took place no earlier than A.D. 4. And since it is very unlikely that he was younger than 20, A.D. 14 can be set as the latest possible date for his birth. This conclusion is supported by the knowledge that Paul studied under the famous Gamaliel I (Acts 22:3), who according to some scholars became a member of the Sanhedrin about A.D. 20. If Paul was 15 years old when he entered the school, the range of A.D. 4–14 for his birth fits all the information available. So, it can be said with a degree of accuracy that Saul was born in the city of Tarsus about A.D. 9, but any estimates about his age should allow a leeway of 5 years either way.

Upbringing. The city of Tarsus was a major population center in the province of Cilicia in the southeastern region of Asia Minor. Lying on a significant commercial route, Tarsus felt the influence of current cultural movements, particularly Stoic philosophy. It is difficult to determine to what extent Greek thought affected Paul as a child. There is a possibility that his family had become "Hellenized"—after all, Paul was born a Roman citizen (we do not know how his father or ancestors acquired citizenship, though military or other notable service is a strong possibility); accordingly, he was given not only a Hebrew name (*Shaul*) but also a Roman cognomen (*Paulus*, though some have argued that he adopted this Roman name at a later point). At any rate, the fact that in his letters he shows great ease in relating to Gentiles suggests that he obtained a Greek education while in Tarsus.

On the other hand, he describes himself as one "circumcised on the eighth day, of the people of Israel, of the tribe of Benjamin, a Hebrew born of Hebrews" (Phil 3:5), and such a characterization, particularly the last phrase, perhaps served to distinguish him from those Jews in the Dispersion who freely adopted Greek ways. Moreover, according to Acts 22:3, he was actually brought up in Jerusalem (possibly in his sister's house, cf. Acts 23:16), and some scholars infer from that statement that Paul was brought up in a totally Jewish environment from earliest childhood.

With regard to Paul's pre-Christian attitude to the gospel, one thing is certain—he was opposed to it with his whole heart. In his apostolic letters he speaks of his previous hatred for the church (e.g., Gal 1:13; Phil 3:6). Paul does not say explicitly why he felt this way, but there are some hints. In 1 Corinthians 1:23, for example, he speaks of the crucifixion of Christ as a stumbling block to the Jews; and in Galatians 3:13 he quotes Deuteronomy 21:23 ("Cursed is everyone who is hung on a tree") as evidence that Christ, by dying on the cross, became a curse for us. It seems reasonable to infer that Paul, along with many other Jews, viewed the preaching of the gospel as blasphemy. How could these Christians regard as Messiah (God's anointed) a lowly man who suffered a criminal's death and received the divine curse itself? Not surprisingly, this theme would become a basic one in Paul's own proclamation of the gospel.

Conversion. At any rate, Paul did become a Christian, and thanks to the Book of Acts we are well informed regarding this event. According to chapter 8, not only did he give approval to Stephen's stoning, but soon after that he "began to destroy the church. Going from house to house, he dragged off men and women and put them in prison" (vv 1, 3). Not satisfied, he decided to pursue the disciples as far away as Damascus. The sequel is familiar to all Bible students. As he and his traveling party approached Damascus, a light flashed and a voice said to him, "Saul, Saul, why do you persecute me?" The One speaking identified himself as "Jesus, whom you are persecuting" (Acts 9:1–5; cf. also 22:4–8 and more fully 26:9–18). Unable to see anything, he followed the Lord's instructions and waited in Damascus. Ananias, a disciple, was sent to speak to Paul, restore his sight, and baptize him (Acts 9:6–19).[2]

Gal 1:1. Paul opens his salutation and greeting by mentioning that the greeting came from himself as an apostle, and from others who were with him and who apparently agreed with his views. His apostleship stressed his authority which he immediately addressed in considerable detail. That the greeting came also from others *"who are with me,"* indicated that his concerns for the Galatian Christians and the gospel of Christ were shared by others, most likely a reference to Barnabas who had accompanied him on his first missionary journey, and possibly also the church in Antioch, who empowered by the Holy Spirit, had commissioned him on his first missionary journey (Acts 13:1-3). The epistle was clearly intended for the Gentile Christians whom Paul and Barnabas had converted in Pisidian Antioch, Iconium, and Lystra.

The term *apostle*, Greek ἀπόστολος, *apóstolos*, carries the double sense of *one who is sent*, and *one who is commissioned*

---

[2] Moises Silva, *Baker Encyclopedia of the Bible*, vol. 2, pp. 1621ff.

with authority to carry a message such as an ambassador.³ In our present-day church terminology, it would be the equivalent of the term *missionary* who is one *sent out by a church and commissioned* with a *mission*. By using the theologically charged technical term *apostle* Paul was aligning himself alongside the "12" Apostles chosen and commissioned by Jesus, himself (Matt 10:2; Matt 28:18-20; Acts 1:8). This thought is key to the argument Paul makes in the next verse. He was not an apostle *"from men nor through man, but through Jesus Christ and God the Father, who raised him from the dead."* He repeats this point in his lengthy argument at Gal 1:11-22 (see below) regarding the divine origin and authority of his apostleship.

The reference to the theme concerning God *"who raised him from the dead"* is central to the argument Paul makes in this epistle that the death of Jesus cancelled or annulled the Law of Moses and circumcision as a marker of one who was in a right relationship with God. The point is that those, Jew and Gentile alike, who through faith are baptized into Christ are also baptized into his death and resurrection and thus raised to become children of God and co-heirs of the promises to Abraham (Gal 3:23-29; Rom 6:1-11; Col 2:10-15).

Additional Comments on the Meaning of the Term Apostle

The reason Paul was at great length in Galatians to define his divine office and apostleship lay in the fact that the Greek term *apóstolos* had a common usage far broader than the Christian use found in the New Testament regarding the Apostles of Christ.

The term *apóstolos* was used in general to imply *any messenger, or one who was sent out with a message.* In the New

---

³ ἀπόστολος *apóstolos*; from *apostéllō* ... to send ... one sent, apostle, ambassador. Sometimes used synonymously to ambassador ... to act as an ambassador (2 Cor. 5:20; Eph. 6:20). The messenger or ambassador ... can never be greater than the one who sends him (John 13:16; Sept.: 1 Kgs. 14:6). The Lord chose the term *apóstoloi* to indicate the distinctive relation of the Twelve Apostles whom He chose to be His witnesses because in Class. Greek the word was seldom used (Luke 6:13; Acts 1:2, 26). Therefore, it designates the office as instituted by Christ to witness of Him before the world (John 17:18). It also designates the authority which those called to this office possess. Zodhiates, S. *The Complete Word Study Dictionary: New Testament*, 2000.

Testament, it was used as a general term simply meaning a *missionary* or for *one sent out*, but also in a narrower theologically technical sense as one specifically chosen by Christ.

Hans Dieter Betz in the *Anchor Bible Dictionary* observes:

> The early Christian title of apostle, although well attested in the NT and other early Christian sources, presents a number of still unresolved problems. The noun "apostle" (*apostolos*) is originally an adjective derived from the verb *apostellō* ("send"), found in the NT with a considerable range of meanings. The basic concept is that of the sending of messengers or envoys; an apostle can also be called *angelos* ("messenger," e.g., Luke 7:24; 9:52) or *kērux* ("herald," e.g., 1 Tim 2:7, 2 Tim 1:11; cf. Mark 1:45; 2 Cor 5:20). Apostles can be human or divine, sent by human or divine authorities.
>
> The basic definition given by Origen … is simple: "Everyone who is sent by someone is an apostle of the one who sent him." The concept involves legal and administrative aspects and is basic to all types of representatives, envoys, and ambassadors. In the area of Christian religion, the term "apostle" can refer to a messenger, human or divine, sent by God or Christ to reveal messages or to reveal *the* message of the gospel.[4]

The *Baker Encyclopedia of the Bible* adds:

> *The Greek Usage.* The Greek word for "apostle" is not used outside the NT in the same sense as it is in the NT. It is derived from the verb "to send" and is at home in the language of the sea meaning a particular "ship" or "group of ships," a "marine expedition" or "the leader" of such. Its usage is almost always impersonal and thoroughly passive. There is no hint of personal initiative or authorization, merely the connotation of something being sent. Later papyri use the word to mean "bill" or "invoice" or even a "passport," continuing to reflect the vocabulary of maritime affairs.[5]

---

[4] Hans Dieter Betz, "Apostle," *Anchor Bible Dictionary*, Vol 1, p. 309.
[5] *Baker Encyclopedia of the Bible*, vol. 1, p. 131.

Spiros Zodhiates provides a detailed definition of the Greek word Apóstolos:

> ἀπόστολος *apóstolos* ... noun from *apostéllō* ... to send. Used as a subst., one sent, apostle, ambassador. Sometimes used syn. with *presbeutés*, ambassador, related to *presbeúō* ... to act as an ambassador (2 Cor. 5:20; Eph. 6:20). The messenger or ambassador (Phil. 2:25 [see also Phil. 4:18]) can never be greater than the one who sends him (John 13:16; Sept.: 1 Kgs. 14:6). The Lord chose the term *apóstoloi* to indicate the distinctive relation of the Twelve Apostles whom He chose to be His witnesses because in Classical Gr. the word was seldom used (Luke 6:13; Acts 1:2, 26). Therefore, it designates the office as instituted by Christ to witness of Him before the world (John 17:18). It also designates the authority which those called to this office possess. See the verb *apostéllō* in Rom. 10:15. Paul combines both these meanings (Rom. 1:1; 11:13; 1 Cor. 1:1; 9:1, 2; 15:9; 2 Cor. 1:1; 12:12; Gal. 1:1). It was the distinctive name of the Twelve Apostles originally (Matt. 10:2; Luke 6:13; 9:10; 22:14; Rev. 21:14) or the eleven later, with whom Paul himself was reckoned, as he says in 1 Cor. 15:7, 9; Acts 1:26. Paul justified his being counted as an apostle by the fact that he had been called to the office by Christ Himself. However, the denomination seems from the very beginning to have been applied, in a much wider sense, to all who ministered as colleagues of the Twelve and bore witness of Christ (Acts 14:4, 14 of Paul and Barnabas; Acts 15:2; Rom. 16:7 of Andronicus and Junias; 2 Cor. 8:23) and even by Paul (2 Cor. 11:13; 1 Thess. 2:6). This general meaning of the word held its place alongside its special and distinctive application.[6]

Richard Longenecker enlarges on how the term was used in Galatians:

> ἀπόστολος, "apostle," is the term Paul uses in Galatians, as well as in all his letters, to epitomize his

---

[6] Zodhiates, *op. cit.,* pp. 2, 3.

consciousness of having been commissioned by God to proclaim with authority the message of salvation in Jesus Christ. In the NT the noun ἀπόστολος connotes personal, delegated authority; it speaks of being commissioned to represent another. It is used broadly of anyone sent by another (cf. John 13:16, "an ἀπόστολος is not greater than the one who sent him"), of Christian brothers sent from Ephesus to Corinth (cf. 2 Cor 8:23, "They are ἀπόστολοι of the churches"), of Epaphroditus sent by the Philippian church to Paul (cf. Phil 2:25, "he is your ἀπόστολον"), and even of Jesus sent by God (cf. Heb 3:1, "the ἀπόστολον and high priest whom we confess"). More narrowly, it is used of a group of believers in Jesus who had some special function (e.g., Luke 11:49; Acts 14:4, 14; Rom 16:7; Gal 1:19; Eph 3:5; Rev 18:20), with particular reference to the twelve disciples (Matt 10:2; Mark 3:14 ... Luke 6:13; 9:10; 17:5; 22:14; Acts 1:2, 26; passim). This narrower usage is how the term is usually used in its approximately seventy-six occurrences in the NT, and that is how Paul uses it of himself in all his letters: one with personal, delegated authority from God to proclaim accurately the Christian gospel.

This is not, however, the way in which ἀπόστολος was commonly understood by either Greeks or Hellenistic Jews of the day. Classical Greek writers usually used the term in an impersonal way, most often to refer to a naval expedition for military purposes—even, at times, of the boat used to transport such an expedition. Josephus' one clear use of ἀπόστολος in *Ant.* 17.300 (the occurrence in *Ant.* 1.146 is textually uncertain) carries the verbal sense of "to send out" (πρεσβεία is the noun in this passage for "delegation"). In fact, there are only a few references in all the extant Greek and Jewish Greek writings from the fifth century B.C. through the second century A.D. where the term means, or could be taken to mean, something like "envoy," "messenger," or "delegate," and so to signal the idea of personal, delegated authority ... [7]

The Apostle Paul, himself, enlarges on his understanding of his apostolic office or ministry at Rom 1:1-3. He added to his apostolic mission by specifying the nature of his calling and the message he was to convey:

> *Paul, a servant of Jesus Christ, called to be an apostle, set apart for the gospel of God* [2] *which he promised beforehand through his prophets in the holy scriptures,* [3] *the gospel concerning his Son ...*

Paul and the New Testament writers understood that there were other Christians sent out as *missionaries* (*apóstoloi*) to spread the message. Consider Barnabas and Silas (Acts 13:1ff), Epaphroditus (Phil 2:25), Titus (2 Cor 8:22, 23), Andronicus and Junias (Rom 16:7).

The point is that Paul, while recognizing the legitimacy of the missionary activity of others as *apóstoloi,* separated himself from them, aligning himself with the 12 apostles commissioned by Jesus himself to take the gospel out to all nations. He was not only a missionary apostle, but one like the 12 apostles carrying a divine commission and authority.

Paul was also aware of the fact that there were others claiming to be apostles of Christ who did not have the divine calling and apostolic commission, who were not qualified to be apostles of Christ. Note 2 Cor 11:12ff:

> *And what I do I will continue to do, in order to undermine the claim of those who would like to claim that in their boasted mission they work on the same terms as we do.* [13] *For such men are false apostles, deceitful workmen, disguising themselves as apostles of Christ.* [14] *And no wonder, for even Satan disguises himself as an angel of light.* [15] *So it is not strange if his servants also disguise themselves as servants of righteousness. Their end will correspond to their deeds.*

---

[7] Longenecker *op. cit.*, pp. 2, 3.

Note also in the same Corinthian context that Paul refers to the signs of a true apostle that false apostles could not produce (2 Cor 12:112ff):

> *I have been a fool! You forced me to it, for I ought to have been commended by you. For I was not at all inferior to these superlative apostles, even though I am nothing. [12] The signs of a true apostle were performed among you in all patience, with signs and wonders and mighty works. [13] For in what were you less favored than the rest of the churches, except that I myself did not burden you? Forgive me this wrong!*

In a completely different yet related context at Mark 16:14-20 Mark records Jesus' commission of the "eleven":

> *Afterward he appeared to the eleven themselves as they sat at table; and he upbraided them for their unbelief and hardness of heart, because they had not believed those who saw him after he had risen. [15] And he said to them, "Go into all the world and preach the gospel to the whole creation. [16] He who believes and is baptized will be saved; but he who does not believe will be condemned. [17] And these signs will accompany those who believe: in my name they will cast out demons; they will speak in new tongues; [18] they will pick up serpents, and if they drink any deadly thing, it will not hurt them; they will lay their hands on the sick, and they will recover."*
>
> *[19] So then the Lord Jesus, after he had spoken to them, was taken up into heaven, and sat down at the right hand of God. [20] And they went forth and preached everywhere, while the Lord worked with them and confirmed the message by the signs that attended it. Amen.*

A significant Scripture in understanding the qualities desired in the theological technical ministry of an Apostle of Christ is Acts 1:15-26. On this occasion, shortly after Jesus' ascension, Peter was addressing the disciples regarding the selection of someone to take Judas Iscariot's place among the 12 apostles. Judas had just hanged himself in shame and remorse for denying Jesus to the authorities. Luke records the event in some detail stressing that although the disciples were to be involved in the selection it was God and the Holy Spirit who were making the decision through the disciples.

> *In those days, Peter stood up among the brethren (the company of persons was in all about a hundred and twenty), and said,* [16] *"Brethren, the scripture had to be fulfilled, which the Holy Spirit spoke beforehand by the mouth of David, concerning Judas who was guide to those who arrested Jesus.* [17] *For he was numbered among us, and was allotted his share in this ministry.* [18] *(Now this man bought a field with the reward of his wickedness; and falling headlong he burst open in the middle and all his bowels gushed out.* [19] *And it became known to all the inhabitants of Jerusalem, so that the field was called in their language Akeldama, that is, Field of Blood.)* [20] *For it is written in the book of Psalms,*
> *'Let his habitation become desolate,*
> *and let there be no one to live in it';*
> *and 'His office let another take.'*
> [21] *So one of the men who have accompanied us during all the time that the Lord Jesus went in and out among us,* [22] *beginning from the baptism of John until the day when he was taken up from us—one of these men must become with us a witness to his resurrection."* [23] *And they put forward two, Joseph called Barsabbas, who was surnamed Justus, and Matthias.* [24] *And they prayed and said, "Lord, who knowest the hearts of all men, show which one of these two thou hast chosen* [25] *to take the place in this ministry and apostleship from which Judas turned aside, to go to his own place."* [26] *And they cast lots for them, and the lot fell on Matthias; and he was enrolled with the eleven apostles.*

What do we learn from this interesting text? As an apostle of Jesus, Peter was leading the disciples through the process of another Apostle being selected by God. The Holy Spirit worked through the disciples in making the choice. The Holy Spirit was working through the disciples. The choice was not that of the disciples, but of the Holy Spirit. We also learn that an Apostle had to be a witness to the teaching and ministry of Jesus, and a witness to his resurrection.

Although Paul was not a disciple of Jesus, he certainly had been in Jerusalem during the ministry of Jesus and would have witnessed his miracle and his teaching. Furthermore, he certainly was a witness to Jesus' resurrection, cf. Acts 9:1-9!

Gal 1:3. Paul's greeting continues with a formula that would become, especially in Pauline usage, a primary Christian epistolary greeting, *"Grace to you and peace from God the Father and our Lord Jesus Christ ..."* *Grace*, from the Greek χάρις, *cháris*, primarily means *favor, something that produces a blessing and joy."* In the context of Paul's doctrine of justification, grace carries a far richer meaning. It refers to a gift that God gives that cannot be earned by human effort, but which flows directly out of his love and mercy. Note Zodhiates' excellent comment regarding grace:

> Χάρις *cháris*; "primarily means" to rejoice. "It signifies" grace, particularly that which causes joy, pleasure, gratification, favor, acceptance, for a kindness granted or desired, a benefit, thanks, gratitude. A favor done without expectation of return; the absolutely free expression of the loving kindness of God to men finding its only motive in the bounty and benevolence of the Giver; unearned and unmerited favor. *Cháris* stands in direct antithesis to *érga* ... works, the two being mutually exclusive.[8]

In the New Testament, peace implies a spiritual condition which is derived from both Greek and Hebrew backgrounds.

> The Greek εἰρήνη, *eirēnē* primarily means *peace* ... Particularly in a single sense, the opposite of war and dissension ... Among individuals, peace, harmony ... Metaphorically peace of mind, tranquility, arising from reconciliation with God and a sense of a divine favor ... By implication, a state of peace, tranquility ... Peace, meaning health, welfare, prosperity, every kind of good ... In the OT Hebrew, *peace* is the equivalent word to

---

[8] Zodhiates, *op. cit.*

> *shalom* which meant wholeness, soundness, hence health, well–being, prosperity ...⁹

Peace, thus, in the Christian sense means *a condition of spiritual tranquility and harmony with God.* This *peace* comes primarily from an awareness of God's grace and forgiveness, his declaration of being "not guilty," and thus from a sense of justification and righteousness. This peace lies rooted in an awareness of the grace of God, our faith or trust in Jesus Christ's atoning death on the cross, and our being baptized into Christ's death and resurrection. Paul argues clearly in his Epistle to the Romans, *passim,* that humankind will never have this peace with God through works of Law since no one has ever kept the Law perfectly! Note Rom 7:24-8:2 where Paul emphasizes that Law-keeping results only in frustration and guilt:

> *Wretched man that I am! Who will deliver me from this body of death?* ^{25} *Thanks be to God through Jesus Christ our Lord! So then, I of myself serve the law of God with my mind, but with my flesh I serve the law of sin.*
>
> ^{1}*There is therefore now no condemnation for those who are in Christ Jesus.* ^{2} *For the law* (principle, IAF) *of the Spirit of life in Christ Jesus has set me free from the law of sin and death.* (The Greek *nomos* can also be translated *principle*, IAF)

The weight of this greeting, "grace and peace" is that it comes exclusively from *"God the Father and our Lord Jesus Christ"* and not from Law-keeping!

Gal 1:4. Paul continues with the pivotal point that focuses immediately on Jesus Christ, *"who gave himself for our sins to deliver us from the present evil age, according to the will of our God and Father."* Note the statement that all of the narrative or theology of justification and righteousness was *according to the will of our God and Father*! Paul underscored the fact that the Christian theology of atonement, justification, and of a right relationship with God comes singularly and solely through the will of God and the death of Jesus Christ, and not through Law-

---

⁹ Zodhiates, *ibid.*

keeping or any human effort or moral quality other than through trusting in God and his grace. The death and resurrection of Jesus were not an afterthought to the giving of the Law to Moses in the Sinai desert! They were the predestined and decisive theme of God's plan which he had predetermined in Christ, not the Law, before creation!

Note the profound viewpoint of Paul in his Epistle to the Ephesians at Eph 1:3ff below. The giving of Christ was the *predestined* plan of God, formed before creation. The Law of Moses was a *codicil* introduced because of the sinful nature of man (cf. Paul's statement regarding the Law being added because of transgressions, Gal 3:15-19). Paul's overriding theology of atonement and justification was rooted in the giving of Christ in his death and resurrection, and not in the subsequent temporary giving of the Law. We will discuss the temporary nature of the Law later at Gal 3:19-25:

Blessed be the God and Father of our Lord Jesus Christ, who has blessed us in Christ with every spiritual blessing in the heavenly places, [4] even as he chose us in him before the foundation of the world, that we should be holy and blameless before him. [5] He destined us in love to be his sons through Jesus Christ, according to the purpose of his will, [6] to the praise of his glorious grace which he freely bestowed on us in the Beloved. [7] In him we have redemption through his blood, the forgiveness of our trespasses, according to the riches of his grace [8] which he lavished upon us. [9] For he has made known to us in all wisdom and insight the mystery of his will, according to his purpose which he set forth in Christ [10] as a plan for the fulness of time, to unite all things in him, things in heaven and things on earth.

[11] In him, according to the purpose of him who accomplishes all things according to the counsel of his will, [12] we who first hoped in Christ have been destined and appointed to live for the praise of his glory. [13] In him you also, who have heard the word of truth, the gospel of your salvation, and have believed in him, were sealed with the promised Holy Spirit, [14] which is the guarantee of our

inheritance until we acquire possession of it, to the praise of his glory.[10]

Gal 1:5. Paul closes his greeting and salutation with a doxological statement regarding God our Father, *"to whom be the glory for ever and ever. Amen."* Paul's closing thought in this remarkably theologically loaded salutation draws attention to the whole purpose of man, to bring *"glory to God for ever and ever, Amen." We live for the glory of God!*

The expression *Amen*, Greek, ἀμήν, *amĕn*; is transliterated from the Hebrew ... *ʾāmēn* ... *implies* to be firm, steady, truthworthy.[11] The meaning or implication of *amen* is that the preceding statement is genuine and truthful! *We love for the glory of God*, not of man! Cf. Gal 1:10,11, *"Am I now seeking the favor of men, or of God? Or am I trying to please men? If I were still pleasing men, I should not be a servant of Christ.* [11] *For I would have you know, brethren, that the gospel which was preached by me is not man's gospel."*

Finally, a thought; we do not say *amen* at the close of a prayer to imply that the prayer is over. We say this to stress that the words of the prayer are *true* and *genuine*.

The Quasi-Laudatio

I have referred to this section as the *Quasi-Laudatio* for it is in this section of Paul's letters we would find his introductory prayer and praise section. However, in Galatians he has no praise for the Galatians, nor a prayer, but only a stern rebuke.

The Text: Gal 1:6-9

I am astonished that you are so quickly deserting him who called you in the grace of Christ and turning to a different gospel— [7] *not that there is another gospel, but there are some who trouble you and want to pervert the gospel of Christ.* [8] *But even if we, or an angel from heaven, should preach to you a gospel contrary to that which we preached to you, let him be accursed.* [9] *As we*

---
[10] Eph 1:3-14.
[11] Zodhiates, *op cit*.

have said before, so now I say again, If any one is preaching to you a gospel contrary to that which you received, let him be accursed.

Gal 1:6. Paul wastes no time getting to his main point! He immediately stresses his astonishment that the Galatians are straying from the gospel of Christ! First, he expresses his astonishment that this was occurring. Almost in shock he cries out, "*I am astonished ...*" The word *astonished* carries several meanings, all of which are appropriate!

The Greek θαυμάζω, *thaumázō* means "to wonder, to marvel, to be struck with admiration or astonishment, to be amazed, to be surprised."[12]

Georg Bertram in Kittel observes in the original Greek θαυμάζω, *thaumázō* meant "in the first instance the verb means 'to be astonished,' and it often expresses an attitude of criticism, doubt or even censure and rejection, though it may also express inquisitiveness and curiosity. It can imply a sense of *offence*. There is also a sense of *fear* regarding what has taken place."[13]

It is obvious that Paul was pouring out his utter astonishment and disbelief at what was taking place.

To emphasize the seriousness of the behavior of the Galatians, Paul accentuates the ease and rapidity and the extent in which the Galatian's action was taking place, "*you are so quickly deserting him.*" *Quickly*, like many Greek words, has a range of meanings or translations depending on context. Primarily, "ταχέως *tachéōs* ... from *tachús* ... means *prompt, swift, quickly, speedily*. In the NT, it is an equivalent to *soon, shortly, quickly, hastily.*"[14] Furthermore, it can be rendered "*at once, soon ... too hastily, too quickly.*"[15]

---

[12] Zodhiates, *ibid.*
[13] Georg Bertram, Kittel's *Theological Dictionary of the New Testament.* 1964- , vol. 3, p. 28.
[14] Zodhiates, *op cit.*
[15] Newman, B. M., Jr. *A Concise Greek-English Dictionary of the New Testament,* Stuttgart, Germany: Deutsche Bibelgesellschaft; United Bible Societies, 1993, p. 179.

In keeping with what Paul is charging the Galatians, it is not stretching the point to translate quickly as either *hastily*, or *too quickly*. For some reason, which we may fix on the pressure of the Jews that caused Peter and Barnabas to act hypocritically as referenced by Paul in Gal 2:11-13, the Galatians were in a hurry to revert to Law keeping. How easy it is to compromise faith and faithfulness when danger threatens!

But Paul is not through with the Galatians yet! He accuses them of *"deserting him who called you in the grace of Christ"*! The impact and severity of this charge would not have been lost by the Galatians! Several Lexicons state that in certain contexts such as Gal 1:6 the Greek implies a perversion taking place in the action of change. Μετατίθημι, *metatíthēmi* literally means to change the place where one stands. In Paul's connotation, it implies a change in loyalty and commitment from Christ to the Law of Moses. For instance, this can be seen in the priesthood being transferred from Aaron to Christ or from Levi to the tribe of Judah, cf. Acts 7:16; Heb. 7:11, 14.

Zodhiates observes that in the middle voice, as in Gal 1:6, it carries the sense "to transfer oneself, to change sides or parties, turn away from someone, Gal. 1:6. Metaphorically, to transfer to another use or purpose, to pervert, to abuse as in Jude 1:4, "perverting the grace of God into licentiousness." Friberg adds, "changing one's loyalty as a follower, to turn from, to desert, *to* become apostate, Gal 1:6."[16]

They were deserting the *one calling them in the grace of Christ*. This can only mean they were deserting God who was calling them! Longenecker, with Bruce concurring, observes:

> Paul's reference elsewhere in Galatians to God as the one who calls (cf. 1:15, "the one who called me by his grace"; 5:8, "the one who calls you") and his continuance of this practice in his other letters (cf. Rom 4:17; 8:30; 9:12, 24; 11:29; 1 Cor 1:9, 26; 7:15, 17-24; Eph 1:18; Phil 3:14; 1 Thess 2:12; 4:7; 5:24; 2 Thess 1:11; 2:14; 2 Tim

---

[16] Zodhiates, op cit.; Friberg, Timothy and Barbara, and N. F. Miller, *Analytical Lexicon of the Greek New Testament*, Grand Rapids: Baker's Greek New Testament Library, 2000, vol. 4, p. 261. Cf also Longenecker, *op cit*, p. 14.

1:9)—with never, except in cases of someone "naming" or "inviting to a feast," anyone else in view—make it reasonably certain that he is here referring to God.[17]

J. Louis Martyn observes that "Paul does not use the verb *metatíthēmi* in 1:6 to refer to the Galatians defecting from him. He says they were *defecting* from *the God who called them into existence as part of his new creation, the church*"![18]

Bruce suggests that the expression *in the grace of Christ* refers to "God's saving act in the death of Christ, by which the undeserving, the ungodly (Rom 5:6), are redeemed, justified, and reconciled." Nothing highlights or emphasizes the grace of God more than his gracious act of giving Jesus for the ungodly![19]

Gal 1:6b, 7. Paul adds to his indictment by charging that the Galatians were "turning to a different gospel— ⁷ not that there is another gospel, but there are some who trouble you and want to pervert the gospel of Christ." The turning implies a turning away from something to something else. In this case, Paul charges the turning is to a different gospel.

The sense of this deserting from and turning to is strengthened by Paul's use of two prepositions, ἀπὸ, *apo*, and εἰς, *eis*. *Apo* with the genitive noun means *from*, or *away from*, and *eis* with the accusative case noun implies *direction*. In the *turning* (implied in the Greek use of the two prepositions) Paul is openly accusing the Galatians of taking a new direction away from the grace of God and Christ to something else, in the case of the Galatians, turning *from* Christ *to* Law-keeping which he charges elsewhere will only kill the one putting hope in the Law (Rom 3:20, the law indicts one; Rom 7:7-13, the Law is good, but when working with sin kills one; 2 Cor 3:6, the written code kills).

A *different gospel* (ἕτερον εὐαγγέλιον, *héteron euaggélion*) means a gospel of another kind which in the case of "a gospel" of Law-keeping is no gospel at all! Not only is this not a gospel, it is a totally different kind of gospel from the gospel of Christ. In

---

[17] Longenecker, *op. cit*, p. 15; Bruce, *op. cit*, p. 80.
[18] Martyn, *op. cit*, p. 117. Emphasis added, IAF.
[19] Bruce *op. cit*, p. 80.

fact, it is bad news not good news in that it removes one from the reach of the saving grace of God. Paul plays on the Greek word ἕτερος, *héteros, which means another of a totally different kind, not just another gospel.*[20] The Fribergs add, something "*qualitatively another* of a different kind, *different, not identical* with what was previously referred to."[21]

Accentuating up his charge, Paul adds that this *other* gospel is *a perverted gospel*, not the gospel of Christ.

The term *trouble* implies that the Galatians had not yet completely bought into this new perverted gospel but were inclining that way. They were troubled and perplexed by the new ideas they were hearing and were already questioning the gospel preached by Paul. *The situation was obviously serious*!

Regarding *troubled*, ταράσσω, *tarássō,* Zodhiates adds:

> ταράσσω *tarássō,* To stir up, to trouble, agitate ... Figuratively used of the mind, to stir up, trouble, disturb with various emotions such as fear, put in trepidation. In the pass., to be in trepidation (Matt. 2:3; 14:26; Mark 6:50; Luke 1:12; 24:38; 1 Pet. 3:14). In Acts 17:8 in the act. and with the acc., to stir up or trouble with questions, meaning to disquiet. Used in the pass. (John 12:27; 13:21; 14:1, 27). John 11:33, "He disturbed himself" (a.t.) in the act. is equal to the pass., "He was troubled in the spirit" in 13:21. It also is used in reference to doubt or perplexity, with the acc. (Acts 15:24), "He perplexed you with his words" (a.t. [Gal. 1:7; 5:10]).[22]

Gal 1:8. To show the extent Paul goes to make his argument that there can be no other gospel than the one he preached to the Galatians, he opens his next statement with the adversative particle, "*But ...*" Zodhiates observes regarding the adversative particle *but*:

> ἀλλά *allá*; an adversative particle originally the neuter plural of *állos, other*. A particle implying in speech some

---

[20] Zodhiates, *op. cit.*
[21] Friberg, *op. cit*, p. 176.
[22] Zodhiates, *op. cit.*

diversity or superaddition to what preceded. It serves, therefore, to mark opposition, antithesis, or transition.[23]

Paul adds, *"But even if we, or an angel from heaven, should preach to you a gospel contrary to what we preached to you, let him be accursed."* Note the emphasis on contrary, in other words, different or in opposition to what they had heard.

Paul wastes no words in getting to his critical point! *"But even if we, or an angel from heaven, should preach to you a gospel contrary to that which we preached to you, let him be accursed."*

Referencing an *angel from heaven* would be clearly understood in a Jewish culture since angels were considered messengers from God who carried important messages. Later, at Gal 3:19, Paul refers to the giving of the Law to Moses and states clearly that *angels were an intermediary* factor in the passing of the Law to Moses!

The Jewish tradition in both Jerusalem and Diaspora Judaism had high regard for angels who they saw as *divine servants of God* who often communicated to his people or passed on vital instruction to them through angels. Cole observes:

> … it was a common Jewish belief that the law had been given through angelic mediators, and these new teachers may have stressed this point when urging the simple Gentile Christians to keep the law.[24]

Longenecker, when discussing the role of angels in this text, comments:

> The reference to ἄγγελος ἐξ οὐρανοῦ, "an angel from heaven," carries a note of irony. Probably it is in response to the Judaizers' claim either (1) to have impeccable credentials as members in good standing in the Jerusalem church, or (2) to have the authority of the Jerusalem apostles supporting them—or both (cf. Paul's rather ironic references to the Jerusalem apostles in 2:6-10 and his opposition to Peter in 2:11-14). Paul saw the preacher's authority as derived from the gospel, and not vice versa.

---

[23] Zodhiates, *ibid.*
[24] Cole, op. cit, p. 41,

So he was not prepared to allow any change in the focus or content of that gospel on the basis of someone's credentials or by an appeal to some more imposing authority.[25]

In the *Anchor Bible Dictionary*, Carol A. Newsom points out:

> In addition to the various roles that the angelic beings play as a group, there are many texts which describe the actions of a single angelic figure. Almost always in these instances the term *mal'āk* ("messenger") ... is used. The term "messenger" should not be construed too narrowly, however, for these divine beings carry out a variety of tasks. They do announce births (of Ishmael, Gen 16:11-12; Isaac, Gen 18:9-15; Samson, Judg 13:3-5), give reassurances (to Jacob, Gen 31:11-13), commission persons to tasks (Moses, Exod 3:2; Gideon, Judg 6:11-24), and communicate God's word to prophets (Elijah, 2 Kgs 1:3, 15; a man of God, 1 Kgs 13:18; cf. 1 Kgs 22:19-22; Isaiah 6; Jer 23:18, 23). But the angel may also intervene at crucial moments to change or guide a person's actions (Hagar, Gen 16:9; Abraham, Gen 22:11-12; Balaam, Num 22:31-35; the people of Israel, Judg 2:1-5) and may communicate divine promises or reveal the future in the course of such intervention.[26]

Commenting on Paul's statement regarding the preaching of a different gospel either by Paul himself, by another apostle, or by an angel from heaven, Bruce observes:

> It is the message, not the messenger, that ultimately matters. The gospel preached by Paul is not the true gospel because it is Paul who preaches it; it is the true gospel because the risen Christ gave it to Paul to preach. If Paul himself, or any other apostle, even an angel were to bring a different message from that which had proved its saving power to the Galatians when they heard and

---

[25] Longenecker, *op. cit.* p. 17.
[26] Newsom, C. A., "Angels: Old Testament," *The Anchor Yale Bible Dictionary,* vol. 1, pp. 249-250.

believed it, both the messenger and his counterfeit message should be rejected. The authority and character of the preacher are important, no doubt, but their importance is secondary; more important is the content of what is preached. Luther expressed the idea in his own paradoxical style: 'that which does not preach Christ is not apostolic, even if Peter and Paul be the teachers. On the other hand, that which does preach Christ is apostolic, even if Judas, Annas, Pilate, or Herod should propound it' (Preface to the Epistle of James ... 7.384f.) By 'teaching Christ' Luther meant nothing other than preaching the gospel of justification by faith alone.[27]

The point Bruce makes is that though the authority of Paul may be questioned, the ultimate danger was not to Paul but to the gospel Paul preached which had divine origin and ultimate significance in the message of Christ's death and resurrection.

The preaching of a *different* gospel results in being *accursed*. In Biblical terms, accursed means *being cursed by God*! Even in English the equivalent word to the Greek used by Paul, ἀνάθεμα, *anáthema,* can refer to a "ban or curse solemnly pronounced by ecclesiastical authority and accompanied by excommunication ... or something denounced as evil or accursed."[28] Notably in the nascent Christian religious context of Galatia it would be understood as a *rebuke* of the most *serious nature*, even condemnation. Zodhiates observes:

> ἀνάθεμα *anáthema* ... given up or devoted to destruction for God's sake (Septuagint, Num. 21:1-3; Deut. 13:16-18); therefore, given up to the curse and destruction, accursed (1 Cor. 12:3; 16:22; Gal. 1:8, 9). In Rom. 9:3, estrangement from Christ and His salvation. The word does not denote punishment intended as discipline but something being given over or devoted to divine condemnation. It denotes an indissoluble vow.[29]

---

[27] Bruce, *op. cit*, p. 83.
[28] Oxford and Miriam-Webster Dictionaries.
[29] Zodhiates, *ibid.*

Johannes Behm in Kittel's *Theological Dictionary of the New Testament* has this reflection:

> The Pauline use of ἀνάθεμα is along the lines of the LXX. For Paul, the word denotes the object of a curse. 1 C. 12:3: οὐδεὶς ἐν πνεύματι θεοῦ λαλῶν λέγει· ἀνάθεμα Ἰησοῦς, "Accursed be Jesus!" It would be a self-contradiction for the Christian pneumatic to curse Jesus, i.e., to deliver Him up to destruction by God. The curse formula is also used in 1 C. 16:22: εἴ τις οὐ φιλεῖ τὸν κύριον, ἤτω ἀνάθεμα, cf. Gl. 1:8: ἀνάθεμα ἔστω; Rom 9:3: ηὐχόμην ἀνάθεμα εἶναι αὐτὸς ἐγὼ ἀπὸ τοῦ χριστοῦ, "I could wish myself accursed from Christ and expelled from fellowship with Him." The controlling thought here is that of the delivering up to the judicial wrath of God of one who ought to be ἀνάθεμα because of his sin. We can hardly think of an act of Church discipline, since the apostle uses the phrase ἀπὸ τοῦ χριστοῦ (R. 9:3) and also considers that an angel from heaven (Gl. 1:8) or even Jesus Himself (1 C. 12:3) might be accursed. That he would willingly see himself separated from Christ and given up to divine judgment ὑπὲρ τῶν ἀδελφῶν μου τῶν συγγενῶν μου κατὰ σάρκα (R. 9:3) is a supreme expression of the readiness of Paul for redemptive self-sacrifice for the people which excludes itself from the divine revelation of salvation (Ex. 32:32).[30]

Gal 1:9. Driving home the accursed nature of preaching a different gospel, Paul repeats his anathema! *"As we have said before, so now I say again, If any one is preaching to you a gospel contrary to that which you received, let him be accursed."* It would be difficult for the Galatians to miss Paul's irritation and even anger.

Paul's expression *you received* raises an interesting point. The word παρελάβετε, *paralabete* from παραλαμβάνω, *paralambánō* can simply mean to receive to oneself. However, it

---

[30] Johannes Behm, Kittel's *Theological Dictionary of the New Testament*. 1964- , vol 1. pp. 354-355.

also carries with it a technical and judicial meaning. Bruce points out that *paralabete* is often used to refer to a *formal* and authoritative tradition handed down through the teaching process.[31] Longenecker observes:

> The use of παρελάβετε, "you accepted," signals the passing on of an authoritative tradition (cf. 1 Cor 11:23; 15:3; Gal 1:12; 1 Thess 2:13; 2 Thess 3:6), which Paul had received "by revelation from Jesus Christ" (1:12) and proclaimed to the Galatians. If, then, anyone proclaims something different, he comes under the judicial wrath of God![32]

Cole builds on this, observing regarding the use of this term in the Jewish tradition, which Paul readily applies to the Christian tradition, and in the case of the Galatians, implies rejecting the instruction or word of God; the doctrine concerning the atonement in Christ. Disregarding or rejecting the apostolic doctrine or *tradition* regarding the gospel of Christ *comes under utter condemnation*, hence Paul's second *anathema* condemnation.[33]

Discussion Questions and Thoughts
1. What are the Scriptural qualities of an Apostle of Jesus?
2. What do you see as the central themes of Paul's salutation and greetings? Suggest at least three points!
3. What is the driving point to atonement and justification indicated in this salutation? Note verse 3!
4. Where does the Law of Moses fit into this discussion? What we imply is where is it mentioned in this greeting and salutation, and to the contrary what is stressed in this pericope regarding atonement and justification.

---

[31] Bruce, *op cit*, p. 84.
[32] Longenecker, *op cit*, p.18.
[33] Cole, *op. cit*, p. 43.

Chapter 3: Gal 1:10-24 – Paul's Apostolic Authority

Although our English translations keep verse 10 in the same pericope as 1:9, it is more in keeping with the argument of chapter 1:11 ff concerning Paul's apostolic authority. It is best considered the lead into his argument regarding his apostolic authority and the divine authority of the gospel he preached. The Nestle Aland Greek New Testament places 1:10 with 1:11ff as suggested above!

The Text

Am I now seeking the favor of men, or of God? Or am I trying to please men? If I were still pleasing men, I should not be a servant of Christ.
[11] For I would have you know, brethren, that the gospel which was preached by me is not man's gospel.
[12] For I did not receive it from man, nor was I taught it, but it came through a revelation of Jesus Christ. [13] For you have heard of my former life in Judaism, how I persecuted the church of God violently and tried to destroy it; [14] and I advanced in Judaism beyond many of my own age among my people, so extremely zealous was I for the traditions of my fathers. [15] But when he who had set me apart before I was born, and had called me through his grace, [16] was pleased to reveal his Son to me, in order that I might preach him among the Gentiles, I did not confer with flesh and blood, [17] nor did I go up to Jerusalem to those who were apostles before me, but I went away into Arabia; and again I returned to Damascus.
[18] Then after three years I went up to Jerusalem to visit Cephas[1], and remained with him fifteen days. [19] But I

---

[1] There is some discussion, with little agreement, as to why Paul refers to Peter as Cephas in this epistle. Grant Osborne in the *Baker Encyclopedia of the Bible*, vol. 2, pp 1659f, comments; Peter was the name given by Jesus to one of his 12 disciples, who rose to preeminence both among the disciples during Jesus' ministry and among the apostles afterwards. There are actually four forms of his name in the NT: the Hebrew/Greek Simeon/Simon and the Aramaic/Greek Cephas/Petros. His given name was Simon bar-Jonah (Mt 16:17;

saw none of the other apostles except James the Lord's brother. ^{20} (In what I am writing to you, before God, I do not lie!) ^{21} Then I went into the regions of Syria and Cilicia. ^{22} And I was still not known by sight to the churches of Christ in Judea; ^{23} they only heard it said, "He who once persecuted us is now preaching the faith he once tried to destroy." ^{24} And they glorified God because of me.

Chapter 2

^{1} Then after fourteen years I went up again to Jerusalem with Barnabas, taking Titus along with me. ^{2} I went up by revelation; and I laid before them (but privately before those who were of repute) the gospel which I preach among the Gentiles, lest somehow I should be running or had run in vain. ^{3} But even Titus, who was with me, was not compelled to be circumcised, though he was a Greek. ^{4} But because of false brethren secretly brought in, who slipped in to spy out our freedom which we have in Christ Jesus, that they might bring us into bondage— ^{5} to them we did not yield submission even for a moment, that the truth of the gospel might be preserved for you. ^{6} And from those who were reputed to be something (what they were makes no difference to me; God shows no partiality)—those, I say, who were of repute added nothing to me; ^{7} but on the contrary, when they saw that I had been entrusted with the

---

cf. Jn 1:42), "Simon the son of John," which was common Semitic nomenclature. It is most likely that "Simon" was not merely the Greek equivalent of "Simeon" but that, having his home in bilingual Galilee, "Simon" was the alternate form which he used in dealings with Gentiles. In fact, it was quite common for a cosmopolitan Jew to employ 3 forms of his name depending on the occasion: Aramaic, Latin, and Greek. The double name "Simon Peter" (or "Simon called Peter") demonstrates that the second name was a later addition, similar to "Jesus, the Christ," The number of times that the Aramaic equivalent "Cephas" is used (once in Jn, 4 times each in Gal and 1 Cor) and its translation into the Greek (not common with proper names) indicates the importance of the secondary name. Both Aramaic and Greek forms mean "the rock," an obvious indication of Peter's stature in the early church (see below on Mt 16:18). It is obvious that he was called "Simon" throughout Jesus' ministry but came to be known as "Peter" more and more in the apostolic age. For example, Paul never uses the patronym, not even in the form of the double name "Simon Peter," but always uses "Peter" (twice) or "Cephas" (8 times).

> *gospel to the uncircumcised, just as Peter had been entrusted with the gospel to the circumcised* [8] *(for he who worked through Peter for the mission to the circumcised worked through me also for the Gentiles),* [9] *and when they perceived the grace that was given to me, James and Cephas and John, who were reputed to be pillars, gave to me and Barnabas the right hand of fellowship, that we should go to the Gentiles and they to the circumcised;* [10] *only they would have us remember the poor, which very thing I was eager to do.*

Gal 1:10. Paul opens his argument with the question, *"Am I now seeking the favor of men, or of God?"* The Greek framing of this question is helpful, Ἄρτι γὰρ ἀνθρώπους πείθω ἢ τὸν θεόν..." *"Arti gar anthrōpous peithō, ē to theon ..."* *"What now[2], am I pleasing, placating, or trying to win over[3] men to my side of the argument, or pleasing God?"*

Paul's argument was that in his preaching Christ, he was not seeking to be pleasing to men. His preaching was commissioned by God and the Holy Spirit and centered on Christ crucified. His gospel, based on the death, burial, and resurrection of Jesus was shunned by both Greeks and Jews, but Paul was not interested in pleasing Jews and Greeks, but only God! Cf 1 Cor 1:17-25:

> [17] *For Christ did not send me to baptize but to preach the gospel, and not with eloquent wisdom, lest the cross of Christ be emptied of its power.* [18] *For the word of the cross is folly to those who are perishing, but to us who are being saved it is the power of God.* [19] *For it is written, "I will destroy the wisdom of the wise, and the cleverness*

---

[2] Γάρ, *gár*; a causative particle standing always after one or more words in a clause and expressing the reason for what has been before, affirmed or implied ... Elliptically and in common usage *gár* is also simply intensifying, and merely serves to strengthen a clause ... What then? Zodhiates, *op cit*.

[3] Πείθω, *peithō*; to persuade, particularly to move or affect by kind words or motives ... to conciliate, generally, to persuade another to receive a belief, meaning to convince ... to win over, gain the favor of, make a friend of, with the acc. of person. Zodhiates, *op. cit*; Kittel, *Theological Dictionary of the New Testament*; Balz and Schneider, *Exegetical Dictionary of the New Testament*.

> *of the clever I will thwart."* ²⁰ *Where is the wise man? Where is the scribe? Where is the debater of this age? Has not God made foolish the wisdom of the world?* ²¹ *For since, in the wisdom of God, the world did not know God through wisdom, it pleased God through the folly of what we preach to save those who believe.* ²² *For Jews demand signs and Greeks seek wisdom,* ²³ *but we preach Christ crucified, a stumbling block to Jews and folly to Gentiles,* ²⁴ *but to those who are called, both Jews and Greeks, Christ the power of God and the wisdom of God.* ²⁵ *For the foolishness of God is wiser than men, and the weakness of God is stronger than men.*

In this text at Gal 1:10 Paul emphasizes categorically to the Galatians, who needed to know without mistake or alternate option, that he was a messenger of Christ and the gospel of Christ, and not a messenger commissioned by men or trying to please men.

> *Am I now seeking the favor of men, or of God? Or am I trying to please men? If I were still pleasing men, I should not be a servant of Christ.*

Paul's closing thought to this verse, his being a *servant* is better translated as bonded servant or slave. The Greek δοῦλος, *doulos*, is often translated as *servant* but it refers to a certain kind of servant, not a free servant, but a bonded servant or slave.[4] Paul had given himself fully over to Christ and his gospel. Note Gal 2:19ff:

> *For I through the law died to the law, that I might live to God.* ²⁰ *I have been crucified with Christ; it is no longer I who live, but Christ who lives in me; and the life I now live in the flesh I live by faith in the Son of God, who loved me and gave himself for me.* ²¹ *I do not nullify the grace of God; for if justification were through the law, then Christ died to no purpose.*

---

[4] δοῦλος, *doúlos*; a slave, one who is in a permanent relation of servitude to another, his will being altogether consumed in the will of the other (Matt. 8:9; 20:27; 24:45, 46). Generally, one serving, bound to serve, in bondage (Rom. 6:16, 17). Zodhiates, *op. cit*; Kittel, *op cit*.

In a slightly different context, Paul argued that in Christ all men are free, yet because of the death of Jesus Christians have all been bought with a price, the death of Christ, and belong to Christ,1 Cor 7:22, 23:

> *for he who was called in the Lord as a slave is a freedman of the Lord. Likewise, he who was free when called is a slave of Christ. ^{23} You were bought with a price; do not become slaves of men. ^{24} So, brethren, in whatever state each was called, there let him remain with God.*

Paul is keenly aware of the dramatic change that took place in his life on the road to Damascus (Acts 9). How better to explain than that he now belonged wholly to Christ, and to refer to himself as a *slave* of Christ, rather than a free Roman citizen. Paul was acutely conscious of his freedom as a Roman citizen, yet acutely conscious that he was a slave of Christ's. On other dramatic occasions Paul reminded a magistrate in Philippi, and a Roman tribune and centurion in Jerusalem, that he was a free Roman citizen who had not purchased his freedom but had inherited it through his father. Cf Acts 16:37, Acts 22:25-27. But more significant to Paul was the reality of the irony that he was now redeemed by Christ and belonged to Christ as a slave!

Gal 1:11. *For I would have you know, brethren, that the gospel which was preached by me is not man's gospel.* Like a bulldog, Paul does not let go of his theme of the divine nature of the gospel. The word *for, gar,* is a causative particle or conjunction that connects back to the previous clause or thought expressing the emphasis in the following statement. Paul was not preaching his gospel to please men, *for* (citing the reason) his gospel was not a human gospel; it came by the revelation of Jesus as the risen Lord by the power of God. Jesus spoke to him, personally on the road to Damascus. Note Luke's account of this remarkable revelation at Acts 9:3-6:

> *Now as he journeyed he approached Damascus, and suddenly a light from heaven flashed about him. ^{4} And he fell to the ground and heard a voice saying to him, "Saul, Saul, why do you persecute me?" ^{5} And he said, "Who are*

you, Lord?" And he said, "I am Jesus, whom you are persecuting; ⁶ *but rise and enter the city, and you will be told what you are to do.* ⁵

Paul built his argument regarding the divine nature of the gospel he preached by explaining that he did not receive the gospel from men, it had come by the revelation of Jesus Christ.

Gal 1:12. *For I did not receive it from man, nor was I taught it, but it came through a revelation of Jesus Christ.* The next two clauses are carefully constructed around two negative conjunctions *neither - nor*. The argument is again introduced by that interesting and informative causal particle γάρ, *gár* which gives the reason he did not receive his gospel from man; "neither did he receive it from man nor was he taught it by man," *for* (but) he received it by revelation, which implies a divine supernatural activity. This interesting construction needs a little further discussion to appreciate the full strength of Paul's assertion, and the force of his argument.

Paul's argument against those challenging the authority of his gospel was opened in the Greek with the coordinating conjunction οὐδέ *oudé, nor, neither*. The sentence, however, was actually introduced with the causal particle *gár/for* which although standing second in line in the sentence actually precedes it in syntax or application⁶ by explaining the continuity or reason for his gospel not being human, *for* it was *neither* received *nor* taught by man *but* was received by revelation! Note the four connective parts of speech, *for, neither, nor, but*! The strength of Paul's statement is empowered by the coordinating conjunction οὐδέ *oudé, neither,* implying a different source of Paul's gospel than a human source. Zodhiates observes regarding this negative connotation of *neither* that "*oudé* is continuative, meaning and not, also not, and hence, not, neither, not even, ... In continued negation, at the beginning of a subsequent clause."⁷ *Nor* was he

---

⁵ Acts 9:3–6.
⁶ Zodhiates, *op cit*, γάρ, *gár*, a causative particle standing always after one or more words in a clause and expressing the reason for what has been before, affirmed or implied.
⁷ Zodhiates, *ibid*.

taught it by man, possibly implying one or more of the apostles in Jerusalem, *but[8]*, in contrast to this, he received his gospel by divine revelation of Jesus Christ.

The claim that Paul's gospel "came through a revelation of Jesus Christ" obviously implies something other than a human source! It was through a divine supernatural revelation. However, the words *of Christ*, Ἰησοῦ Χριστοῦ, in Greek are in a genitive construction which could be either a subjective genitive meaning that Jesus was the *source* of the revelation, or an objective genitive meaning that Jesus was the *object* of the revelation or the object revealed! Often Paul and others would use this construction to imply a double meaning.[9]

Paul is either maintaining that his apostleship is real because he had personally witnessed the resurrection of Jesus, or that in some form of revelation Jesus had revealed to Jesus the fact of his resurrection.

Regarding Jesus as the *object* of the revelation, Paul himself wrote at Gal 1:16 that God had been pleased to reveal the risen Jesus to Paul to confirm his resurrection from the dead, completing the impact of Jesus' crucifixion as the headstone of God's eternal plan of salvation. Note Gal 1:16:

> *But when he who had set me apart before I was born, and had called me through his grace, [16] was pleased to reveal his Son to me, in order that I might preach him among the Gentiles ...*

The experience of witnessing Jesus alive and resurrected from the dead made such an impression on Paul that it turned his life around 180° and became the foundation of his theology. There can be little question that the resurrected Jesus is the focus of his gospel message. We see this played out in each of his

---

[8] Zodhiates, ibid, ἀλλά, *allá*; an adversative particle, *but, other*. A particle implying in speech some diversity or superaddition to what preceded. It serves, therefore, to mark opposition, antithesis, or transition.

[9] Dana, H. E. and Julius R. Mantey, *A Manual Grammar of the Greek New Testament*, New York: MacMillan Company, 1966, pp. 78f; James Hope Moulton, *A Grammar of New Testament Greek*, Edinburgh, T. and T. Clark, 1963, pp. 210f.

epistles, notably Romans and 1 Corinthians. Note Paul's comment at 1 Cor 15:1-5:

> *Now I would remind you, brethren, in what terms I preached to you the gospel, which you received, in which you stand, ² by which you are saved, if you hold it fast—unless you believed in vain.*
>
> *³ For I delivered to you as of first importance what I also received, that Christ died for our sins in accordance with the scriptures, ⁴ that he was buried, that he was raised on the third day in accordance with the scriptures, ⁵ and that he appeared to Cephas, then to the twelve.*

Bruce favors the objective genitive of Jesus actually being the object of the revelation:

> That Ἰησοῦ Χριστοῦ here is an objective genitive is rendered most probably by the wording of vv. 15f: God "was pleased to reveal his Son to me (ἀποκαλύψαι τὸν υἱὸν αὐτοῦ ἐν, apokalupsai ton hion auto)". That is to say, God the Father was the revealer, it was Jesus Christ who was revealed, and in that revelation Paul received his gospel together with the command to make it known in the Gentile world. The gospel and the risen Christ were inseparable; both were revealed to Paul in the same moment. To preach the gospel (v11) was to preach Christ (v16).[10]

Cole has a keen perspective regarding this revelation of Jesus and its impact on Paul:

> Is the *Iēsou Christou* subjective or objective genitive? Is this a revelation made by Christ to Paul, or a revelation of the true meaning of the Christ, made by God to Paul? Perhaps it is better to leave the ambiguity in the English as it is in the Greek. Of the alternatives, the second seems slightly better, but it need not rule out the first. On the road to Damascus Paul received a transforming revelation. The source of the revelation is God; and the content was Christ. From that moment, the veil that had obscured the Messiahship of Jesus was drawn away, and

---

[10] Bruce, *op cit*, p. 89.

> Paul saw clearly the true meaning of the facts with which he had long been acquainted. It seems impossible that Paul could have lived in Jerusalem from boyhood ... without knowing at least the outline story of the life of Jesus.[11]

I am in agreement with Cole. It is possible to read *Iēsou Christou* as both an objective and subjective genitive at the same time! The Greek appears to maintain that opportunity and our New Testament writers were well aware of this. Note the similar construction at 2 Cor 7:14 *"For the love of Christ controls us, because we are convinced that one has died for all; therefore all have died."* Here the context implies that Christians are controlled by both Christ's love for us and our love for Christ.

The leading point of this text is that Paul had received his apostleship as a result of a divine revelation, the revelation of the resurrected Christ, and not as a result of a human source or opinion.

Gal 1:13, 14. Paul highlights the absurdity of his Christian ministry unless something had not changed his direction in life and mission. Most Jews knew of his former life, commissioned by the Sanhedrin to root out and destroy the Christian faith. He had been an approving witness at the stoning of Steven (Acts 7:1ff) and commissioned with letters of appointment to go to Damascus and seek out and arrest Christians (Acts 9).

> *For you have heard of my former life in Judaism, how I persecuted the church of God violently and tried to destroy it;* [14] *and I advanced in Judaism beyond many of my own age among my people, so extremely zealous was I for the traditions of my fathers.*[12]

Gal 1:15-17. But God had a different plan for Paul! To his utter amazement, God called him out of his past life of being a persecutor of Christ into a new life of being an apostle for Jesus Christ!

---

[11] Cole, *op cit*, pp. 46f.
[12] Gal 1:13-14.

> *But when he who had set me apart before I was born, and had called me through his grace, ¹⁶ was pleased to reveal his Son to me, in order that I might preach him among the Gentiles, I did not confer with flesh and blood, ¹⁷ nor did I go up to Jerusalem to those who were apostles before me, but I went away into Arabia; and again I returned to Damascus.* [13]

Paul's comment that God, in his eternal plan of redemption[14], had set him apart for his ministry was not that surprising, but the statement that God had done this before Paul was born certainly captures one's attention, which Paul was overtly and intentionally doing! But Paul was well within biblical prophetic limits in this statement, for Jeremiah and Isaiah had made similar claims. Isaiah's statement was more in keeping with the servant mindset of Isa 49:1-5:

> *Listen to me, O coastlands,*
>   *and hearken, you peoples from afar.*
> *The* L<small>ORD</small> *called me from the womb,*
>   *from the body of my mother he named my name.*
> *² He made my mouth like a sharp sword,*
>   *in the shadow of his hand he hid me;*
> *he made me a polished arrow,*
>   *in his quiver he hid me away.*
> *³ And he said to me, "You are my servant,*
>   *Israel, in whom I will be glorified."*
> *⁴ But I said, "I have labored in vain,*
>   *I have spent my strength for nothing and vanity;*
> *yet surely my right is with the* L<small>ORD</small>,
>   *and my recompense with my God."*
> *⁵ And now the* L<small>ORD</small> *says,*
>   *who formed me from the womb to be his servant,*
> *to bring Jacob back to him,*
>   *and that Israel might be gathered to him,*
> *for I am honored in the eyes of the* L<small>ORD</small>,

---

[13] Gal 1:15-17.
[14] Cf. Eph 2:3-11 for Paul's theology of predestination, God's calling, and God's plan of redemption in Christ.

> *and my God has become my strength ...* [15]

Jeremiah's statement at Jer 1:5 is more directed toward his own prophetic ministry:
> *Now the word of the* LORD *came to me saying,*
> *⁵ Before I formed you in the womb I knew you,*
>   *and before you were born I consecrated you;*
>   *I appointed you a prophet to the nations.* [16]

Gal 1:15. A major and profound principle in Paul's self-understanding of his apostleship was that he did not achieve his apostleship and calling based on his knowledge and development in Judaism, or of his zeal. His calling was solely a gift of God's grace and purpose for him. Note his statement at 1 Cor 15:83ff. Note the emphasis in Paul's motivation. It was not his giftedness or position as an apostle that motivated him in his mission and ministry, although his apostleship was important it was secondary. What drove Paul was the realization of the magnitude of the gift of God's grace in calling him that was his primary motivating influence:

> *For I delivered to you as of first importance what I also received, that Christ died for our sins in accordance with the scriptures, ⁴ that he was buried, that he was raised on the third day in accordance with the scriptures, ⁵ and that he appeared to Cephas, then to the twelve. ⁶ Then he appeared to more than five hundred brethren at one time, most of whom are still alive, though some have fallen asleep. ⁷ Then he appeared to James, then to all the apostles. ⁸ Last of all, as to one untimely born, he appeared also to me. ⁹ For I am the least of the apostles, unfit to be called an apostle, because I persecuted the church of God. ¹⁰ But by the grace of God I am what I am, and his grace toward me was not in vain. On the contrary, I worked harder than any of them, though it was*

---

[15] Isa 49:1-5.
[16] Jer 1:4-5.

not I, but the grace of God which is with me. [11] Whether then it was I or they, so we preach and so you believed.[17]

Gal 1:18. Paul stressed that he was independent of the other apostles. His introductory statement, *Then after three years I went up to Jerusalem to visit Cephas, and remained with him fifteen days ...* has introduced an interesting and challenging thought into the discussion. How are we to read and apply the *then*? We are reminded that Paul was not interested in diagramming a timetable of his movements, and the difficulty of harmonizing Luke's account of Paul's ministry, yet we face the temptation of linking the *then* as a sequential time connection. *Then* does not point to the next thing Paul did after returning from Arabia and Damascus, but points to the next point in his argument of independence from Jerusalem. He was merely indicating the high points of his discussion. He visited Arabia, Damascus, without consulting any men or the apostles, and then likewise visited Cephas/Peter in Jerusalem, staying with him for 15 days.

Gal 1:19. *But I saw none of the other apostles except James the Lord's brother. [20] (In what I am writing to you, before God, I do not lie!)* The word *but*, δὲ, is an adversative particle basically meaning *on the contrary*.[18] What raises some interest in this text is that our English translations indicate that Paul mentions that he saw none of the other apostles *except* James the Lord's brother. This has been interpreted by some that James the Lord's bother was an apostle of Christ along with Paul and the twelve. The RSV and ESV translate this as indicated above *as "But I saw*

---

[17] 1 Co 15:3-11.
[18] Zodhiates, *op. cit*; Balz, *op. cit.*'; Walter Bauer, William F. Arndt, and F. Wilbur Gingrich, *A Greek-English Lexicon of the New Testament*, Chicago: Univ. of Chicago Press, 1979, "δέ ... one of the most commonly used Gk. particles, used to connect one clause w. another when it is felt that there is some contrast between them, though the contrast is often scarcely discernible. Most common translations: *but,* when a contrast is clearly implied; *and,* when a simple connective is desired, without contrast; frequently it cannot be translated at all."

none of the other apostles except James the Lord's brother..." The KJV renders this as *"But other of the apostles saw I none, save James the Lord's brother."* The Greek word order is different from the English word order. Translated literally this would read *but other than of the apostles I did not see except for Jakobus the brother of the Lord.*

The question is whether Paul was listing James, the Lord's brother, as an apostle along with the twelve, or whether he was merely recognizing James as one of the leaders, possibly as an ambassador, in the early church in Jerusalem. We had noted above that the word *apostle*, ἀπόστολος, had a wider usage than the usual meaning we associate with the word. It was a word used generally in Greek to refer to *one sent out, one sent out and commissioned*, and *an ambassador*, or *a missionary*. We noted that Barnabas was referred to as an apostle, Acts 14:14, in the sense that he, with Paul, was a missionary, one sent out to do mission work. Likewise, it is possible that Andronicus and Junias were referred to as apostles in the sense that they too were persons sent out as missionaries, Rom 16:7.

Bruce observes regarding Paul's reference to James as an apostle that he was using the term in the general sense:

> Probably few would have questioned the rendering here preferred but for misgivings about the designation of James as an apostle. But there is nothing anomalous in the designation, so far as Paul's usage of apostolos is concerned. He clearly did not restrict the designation to the twelve.[19]

It would seem best in this text, Gal 1:19, that Paul was referencing James as a leader, or ambassador, or significant person in the church in Jerusalem. James was early recognized as one of the leading men in the Jewish churches.

Florence Gillman in the *Anchor Bible Dictionary* has the following observation about James and his role in the Jerusalem church:

> Paul's description of James as a pillar occurs in the context of a discussion in Gal 2:1-10 about a conference

---

[19] Bruce, *op. cit*, p, 101.

in Jerusalem. James figures prominently also in the conference concerning Paul's work detailed in Acts 15:1-29. The two accounts are difficult to harmonize and discussion continues as to whether Galatians and Acts refer to the same meeting (see e.g. Catchpole 1976-77: 432-38).[20]

If we adopt the early date for Galatians and the Southern theory, then it is most unlikely that the conference referred to in Gal 2:1-10 and the conference in Acts 15 are the same conference or meeting, but that has little to say about James being an ambassador, pillar in the church, a missionary or apostle! The point is that James was highly regarded in Jerusalem and by Paul as a leading person in the church.

The point Paul is making in Gal 1:19 was that he had visited with some of the apostles in Jerusalem, as well as James the Lord's brother. They had added nothing to his gospel, reinforcing Paul's point that his gospel was not from or of men, but one he received by divine intervention by God who called him before he was born to be an apostle to the Gentiles.

Gal 1:20. Paul was concerned that the Galatians understood that he was speaking the truth, so he included an "oath" reinforcing his point, *In what I am writing to you, before God, I do not lie!*

Gal 1:21-24. Paul again recounts one of his travels outside of Judea and Jerusalem. *Then I went into the regions of Syria and Cilicia. [22] And I was still not known by sight to the churches of Christ in Judea; [23] they only heard it said, "He who once persecuted us is now preaching the faith he once tried to destroy." [24] And they glorified God because of me.*

Paul does not explain his reason for his journey through Syria to Cilicia, but one can only assume that on this trip he paid a visit to his hometown, Tarsus, in Cilicia. It is possible that this visit relates to Acts 9:26-30, *"And when he had come to Jerusalem he attempted to join the disciples; and they were all afraid of him, for they did not believe that he was a disciple.*

---

[20] Gillman, F. M. "James," *The Anchor Bible Dictionary,* vol. 3, p. 620.

²⁷ But Barnabas took him, and brought him to the apostles, and declared to them how on the road he had seen the Lord, who spoke to him, and how at Damascus he had preached boldly in the name of Jesus. ²⁸ So he went in and out among them at Jerusalem, ²⁹ preaching boldly in the name of the Lord. And he spoke and disputed against the Hellenists; but they were seeking to kill him. ³⁰ And when the brethren knew it, they brought him down to Caesarea, and sent him off to Tarsus."

Paul does add that he was not known to the churches of Christ in Judea which implies that he had not spent much time there and consequently did not learn anything about the gospel from these churches. He obviously was aware of the spread of the gospel in Judea where many Christians in Jerusalem had fled to escape the persecution after the stoning of Stephen, Acts 8:1-5:

And Saul was consenting to his death. And on that day a great persecution arose against the church in Jerusalem; and they were all scattered throughout the region of Judea and Samaria, except the apostles. ² Devout men buried Stephen, and made great lamentation over him. ³ But Saul was ravaging the church, and entering house after house, he dragged off men and women and committed them to prison. ⁴ Now those who were scattered went about preaching the word. ⁵ Philip went down to a city of Samaria, and proclaimed to them the Christ.

However, the Christians in Judea knew of Paul from the spreading word of his conversion, and they glorified God for Paul's conversion.

Paul's purpose in mentioning the three-year period after his conversion was not to establish any timetable, but to stress that he had not heard the gospel from the apostles or Christians in Jerusalem, but nevertheless, he had been preaching the gospel of Christ in Syria and Cilicia.

Paul continues his argument stressing his independence of the other apostles and the Jerusalem church in Gal 2:1ff, *"Then after fourteen years I went up again to Jerusalem with Barnabas, taking Titus with me."* As we will learn that on this private visit (Gal 2:2) he was accepted by Peter, and James the Lord's brother.

Discussion Questions and Thoughts
1. How had Paul received his Gospel message? Comment on the two possible explanations of this revelation.
2. What was Paul's purpose in describing his visit to Jerusalem (Gal 1:18)?
3. What was Paul's purpose in describing the events of this section?
4. How does Paul explain the eternal nature of his calling by God?
5. What do you think Paul was doing in his visit to Syria and Cilicia?

Chapter 4: Gal 2:1-10 – Paul was Accepted by the Leaders of the Jerusalem Church

Paul continues to demonstrate that his gospel was not something new and different from the gospel preached by the other apostles. Scholars differ when trying to date this event or journey by adding the three years of Gal 1:18 to the fourteen years of Gal 2:1. We need to remember that attempting to reconcile Luke's account of Paul's movements with Paul's in Galatians is going in the wrong direction for neither Luke nor Paul was primarily concerned with chronology or history. Both were making different theological statements regarding Paul's activities.

Luke was writing to convince Theophilus and a Gentile readership that the gospel of Christ was intended for all nations, not only the Jews, and that the gospel had in fact reached Rome (the end of the earth, Acts 1:8!) during Paul's ministry.

Paul was writing to convince the churches in Galatia, including Jews and Gentiles, that his gospel had divine approval, and that he had not learned this gospel from men. His gospel originated before the foundation of the earth (Eph 1:2-11), was authorized by God's calling Paul as an apostle to preach the gospel to the Gentiles, and was accepted by Peter and James in Jerusalem.

The Text

> *Then after fourteen years I went up again to Jerusalem with Barnabas, taking Titus along with me. ² I went up by revelation; and I laid before them (but privately before those who were of repute) the gospel which I preach among the Gentiles, lest somehow I should be running or had run in vain. ³ But even Titus, who was with me, was not compelled to be circumcised, though he was a Greek. ⁴ But because of false brethren secretly brought in, who slipped in to spy out our freedom which we have in Christ Jesus, that they might bring us into bondage— ⁵ to them we did not yield submission even for a moment, that the truth of the gospel might be preserved for you. ⁶ And from those who were reputed to be*

> *something (what they were makes no difference to me; God shows no partiality)—those, I say, who were of repute added nothing to me; [7] but on the contrary, when they saw that I had been entrusted with the gospel to the uncircumcised, just as Peter had been entrusted with the gospel to the circumcised [8] (for he who worked through Peter for the mission to the circumcised worked through me also for the Gentiles), [9] and when they perceived the grace that was given to me, James and Cephas and John, who were reputed to be pillars, gave to me and Barnabas the right hand of fellowship, that we should go to the Gentiles and they to the circumcised; [10] only they would have us remember the poor, which very thing I was eager to do.*

Gal 2:1. *Then after fourteen years I went up again to Jerusalem with Barnabas, taking Titus along with me.* As mentioned above, scholars debate whether one can reach a calendar of Paul's events by adding the three years and fourteen years in Galatians.[1] That was not Paul's intention.

Some hope to harmonize the Gal 2:1 event with Acts 9:26ff, and Acts 15:1ff, but this attempt faces several problems. *First*, as mentioned above, this was not Paul's purpose. *Second*, we know from Acts that Luke mentioned three visits by Paul and Barnabas to Jerusalem, Acts 9:26ff; Acts 11:30 (the famine visit); and Acts 15, the conference in Jerusalem. Paul only mentions two visits. *Third*, Luke does not mention Titus in any of the visits to Jerusalem he recorded in Acts. This might simply be accidental, but Luke does not do much accidentally! He told Theophilus that he researched everything carefully (Luke 1:1-3)! Most likely, Titus was not present in the three visits, including the Acts 15 conference. One should conclude, therefore, that the conference of Gal 2:1ff where Titus was mentioned was not the conference of Acts 15:1ff. That Titus was not mentioned is significant; he

---

[1] Cf the discussion of this in Bruce, *op it*, and other major commentaries.

was not there! His presence with Paul and Barnabas would have been important to Paul's theology!

The difference between Luke/Acts and Paul/Galatians is not an issue in this discussion, for as we have already mentioned above neither Luke nor Paul were intentionally or specifically chronological. They had different agendas. Paul's was simply that when he did visit Jerusalem and the church leaders in Jerusalem, they added nothing to the gospel he preached. It is important that we keep Paul's visits in the context of his purpose in Galatians.

Paul opens this pericope, as in Gal 1:18, with the adverb Ἔπειτα, *epeita, then ... Epeita* is best translated in this context as *Then after that ...*, as in the RSV and ESV indicating a sequence of events, not time.[2] What Paul has in mind is *then 14 years after preaching this gospel of Christ in Syria and Cilicia he went up to Jerusalem with Barnabas and Titus*. Again, he is not so much interested in setting a chronology to the argument he is making. He was interested only in stating that he had been preaching the gospel of Christ for fourteen years before he went up to Jerusalem with Titus. Again, we should stress that Paul was interested in the sequence of events in his ministry, not in providing a timeline to his ministry. It is misdirected to use these fourteen years to calculate a timeline to Paul's ministry.

The inclusion of Titus in this event was calculated by Paul to make a clear statement to the Galatians that even in the view of the Jerusalem leaders there was no religious or cultic difference between Jews and Gentiles in Christ. I like the statement by Martin Luther: Paul "took [Titus] along then, in order to prove that grace was equally sufficient for Gentiles and Jews, whether circumcised or without circumcision."[3]

---

[2] Zodhiates, *op, cit*, the adverb "Ἔπειτα *épeita*; is an adverb of time and order ... it can be translated as then, moreover then ... afterwards, or next (Luke 16:7; Gal. 1:21; James 4:14). Cf also Balz, *op cit*, notes that "*epeita* ... appears consistently in sequences and enumerations. Along with the function of indicating relationship in subject matter, it is also used to indicate temporal relationship. It can relate separate periods with the aid of ἔπειτα ... *then, after that ...*"

[3] Cited by Bruce, *op. cit.*, p. 108.

Bruce adds:
> In the light of v 7 we may conclude that he (Paul) gave them an account of his gospel ministry to date … The Jerusalem leaders could see that it was basically the same gospel as they themselves preached among the Jews – the gospel summarized in 1 Cor 15:3-7. Of which Paul could say a few years later, 'Whether then it was I or they [Cephas. James, etc.], so we preach and so you believed' (1 Cor 15:11).

Gal 2:2. *I went up by revelation; and I laid before them (but privately before those who were of repute) the gospel which I preach among the Gentiles, lest somehow I should be running or had run in vain.* Paul obviously received instruction from God, most likely through the Holy Spirit, which he refers to as "by revelation, "κατὰ ἀποκάλυψιν, kata apokalupsin." The noun apokalupsin in this place, unlike Gal 1:12, is not followed by a genitive noun so therefore by implication refers directly to God/Holy Spirit who instructed him. Paul is stressing that the Jerusalem visit was within the will and intention of God. Since this visit included Titus we should not jump to the conclusion that it referred to the Acts 15 visit in which Paul was instructed by the church in Antioch to go down to Jerusalem.

> *And when Paul and Barnabas had no small dissension and debate with them, Paul and Barnabas and some of the others were appointed to go up to Jerusalem to the apostles and the elders about this question. ³ So, being sent on their way by the church, they passed through both Phoenicia and Samaria, reporting the conversion of the Gentiles, and they gave great joy to all the brethren.*
> *⁴ When they came to Jerusalem, they were welcomed by the church and the apostles and the elders, and they declared all that God had done with them.*[4]

It is interesting that since Paul took Titus along in the Gal 2:1 reference above because he felt this would make a statement, that on this important visit in Acts 15 Titus was not included and no mention was made of his presence.

---

[4] Acts 15:2-4.

In Acts 15 the whole church in Jerusalem was present (Acts 15:22), but in Gal 2:2 Paul discussed his gospel *in private* (κατ' ἰδίαν, *kat idian*[5]) with only those who were *of repute* (δοκοῦσιν, from δοκέω, *dokéō, able to think, proven reliable, of good reputation*) possibly in this case, Cephas, James, and John. Bruce, T. W. Manson, and others suggest that this visit of Gal 2:1 should be equated with the famine visit of Acts 11:30.[6] The key to this verse is that this visit was not public. Paul laid before *those of repute* the gospel he preached, not for their approval but so that they would understand his mission and his gospel. Bruce has this insightful and profound observation:

> What Paul was concerned about was not the validity of his gospel (of which he had divine assurance) but its practicality. His commission was not from Jerusalem, but it could not be executed effectively except in fellowship with Jerusalem. A cleavage between his Gentile mission and the mother-church would be disastrous: Christ would be divided, and all the energy which Paul had devoted, and hoped to devote, to the evangelization of the Gentile world would be frustrated.[7]

Gal 2:3-5. *But even Titus, who was with me, was not compelled to be circumcised, though he was a Greek. 4 But because of false brethren secretly brought in, who slipped in to spy out our freedom which we have in Christ Jesus, that they might bring us into bondage— 5 to them we did not yield submission even for a moment, that the truth of the gospel might be preserved for you.*

The point made by Paul that Titus was not required to be circumcised indicates two things, *one,* Titus was not circumcised, and *two,* Titus was received by those of repute while not circumcised. This validated Paul's argument he would make later in the epistle that righteousness and fellowship was not based on the Law or circumcision, but on faith in Jesus Christ. Cf Gal 5:2-6:

---

[5] Zodhiates, *op. cit.*, ἴδιος *idios*; properly one's own, as pertaining to a private person and not to the public, private, individual.[5]
[6] Bruce, *op cit*, p. 108.
[7] Bruce, *ibid*, p. 111.

> *Now I, Paul, say to you that if you receive circumcision, Christ will be of no advantage to you. [3] I testify again to every man who receives circumcision that he is bound to keep the whole law. [4] You are severed from Christ, you who would be justified by the law; you have fallen away from grace. [5] For through the Spirit, by faith, we wait for the hope of righteousness. [6] For in Christ Jesus neither circumcision nor uncircumcision is of any avail, but faith working through love.*

Somehow, Paul does not mention how, false brethren secretly slipped into the meeting to challenge Paul's doctrine. Their purpose was to require keeping the Law as a sign of relationship with God. Paul stridently calls this being put back into *bondage*, not *freedom* as he will later argue in Gal 5 where he argues that in Christ we have freedom from the Law. Paul and Barnabas did not yield in submission to these false brethren so that the truth of the gospel of Christ could be preserved for the Galatians.

Gal 2:6-10. *And from those who were reputed to be something (what they were makes no difference to me; God shows no partiality)—those, I say, who were of repute added nothing to me; [7] but on the contrary, when they saw that I had been entrusted with the gospel to the uncircumcised, just as Peter had been entrusted with the gospel to the circumcised [8] (for he who worked through Peter for the mission to the circumcised worked through me also for the Gentiles), [9] and when they perceived the grace that was given to me, James and Cephas and John, who were reputed to be pillars, gave to me and Barnabas the right hand of fellowship, that we should go to the Gentiles and they to the circumcised; [10] only they would have us remember the poor, which very thing I was eager to do.*

Paul was not seeking the approval of the respected leaders of the church, Peter, James, and John, but stressed that these respected leaders added nothing (notably the Law and circumcision) to what Paul was preaching. These leaders understood that Paul had been commissioned to preach to the Gentiles (Acts 9:15; Acts 22:15, 16) just as Peter had been commissioned as an apostle to preach to the Jews. Both commissions and ministries received divine approval by the activity of the Holy Spirit in each case. Paul closes his comments with the strong statement of Jerusalem's recognition of his Gentile mission; *James and Cephas and John, who were reputed to be pillars, gave to me and Barnabas the right hand of fellowship, that we should go to the Gentiles and they to the circumcised.*

Gal 2:10 introduces an interesting point, but apparently to James, Peter, and John, an important point; Paul and Barnabas, and their ministry, should be diligent in taking care of the poor, which Paul observes they were eager to do so. The early activity and example of the Jerusalem church in taking care of the poor (Acts 2:43ff; 4:32ff) established benevolence as a fundamental practice of the Christian church. It is altogether possible that the early church also recognized benevolence as a sign of Jesus' messianic mission, cf, Isa 61:1, 2 and Luke 4:16-19.

That Paul was eager to minister to the poor, even in Jerusalem, is clearly seen in his great ministry of setting up a contribution among the Gentile churches for the poor in Jerusalem (Cf 1 Cor 16:1-5; 2 Cor 8, especially Rom 15:22-29).

Discussion Questions and Thoughts
1. In your own words, what do you see as the high point and purpose of this block of material in Paul's epistle to the Galatians?
2. Name some unique points Paul makes in this material that highlight the agreement between the gospel preached by Peter and the Jerusalem church.
3. Why was it important to include Titus in this discussion?

Chapter 5: Gal 2:11-21 – Confrontation with Peter

We will note how difficult at times it is to carry out our faith in practice, and how easy it is to be hypocritical in this.

The Text

But when Cephas came to Antioch I opposed him to his face, because he stood condemned. [12] For before certain men came from James, he ate with the Gentiles; but when they came he drew back and separated himself, fearing the circumcision party. [13] And with him the rest of the Jews acted insincerely, so that even Barnabas was carried away by their insincerity. [14] But when I saw that they were not straightforward about the truth of the gospel, I said to Cephas before them all, "If you, though a Jew, live like a Gentile and not like a Jew, how can you compel the Gentiles to live like Jews?" [15] We ourselves, who are Jews by birth and not Gentile sinners, [16] yet who know that a man is not justified by works of the law but through faith in Jesus Christ, even we have believed in Christ Jesus, in order to be justified by faith in Christ, and not by works of the law, because by works of the law shall no one be justified. [17] But if, in our endeavor to be justified in Christ, we ourselves were found to be sinners, is Christ then an agent of sin? Certainly not! [18] But if I build up again those things which I tore down, then I prove myself a transgressor. [19] For I through the law died to the law, that I might live to God. [20] I have been crucified with Christ; it is no longer I who live, but Christ who lives in me; and the life I now live in the flesh I live by faith in the Son of God, who loved me and gave himself for me. [21] I do not nullify the grace of God; for if justification were through the law, then Christ died to no purpose.

Gal 2:11-13. *But when Cephas came to Antioch* has generated considerable discussion as to when this took place in the scheme of things discussed in both Acts and Galatians. Cole observes that it is not possible to date the circumstances presented by Paul in Gal 2:11, but does remark that Barnabas was back in Antioch and that Peter must have been present in Antioch for some time for this problem to have arisen.[1] Some would date this discussion after the Jerusalem conference in Acts 15, but if the meeting of Paul, Barnabas, and Titus is to be considered the meeting of Gal 2:1-10, Acts 11:30, then dating Cephas' insincerity with the Jews most likely took place after Paul and Barnabas had returned from their first mission trip. Cephas' error in judgment must have taken place ca. Acts 14.

Paul's frustration surfaced immediately, *I opposed him to his face, because he stood condemned.* *[12] For before certain men came from James, he ate with the Gentiles; but when they came he drew back and separated himself, fearing the circumcision party.*

The word used by Paul for *eating with* in Greek is a compound word, συνεσθίω, *sunesthiō*; which *intensifies* the meaning of eating and involves more than simply eating with. It implies enjoying close fellowship. Zodhiates observes that *sunesthiō* means *to have communion with*. It infers *having close accepting fellowship* with someone.[2]

Longenecker prefers aligning this event with Paul and Barnabas in Antioch after they returned from Paul's first mission trip:

> The temporal particle ὅτε ("when") is indeterminate. Some have proposed that the episode of 2:11-14 should be seen as occurring historically before the events of 2:1-10, and that such a displacement of events is signaled by Paul's use of ὅτε rather than ἔπειτα as in 1:18, 21 and 2:1 (see above on *Form/Structure/Setting*). Most, however, take the Antioch episode as historically following the events described in 2:1-10, whether those verses be understood as Paul's version of the Jerusalem Council (so "North Galatianists") or his account of the earlier famine visit (so contemporary "South Galatianists"). In our view

---

[1] Cole, *op cit*, p. 72.
[2] Zodhiates, *op. cit.*

(see *Introduction*, lxvii–lxxxvii), the Antioch episode most likely took place *after* Paul and Barnabas returned to Syrian Antioch from their mission to Cyprus and Southern Galatia as recorded by Luke in Acts 13:4-14:25, *during* the time when "they stayed there [at Antioch] a long time with the disciples" as told us in Acts 14:26-28, and *before* the Jerusalem Council of Acts 15:1-29. The postpositive δέ functions here both as a mild adversative and as a continuative particle, for it (1) signals a contrast between the unity of 2:7-10 and the confrontation of 2:11-14, yet also (2) continues the narrative as to Paul's nondependence on, but underlying agreement with, the Jerusalem apostles.[3]

In similar vein, Bruce places this visit ca. Acts 14 before the Jerusalem conference of Acts 15:

> The incident of vv 11-14 should probably be dated in the period following Barnabas and Saul's return to Antioch after their mission in Cyprus and South Galatia (Acts 14:26-28). If the demarcation of the two spheres of evangelism in vv 8f had been envisioned as hard and fast, whether territorial or communally, one would have to ask what Cephas was doing in Antioch, the headquarters of Gentile Christianity. He was not confining himself to missionary work among the Jews of the city; he was enjoying table-fellowship with Gentiles--Gentile Christians, presumably. The Jerusalem agreement (Gal 2:1-10 IAF) was flexible enough to accommodate such friendly fellowship as this. It was Cephas' *volte-face* (about face IAF) that made Paul speak out so bluntly, 'because he was wrong'—literally 'condemned' (*kategnōsmenos*), not by any external authority but (as Paul saw it) by the inconsistency of his own conduct.[4]

What added insult to injury was that the issue had surfaced when *certain men came from James*, indicating Jewish Christians from the Jerusalem church. Apparently, the Jerusalem church

---

[3] Longenecker, *op cit*, *Galatians*. Word Biblical Commentary, p. 71.
[4] Bruce, *op cit*, pp. 128f.

had not yet settled in comfortably with fellowshipping Gentile Christians. It seemingly was permissible to evangelize the Gentiles, but sensitivities surfaced in fellowshipping them, notable at meals. Sometimes *religio-cultural* issues impinge on *religio-doctrinal* norms!

But what was the underlying issue in the message coming from James and the Jerusalem church? T. W. Manson[5] comments on this:

> What was their message? It may have been something like this: 'news is reaching us in Jerusalem that you are habitually practicing table-fellowship with Gentiles. This is causing grave scandal to our more conservative brethren here. Not only so: it is becoming common knowledge outside the church, so that our attempts to evangelize our fellow-Jews are being seriously hampered.'

Bruce adds an interesting point that might have been of greater concern to the Jerusalem church. Jewish militancy and opposition to the Roman sovereignty among Jewish freedom fighters was on the rise at the time of this issue, ca. 47 CE. It would burst forth on the Jewish scene in the Roman-Judean War of 66-74 C.E.

> In the eyes of such militants, Jews who fraternized with Gentiles and adopted Gentile ways were traitors, and the leaders of the Jerusalem church may have felt themselves endangered by their colleague's free-and-easy conduct in Antioch.[6]

Whatever lay behind the message from Jerusalem, Peter succumbed to this pressure, thus breaking the Christian custom of open fellowship between Jews and Gentiles in Antioch. Peter's example was such that some of the Jewish Christians in Antioch, including Barnabas, followed his example; *And with him the rest of the Jews acted insincerely, so that even Barnabas was carried away by their insincerity.*

---

[5] Manson, T. W. *Studies in the Gospels and Epistles*, Manchester, 1962, pp. 178-181.
[6] Bruce, *op. cit.*, p. 130.

However, the solution may not have been so simple, for Paul adds stronger language to the discussion for *Peter drew back and separated himself, fearing the circumcision party.* Paul's comment may imply that he separated himself not only from table-fellowship but from the Gentile Christians in general. The Greek language is stronger than the RSV English, *drew back and separated himself,* for it reads that Peter ὑπέστελλεν καὶ ἀφώριζεν ἑαυτὸν, *hupestellen kai aphōridzen eauton, separated and withdrew himself,* out of fear of the circumcision party! The word *aphōridzen, withdrew,* is built of the root word that can be translated as *divorced*[7] *himself* or *cut himself off from,* or *excommunicated himself from* the Gentile Christians. A serious charge under any circumstance, whether from Paul or in general.

However, the reason he withdrew himself and separated himself was out of *fearing of the circumcision party.* I doubt it meant physical opposition from the circumcision party, but it is possible that some such fear may have been present, but that does not sound like the Peter we read of in Acts 3 and 4!

Perhaps Manson's observation above helps us understand that he feared the implications and results of the circumcision party's opposition to his and the Jerusalem church's evangelistic ministry. Whatever conclusion we might come to as to the real reason for Peter's failure, it need not be a doctrinal issue but more likely was of a practical issue. *But Paul took it seriously as a threat to the Gentile evangelistic ministry, and to the life of the mixed church in Antioch!*

The danger of Peter's action was that it had already permeated the life of the Antioch church for *"with him the rest of the Jews acted insincerely, so that even Barnabas was carried away by their insincerity."* The Greek word for insincerity is συνυποκρίνομα, *sunupokrínomai,* which literally means *to play the hypocrite with someone.* Zodhiates observes that the word

---

[7] Zodhiates, *op. cit.,* ἀφορίζω *aphorízō* ... To separate locally (Matt. 13:49; 25:32 [cf. Acts 19:9]; 2 Cor. 6:17; Gal. 2:12; Sept.: Lev. 20:25; Is. 56:3); to separate from or cast out of society as wicked and abominable, to excommunicate (Luke 6:22) ... Cf also Arndt and Gingrich, *op. cit.,* p. 127, ἀφορίζω.

means *to feign, pretend, to play the hypocrite with someone*.⁸ Obviously playing at something when it is a charade means to be hypocritical, a serious accusation.

Gal 2:14. Paul's confrontation with Peter went straight to the point: *But when I saw that they were not straightforward about the truth of the gospel, I said to Cephas before them all, 'If you, though a Jew, live like a Gentile and not like a Jew, how can you compel the Gentiles to live like Jews?'*

The expression *straightforward* about the truth, ὀρθοποδοῦσιν πρὸς τὴν ἀλήθειαν, *orthopodousin pros tēn alēthein*, can be translated as *walking according to orthodox truth*, or *walking straight toward the truth*, or *walking on the right road to the truth*.⁹ Perhaps we can understand Paul as accusing Peter as not walking according to the truth of the gospel of Christ in which there is no distinction socially or theologically between the Jew and Gentile.

Paul's next statement needs some help! *If you, though a Jew, live like a Gentile and not like a Jew, how can you compel the Gentiles to live like Jews?* Precisely, what does he mean by Peter living like a Gentile? It is easy to understand what Paul meant when saying that Peter should not live like a Jew; that is, with all the social prejudices of a Jew. But what does he mean by Peter living like a Gentile? Paul's charge more literally translated reads *since¹⁰ you, being a Judean or descendant of Jacob, live in the manner of a Gentile and not according to the manner of a Judean, how can you now compel the Gentiles to live in the manner of a Jew or Judean*?

Perhaps Paul intended to remind Peter that in the Christian faith both Jew and Gentile do not carry over their ethnic or

---

⁸ Zodhiates, *op. cit.*, ὀρθοποδοῦσιν, *orthopodousin*, is built of two words *orthós* and *poús*, or *podeō*, which literally means *standing upright* or *straight*, hence *orthodox, conforming to what is generally or traditionally accepted as right or true; established and approved*.
⁹ Bruce, *op. cit.*, p. 132.
¹⁰ The conjunction *if* is in a first-class conditional form implying since. Cf. Dana and Mantey, *op. cit.*, εἰ with a verb in the indicative mood implies certainty, since, p. 288f.

religious prejudices from the past. In Christ, Christians live under different circumstances! Paul later with the Gentile Christians argued emphatically at Gal 3:28, 29 that in Christ there are neither Jew nor Greek, for all are children of Abraham together through our faith.

Now, Peter, out of concern or fear of the Jewish prejudices, was living like a Jew in a Gentile community of Christians, setting a bad example for both the Jerusalem Jewish Christians and the Antiochian Gentile and Jewish Christians and Paul will have nothing to do with this hypocrisy. He addresses the false practice both privately and publicly confronting Peter in the sternest manner.

Gal 2:15. *We ourselves, who are Jews by birth and not Gentile sinners, [16] yet who know that a man is not justified by works of the law but through faith in Jesus Christ, even we have believed in Christ Jesus, in order to be justified by faith in Christ, and not by works of the law, because by works of the law shall no one be justified.*

The two cases of *we* in verse 15 and 16 are *emphatic* and are rendered *we ourselves* and *even we*, emphasizing that Paul, Peter, and Barnabas, who are Jews by birth, and not *pagan*[11] Gentile sinners[12], *even we know* that we are all justified by faith in Jesus and not by works of the Law. Paul's point was that Paul and Barnabas *should know well* that justification, or a covenant relationship with God, was not based on Law keeping and circumcision, as the Jews erroneously held. *Peter and Barnabas should know this well!*

---

[11] Zodhiates, *op. cit.*, the Greek word ἔθνος, *éthnos*, "in the Jewish sense, *tá éthnē*, the nations, meaning the Gentile nations or the Gentiles in general as spoken of all who are not Israelites and implying *idolatry* and *ignorance of the true God*, i.e., *the heathen, pagan* nations;" Georg Bertram, Karl Ludwig Schmidt, *Kittel's Theological* Dictionary of the New Testament, pp. 364ff.

[12] Cf. Bruce, *op. cit.*, p. 137. The Jews, being people of the covenant of God considered all Gentiles to be sinners since they lived outside the covenant of God. The Jewish mind saw keeping of the Law as the key to covenant relations with God, but Paul argued in Romans and Galatians that it was not the Law that was a covenant marker, but faith.

Gal 2:17, 18. *But if, in our endeavor to be justified in Christ, we ourselves were found to be sinners, is Christ then an agent of sin? Certainly not!* [18] *But if I build up again those things which I tore down, then I prove myself a transgressor.*

The interpretation of Gal 2:17, 18 and this whole pericope is difficult to translate, interpret, and explain since we do not know precisely what the questions were, or accusations that Paul was answering.

Longenecker observes:

> Verse 17 is complex and has been variously interpreted. It involves three propositions: (1) "we are seeking to be justified by Christ"; (2) "we are found to be sinners"; and (3) "Christ is a minister of sin." The questions that arise are: Is the entire sentence a factual statement or a question? Are all of the sentence's propositions presented as being true, or just the two contained in the sentence's premise or protasis—or perhaps just the first of these two? Is Paul here responding to a charge made by his opponents? If so, what is the truth of their claim and what does Paul counter? How can it be said, on whatever basis, that "Christ is a minister of sin" or "promotes sin"?
>
> The protasis of the sentence contains the first two propositions, both of which are governed by the conditional particle εἰ ("if"). The sentence is a first-class conditional sentence, which grammatically assumes all of the protasis to be true. Obviously, the first proposition of the protasis is true, as clearly stated in vv 15-16 already: "we are seeking to be justified by Christ" …
>
> The crucial question for the interpretation of v 17, however, is, what does Paul mean by the second proposition of the protasis, "we are found to be sinners"? … The conclusion that "Christ is a minister of sin" and so actually "promotes sin" or "furthers sin's interests," however, is assuredly not true.[13]

---

[13] Longenecker, *op. cit.*, pp. 89, 90.

A brief grammatical comment on the word *protasis* will help! Protasis: refers to the first part of a conditional statement beginning with "if" as in "if we are seeking to be justified by Christ." This conditional clause expects an answer or response to follow. Grammatically, the response could be one of the following, or all three of the following clauses, but this raises theological questions:
1. *"we ourselves were found to be sinners,"* which it seems the Judaizers are charging Paul, or
2. *"Christ is an agent of sin,"* which Paul will not consider, and emphatically denies, *certainly not*!
3. *"But if I build up again those things which I tore down, then I prove myself a transgressor."* This was the charge Paul is leveling against Cephas. Paul is not acting like Cephas, a hypocrite by acting contrary to the gospel of Christ!

The following is a possible translation and interpretation of these verses. Paul is still addressing Peter and Barnabas' hypocritical behavior, but also answering challenges brought by the Judaizing Christian opponents from Jerusalem.[14]

---

[14] R. David Rightmire, *Bakers Evangelical Dictionary of Biblical Theology*, Grand Rapids: Baker Books, 1966. "The term "Judaizer" has come to be used in theological parlance to describe the opponents of Paul and Barnabas at the Jerusalem Council (Acts 15) and those who sought to preach "another gospel" in the churches of Galatia (Galatians 2:4 Galatians 2:12; 6:12; cf. Phil 3:2). In this sense, "Judaizers" refers to Jewish Christians who sought to induce Gentiles too serve Jewish religious customs: to "judaize." It appears that these individuals agreed with much of the apostolic kerygma but sought to regulate the admission of Gentiles into the covenant people of God through circumcision and the keeping of the ceremonial law. Insisting that "Unless you are circumcised ... you cannot be saved" (Acts15:1), these "believers who belonged to the party of the Pharisees" (Acts 15:5) posed a serious threat to the gospel of grace and the universality of the Christian mission. Paul's Galatian epistle portrays the Judaizers as having come from the Jerusalem church to his churches in Galatia, stressing the need for Gentiles to be circumcised and keep the law, both for full acceptance by God (legalism) and as the basis for Christian living (nomism) ... They understood keeping the law not only as the means by which the blessings of the Abrahamic covenant could be appropriated, but also as the regulative guide for Christian life within that covenant relationship. Although the Judaizers appear to be concerned with bringing the Galatian Christians to

> But, if on the contrary[15], we ourselves[16] are found to be sinners in the mind of the Jews because we endeavor to be justified in Christ, does that make Christ the cause of sinning? Certainly not! Nor does that imply that we are sinners, inconsistent, by tearing down the gospel which we have built up!" You can hear the indignation in Paul's thinking and response! The Greek expression is one of surprise and certainty! Certainly not![17]

Longenecker observes regarding Paul's expression, "Here, however, he answers emphatically and emotively μὴ γένοιτο, "Absolutely not!"[18]

Paul argues regarding Law keeping as a means of justification, *But if I build up again those things which I tore down, Law keeping, then I am proving myself to be a transgressor by inconsistently tearing down and restoring the practice of Law keeping, which I tore down!* Paul states that he would be, like Cephas, a hypocrite and sinner. If he was still trying to uphold the Law as a means of table fellowship with Gentiles, after preaching contrary to the Law that neither Jew nor Gentile could be justified by Law, he would be a hypocrite like Cephas. On the contrary, Paul teaches emphatically that neither Jew nor Gentile could be justified by Law-keeping, that Law keeping should not be a condition of table-fellowship. Justification and table-fellowship come solely through faith in Christ and his death and resurrection, and certainly not by the Law.

---

perfection through the observance of the law, Paul charges them with being motivated by a desire to avoid persecution (Gal 6:12-13). Amidst the rising pressures of Jewish nationalism in Palestine during the mid-first century, and increased Zealot animosity against any Jew who had Gentile sympathies, it would appear that these Jewish Christians embarked on a judaizing mission among Paul's converts in order to prevent Zealot persecution of the Palestinian church."

[15] Zodhiates, *op. cit.*, "δέ *dé*; a particle standing after one or two words in a clause, *strictly adversative*, meaning but, *on the contrary, on the other hand*."
[16] Καὶ αὐτο, emphasizes the *"we,"* meaning <u>indeed we ourselves</u>.
[17] Bruce, *op. cit.*, "*Far from it!*" "*Perish the thought!*" (μὴ γένοιτο, *mē genoito, emphatically not!*)
[18] Longenecker, *op. cit.*, p. 90.

Practicing, or requiring the Law as a *condition* of *fellowship* with the Gentiles would result in hypocritical behavior on the part of Paul, and also of Cephas and Barnabas! It would make Paul a sinner and transgressor of the gospel of Christ and make Christ an agent of sin! Paul proclaims, *mē genoitō!*

Gal 2:19-21. Paul introduces the key to his understanding and behavior! *For I through the law died to the law, that I might live to God.* ^{20} *I have been crucified with Christ; it is no longer I who live, but Christ who lives in me; and the life I now live in the flesh I live by faith in the Son of God, who loved me and gave himself for me.* ^{21} *I do not nullify the grace of God; for if justification were through the law, then Christ died to no purpose.*

This statement by Paul crystalizes his theology. Through the teaching of the Law itself, he has died to any possibilities of the Law saving or justifying anyone, both Jew and Gentile!

He points out that he, personally, has been crucified with Christ, Rom 6:1-4:

> *What shall we say then? Are we to continue in sin that grace may abound?* ^{2} *By no means! How can we who died to sin still live in it?* ^{3} *Do you not know that all of us who have been baptized into Christ Jesus were baptized into his death?* ^{4} *We were buried therefore with him by baptism into death, so that as Christ was raised from the dead by the glory of the Father, we too might walk in newness of life.*

Note also Col 2:12, 13:

> *you were buried with him in baptism, in which you were also raised with him through faith in the working of God, who raised him from the dead.* ^{13} *And you, who were dead in trespasses and the uncircumcision of your flesh, God made alive together with him, having forgiven us all our trespasses ...*

Paul enlarges on this claim in Gal 3:23-29 which we will enlarge on in the next chapters:

> *Now before faith came, we were confined under the law, kept under restraint until faith should be revealed.* ^{24} *So that the law was our custodian until Christ came,*

> *that we might be justified by faith.* ²⁵ *But now that faith has come, we are no longer under a custodian;* ²⁶ *for in Christ Jesus you are all sons of God, through faith.* ²⁷ *For as many of you as were baptized into Christ have put on Christ.* ²⁸ *There is neither Jew nor Greek, there is neither slave nor free, there is neither male nor female; for you are all one in Christ Jesus.* ²⁹ *And if you are Christ's, then you are Abraham's offspring, heirs according to promise.*

Paul closes this point by stating that in this new Christian experience he lives only for Christ. This new life in which he enjoyed a right-relationship with God and Christ was through Christ's death and resurrection, and not through the Law of Moses, as good and useful as the Law had been. Faith in Christ and Christ's death, and not Law-keeping was the door to the life of freedom for Paul.

Paul was constantly aware of how much he owed to the calling and grace of God in Christ, 1 Cor 15:9-10:

> *For I am the least of the apostles, unfit to be called an apostle, because I persecuted the church of God.* ¹⁰ *But by the grace of God I am what I am, and his grace toward me was not in vain. On the contrary, I worked harder than any of them, though it was not I, but the grace of God which is with me.*

God's grace and faith in Jesus Christ bring freedom from both the Law and sin! If the Law was still binding, or considered a means of justification or limitation of table-fellowship with Gentiles, then Christ died for no purpose, and Paul's preaching and the gospel of Christ are in vain!

Discussion Questions and Thoughts
1. Why was Paul so upset with Cephas that he reprimanded him publicly "to the face"?
2. Why were Cephas and Barnabas acting hypocritically; what were they doing and why were they doing this?
3. When did Paul die to the Law of Moses?

Chapter 6: Gal 3:1-14 – Paul's Doctrine of Justification

At this point in the epistle we get into Paul's doctrine of justification by faith in Christ, not by works of the Law. To open the discussion Paul returns to his opening comments regarding the Galatians being deceived. As a foundation to his theology of justification Paul builds on the Jewish heritage of Abraham, always a pivotal point in Jewish theology.

The Text

O foolish Galatians! Who has bewitched you, before whose eyes Jesus Christ was publicly portrayed as crucified? ² Let me ask you only this: Did you receive the Spirit by works of the law, or by hearing with faith? ³ Are you so foolish? Having begun with the Spirit, are you now ending with the flesh? ⁴ Did you experience so many things in vain? —if it really is in vain. ⁵ Does he who supplies the Spirit to you and works miracles among you do so by works of the law, or by hearing with faith?

⁶ Thus Abraham "believed God, and it was reckoned to him as righteousness." ⁷ So you see that it is men of faith who are the sons of Abraham. ⁸ And the scripture, foreseeing that God would justify the Gentiles by faith, preached the gospel beforehand to Abraham, saying, "In you shall all the nations be blessed." ⁹ So then, those who are men of faith are blessed with Abraham who had faith.

¹⁰ For all who rely on works of the law are under a curse; for it is written, "Cursed be every one who does not abide by all things written in the book of the law, and do them." ¹¹ Now it is evident that no man is justified before God by the law; for "He who through faith is righteous shall live"; ¹² but the law does not rest on faith, for "He who does them shall live by them." ¹³ Christ redeemed us from the curse of the law, having become a curse for us— for it is written, "Cursed be every one who hangs on a tree"— ¹⁴ that in Christ Jesus the blessing of Abraham might come upon the Gentiles, that we might receive the promise of the Spirit through faith.

The Galatians were Deceived

Gal 3:1-5. His charge was that the Galatians had permitted themselves to be deceived by the quasi predilection of Jews for the Law; certainly, a foundation to faithful Jewish theology. However, as he will shortly argue, a mistaken understanding of the purpose of the Law. Paul's point that serves as his discussion of this deception was that the Law was never intended by God to justify anyone, notably the Jews. Paul was driven by a deep commitment to the Law when it was used according to its purpose which was to point out sin, indict those who lived contrary to the Law, and to demonstrate that no one could keep the Law to the degree that it would justify them before God.

Gal 3:1. *O foolish Galatians! Who has bewitched you, before whose eyes Jesus Christ was publicly portrayed as crucified?* Paul charges that the Galatians were *foolish*[1] to permit themselves to be *bewitched* by the Judaizers who had come from Jerusalem claiming to be the curators of the Law. The word *bewitched, baskaínō*[2] is a *hapax* indicating that it is not found anywhere else in the New Testament. It was popular among the classical Greek philosophers. The word is clearly a derogatory term implying something after the nature of *trickery*, or of a *deceptive subversive nature*.

Bruce adds:

---

[1] Zodhiates, *op. cit.*, ἀνόητος *anóētos*, one who acts without mind or rational thinking.
[2] Zodhiates, *ibid.*, βασκαίνω *baskaínō* ... To bewitch as with the eye, to cast an evil eye. A Greek commentator on the work of the poet Theocritus observes that the noun *báskanos* means one who with his eyes kills or destroys. Superstitious people believed that great harm might result from the "evil eye" or from being looked upon with envious and malicious stares. *Baskaínō* and its derivative are frequently used in the Classical Greek authors for envy, and the Septuagint and Apocryphal writers apply the words with the same meaning. In the NT, it means to utter foolish babble, i.e., to mislead by pretenses as if by magic arts, to bewitch (Gal. 3:1).

Their new behaviour was so strange, so completely at odds with the liberating message which they had previously accepted, that it appeared as if someone had put a spell on them.

Paul laid heavy influence on the seriousness and conclusiveness of his preaching of Christ, crucified, resurrected, and openly seen by many. This was the heart of his gospel. We see this in his correspondence with the Corinthian church: *For I decided to know nothing among you except Jesus Christ and him crucified.*[3]

The death, burial, resurrection, and appearance of Jesus formed the basis of Paul's theology. In 1 Cor 15:6-7 Paul explained this to the Corinthians:

> *For I delivered to you as of first importance what I also received, that Christ died for our sins in accordance with the scriptures, ⁴ that he was buried, that he was raised on the third day in accordance with the scriptures, ⁵ and that he appeared to Cephas, then to the twelve. ⁶ Then he appeared to more than five hundred brethren at one time, most of whom are still alive, though some have fallen asleep. ⁷ Then he appeared to James, then to all the apostles.*

Although the above quotation is from the Corinthian correspondence which came a little later than Galatians, note the emphasis on Cephas and James, both of whom were contributors to the Galatian problem!

Longenecker emphasizes Paul's frustration in the following quote:

> … you foolish Galatians!" Not since 1:9 has Paul mentioned the situation in Galatia itself and not since 2:5 has he referred to the Galatians directly, so intent has he been on demonstrating his own apostleship and defending the "truth of the gospel." The twice repeated ἀνόητοι, "foolish" (here and v 3), highlights the sharpness of Paul's address. It is, indeed, biting and aggressive in tone. Yet more than just a reprimand, it expresses Paul's deep

---

[3] 1 Cor 2:2.

concern, exasperation, and perplexity (cf. 4:11, 20). It is not a lack of intelligence on their part that grieves Paul but a failure to exercise even a modicum of spiritual discernment ....[4]

Paul reminded the Galatians that he had carefully and clearly and openly preached the crucifixion to them, which they had apparently accepted, believed, and obeyed. For them now so easily to turn away from that gospel is beyond his understanding and can only be attributed to some ulterior motives among both the false teachers and the Galatians – they had allowed themselves to be "bewitched"! They had been misled by false pretensions regarding the Law which Paul explained and denied in the remainder of Gal 3 by going back to the "father of their faith," Abraham, and explaining the proper purpose of the Law, which the Judaizers had abused and misapplied.

Gal 3:2-5. *O Foolish Galatians, how did you receive the Holy Spirit?*

> *Let me ask you only this: Did you receive the Spirit by works of the law, or by hearing with faith? ³ Are you so foolish? Having begun with the Spirit, are you now ending with the flesh? ⁴ Did you experience so many things in vain? —if it really is in vain. ⁵ Does he who supplies the Spirit to you and works miracles among you do so by works of the law, or by hearing with faith?*

Paul reminded the Galatians of an experience they could hardly deny; they had received the Holy Spirit in a manner that was obvious and open, miraculous works! (Gal 3:5). He challenged them with the pointed question as to how they received the Holy Spirit and had experienced and witnessed the miraculous works; it was by faith in Jesus and not by the works of the Law!

What Paul was doing was arguing that there are not two principles involved: *one*, that you received the Holy Spirit by faith, and, *two*, that you received justification or righteousness by keeping the Law. Both righteousness and the reception of the

---

[4] Longenecker, *op. cit*, p. 99.

Holy Spirit were grounded in the same principle: justification and receiving the Holy Spirit by *hearing the gospel with faith*.

The Greek expression ἀκοῆς πίστεως, *akoēs pisteōs*, hearing with faith or the coupling of *akoē* in this construction was common in classical Greek implying that the two words hearing with faith means *hearing the gospel and believing it,* or *believing what you heard.*[5]

Bruce cites J. D. G. Dunn by saying:

> The gift of the Spirit and justification are two sides of the one coin. The blessing of Abraham is equated with the latter in v.v. 8f., and the former in v. 14. *Both times the means given is faith.*[6]

At Gal 3:3, again Paul refers to the Galatians as being *foolish*, ἀνόητος, anóētos, or *acting without a brain*! They had begun with faith and were now reverting to Law-keeping! In modern parlance, a no-brainer!

Gal 3:4. Referencing the gifts of the Spirit which they had received by believing with faith he asks whether all of their experience was for nothing or amounted to nothing! *"Did you experience so many things in vain? —if it really is in vain."* His clinching argument in vs. 5 sums up his point: *Does he who supplies the Spirit to you and works miracles among you do so by works of the law, or by hearing with faith?* Again, his question was a no-brainer! They knew the answer! Their giftedness came through believing the gospel with faith, and not by Law-keeping!

Comment on the Gifts of the Holy Spirit

There is often considerable misunderstanding surrounding the miraculous gifts of the Spirit, notably among charismatic churches, that a short supplement here on this topic will be helpful in relation to Paul's discussion of the miraculous gifts of the Spirit at Gal 3. There is no question that during the Apostolic age the Holy Spirit was given to certain believers that involved miraculous powers and speaking in tongues. Joel had prophesied

---

[5] Bruce, *op. cit.*, p. 149; Longenecker, *op cit.*, p. 102.
[6] Bruce, *op. cit.*, p. 149; J. D. G. Dunn, *Baptism in the Holy Spirit*, London: SBT, 1970, p. 108.

such at Joel 2:28. Jesus had spoken of such in his apostolic commission at Mark 16:15-20, which we shall shortly examine in some detail. Jesus had also instructed his apostles at Acts 1:8 to wait in Jerusalem for the gift of the Spirit which came powerfully on them on the Day of Pentecost. The New Testament is replete with references to the ministry of the Holy Spirit in situations not related to the impartation of miraculous powers which are often left out in the discussion of the gift of the Holy Spirit. These references to the ministry or the Holy Spirit are in fact far more significant and lasting than miraculous powers.

Nevertheless, the testimony of the miraculous working of the Holy Spirit played a significant role in verifying the validity of the apostolic gospel message of Christ, which in itself was astonishing in the critical religious transformational age of Judaism and paganism of the first century CE.

We should begin by stressing that the miraculous gifts of the Holy Spirit played a critical part in the initial spread of the gospel among both the Jews and the Gentiles. The pouring out of the Holy Spirit testified to the veracity of the gospel message among both Jews and Gentiles. It certainly got their attention! So much so that the Jews present in Jerusalem on the Day of Pentecost thought the Apostles were drunk (Acts 2:1ff). This created an opportunity for Peter to preach his great sermon that resulted in about 3,000 Jews believing, repenting, and being baptized for the remission of their sins (Acts 2:14-42).

In like manner, when Peter preached his gospel sermon to Cornelius and his household in Caesarea the Holy Spirit fell on them, Peter adds, in the same manner that he had fallen on the apostles in Acts 2 (Acts 10, 11). This remarkable experience convinced Peter and the Jews in Jerusalem that God had granted repentance also to the Gentiles.

In both these remarkable instances the pouring out of the Holy Spirit in each instance verified the gospel message of salvation preached by Peter. It must have played the same role for Paul in his ministry to the Galatian churches since Paul in Gal 3 references such.

At this point in our discussion we need to drop back to Jesus' commission of his disciples at Mark 16:15-20, and note carefully what Mark has recorded, Mark 16:14-20:

> *Afterward he appeared to the eleven themselves as they sat at table; and he upbraided them for their unbelief and hardness of heart, because they had not believed those who saw him after he had risen. ^{15} And he said to them, "Go into all the world and preach the gospel to the whole creation. ^{16} He who believes and is baptized will be saved; but he who does not believe will be condemned. ^{17} And these signs will accompany those who believe: in my name they will cast out demons; they will speak in new tongues; ^{18} they will pick up serpents, and if they drink any deadly thing, it will not hurt them; they will lay their hands on the sick, and they will recover."*
>
> *^{19} So then the Lord Jesus, after he had spoken to them, was taken up into heaven, and sat down at the right hand of God. ^{20} And they went forth and preached everywhere, while the Lord worked with them and confirmed the message by the signs that attended it. Amen.*

The Witness of Abraham to Righteousness by Faith

Gal 3:6-9. Paul began his argument of justification through the hearing of the gospel with faith by referring to the Jewish patriarch and hero of faith, Abraham.

Perhaps we need first to comment briefly, by way of a theological definition, on Paul's major doctrine of justification! Obviously, it is expressed clearly at Rom 1:16, 17, but this is also spelled out in many texts throughout Paul's epistles:

> *For I am not ashamed of the gospel: it is the power of God for salvation to everyone who has faith, to the Jew first and also to the Greek. ^{17} For in it the righteousness of God is revealed through faith for faith; as it is written,*
> *'He who through faith is righteous shall live.*

Breaking this down, we see that Paul was asserting that everyone, both Jew and Greek, is justified by God through faith in the death of Jesus Christ. He adds, *through faith for faith*! Paul means by this that it is for the purpose of developing justification by faith that justification is revealed by faith, and not by works of Law.

Making a strong statement regarding attempts to be declared righteous by the Law, at Rom 3:20-26 Paul adds:

> *For no human being will be justified in his sight by works of the law, since through the law comes knowledge of sin. [21] But now the righteousness of God has been manifested apart from law, although the law and the prophets bear witness to it, [22] the righteousness of God through faith in Jesus Christ for all who believe. For there is no distinction; [23] since all have sinned and fall short of the glory of God, [24] they are justified by his grace as a gift, through the redemption which is in Christ Jesus, [25] whom God put forward as an expiation by his blood, to be received by faith. This was to show God's righteousness, because in his divine forbearance he had passed over former sins; [26] it was to prove at the present time that he himself is righteous and that he justifies him who has faith in Jesus.*

At Rom 4:22-5:2, Paul, when commenting on Abraham being declared righteous by faith, adds:

> *That is why his faith was "reckoned to him as righteousness." [23] But the words, "it was reckoned to him," were written not for his sake alone, [24] but for ours also.* It (righteousness) will *be reckoned to us who believe in him that raised from the dead Jesus our Lord, [25] who was put to death for our trespasses and raised for our justification.*
>
> Chapter 5
>
> *[1] Therefore, since we are justified by faith, we have peace with God through our Lord Jesus Christ. [2] Through him we have obtained access to this grace in which we stand, and we rejoice in our hope of sharing the glory of God.*

Gal 3:6-9. *Thus Abraham "believed God, and it was reckoned to him as righteousness." [7] So you see that it is men of faith who are* *the sons of Abraham. ⁸ And the scripture, foreseeing that God would justify the Gentiles by faith, preached the gospel beforehand to Abraham, saying, "In you shall all the nations be blessed." ⁹ So then, those who are men of faith are blessed with Abraham who had faith.*

No Jew, even a Christian Judaizer, if there can be such a person, would argue against Abraham being declared righteous by God. That would almost be blasphemy! With this in mind, Paul drives home his *decisive* point: *Abraham was declared righteous by God by his faith in God.* Consequently, *all men of faith are the sons of Abraham*!

This strong statement regarding all men being sons of Abraham by faith forms the initial statement of an *inclusio*[7] with the closing statement of Gal 3:26-29. These two texts define the context of the discussion lying between them.
We should set these two texts out below to clarify this *inclusio*:

Gal 3:9, *So then, those who are men of faith are blessed with Abraham who had faith.*

Gal 3: 25-29, *But now that faith has come, we are no longer under a custodian; ²⁶ for in Christ Jesus you are all sons of God, through faith. ²⁷ For as many of you as were baptized into Christ have put on Christ. ²⁸ There is neither Jew nor Greek, there is neither slave nor free, there is neither male nor female; for you are all one in Christ Jesus. ²⁹ And if you are Christ's, then you are Abraham's offspring, heirs according to promise.*

Gal 3:8. Paul's gospel of justification by faith was nothing new. Neither was a Gentile mission based on faith anything new or radical. It was rooted in Abraham and testified in the Scriptures, *And the scripture, foreseeing that God would justify the Gentiles by faith, preached the gospel beforehand to Abraham, saying, "In you shall all the nations be blessed."*

---

[7] Richard N. Soulen, *Handbook of Biblical Criticism*, Atlanta: John Knox Press, 1976, p. 82: *Inclusio*: A technical term for a passage of Scripture in which the opening phrase is repeated, paraphrased, or otherwise returned to at the close indicating that the enclosed material is composite in nature.

Note Paul's decisive argument, Gal 3:9, *So then, those who are men of faith are blessed with Abraham who had faith.*

Justification by Faith without Works

Gal 3:10-14. Paul contrasts faith with the Law. Each of them has a role in God's economy, but their role is different.

For all who rely on works of the law are under a curse; for it is written, "Cursed be everyone who does not abide by all things written in the book of the law, and do them." [11] Now it is evident that no man is justified before God by the law; for "He who through faith is righteous shall live"; [12] but the law does not rest on faith, for "He who does them shall live by them." [13] Christ redeemed us from the curse of the law, having become a curse for us—for it is written, "Cursed be everyone who hangs on a tree"— [14] that in Christ Jesus the blessing of Abraham might come upon the Gentiles, that we might receive the promise of the Spirit through faith.

Gal 3:10. This pericope (notably, Gal 3:10-13) has given rise to extended discussion among scholars. Paul was obviously citing Deut 27:15-26, the dodecalogue, the twelve curse commands of Deut 27. We speak of the ten commandments of Exodus as the *decalogue*, meaning *ten* sayings or laws. Here at Deut 27:15-26 we have *twelve* sayings which are referred to by scholars as the *dodecalogue,* the twelve sayings or curse laws of Deut 27. Figuring out exactly what Paul meant by citing Deut 27:26 here at Gal 3:10 has raised some interesting thoughts and discussion among scholars.

Our text, with my comments in parentheses, reads; "For all (both Jew and Gentile) who rely on works of the law (for righteousness) are under a curse; for it is written, "Cursed be everyone who does not abide by all things written in the book of the law, and do them (Deut 27:26)."

It is interesting to note as you read the dodecalogue of Deut 27:15-26 that each statement of a curse ends with the expression, *Amen, that is true*! Paul, and the Jews were well aware of the seriousness of the curses of Deut 27:15ff. So, Paul drew on this to demonstrate the folly of attempting to be justified by keeping the Law, either the decalogue or the dodecalogue!

Paul's comment is consequently unambiguous and blunt: *all who rely on works of the law for righteousness are under a curse*! He adds that this principle has deep roots in Scripture, *for it is written*! In order to escape the curse by keeping the Law one would have to abide by, and keep *all things written in the dodecalogue*, and every sincere Jew and Christian would know that because of our human nature this is not possible, for all men are sinners; Cf. Rom 3:9,10, where Paul speaks to Jew and Gentile and quotes the Old Testament to prove his point:

> *What then? Are we Jews any better off? No, not at all; for I have already charged that all men, both Jews and Greeks, are under the power of sin, [10] as it is written:*
> *"None is righteous, no, not one;*
> *[11] no one understands, no one seeks for God. [12] All have turned aside, together they have gone wrong; no one does good, not even one."*

Paul's argument in both Romans and Galatians is that no human being will be justified by Law-keeping, Rom 3:19, 20:

> *Now we know that whatever the law says it speaks to those who are under the law, so that every mouth may be stopped, and the whole world may be held accountable to God. [20] For no human being will be justified in his sight by works of the law, since through the law comes knowledge of sin.*

Gal 3:11. So, Paul concludes, *Now it is evident that no man is justified before God by the law ...* People may justify themselves by Law-keeping, but before God they will not be justified by the Law. Paul immediately follows his argument up with his major premise, *for 'He who through faith is righteous shall live.'* This was not a new idea thought up by Paul, for he is drawing on Hab 2:4, *Behold, he whose soul is not upright in him shall fail, but the righteous shall live by his faith.*[8]

---

[8] Cf. also Rom 3:20; Heb 10:38 which likewise builds off Hab 2:4.

Gal 3:12. *…but the law does not rest on faith, for "He who does them shall live by them."* The basis of the Law principle is maintaining or keeping the Law. The basis of the faith principle is faith, or trusting in the grace of God and his atoning work in the death of Jesus on the cross. Since justification or righteousness comes through faith in the death of Jesus Christ as the atoning work of God, then the Law principle as an atoning function is out of its league, for all the Law will do is clarify sin and indict the sinner, Rom 3:20:

> *For no human being will be justified in his sight by works of the law, since through the law comes knowledge of sin. [21] But now the righteousness of God has been manifested apart from law, although the law and the prophets bear witness to it, [22] the righteousness of God through faith in Jesus Christ for all who believe.* Paul continues this train of thought at Gal 3:19 *"Why then the law? It was added because of transgressions …"*

Bruce adds an interesting thought to this discussion:
> Paul's confrontation with the risen Christ on the Damascus road after his grounding in Judaism, and the new understanding of salvation-history which sprang from that confrontation, compelled him to see the legal path to salvation closed by a barrier … which carried a notice reading: 'No road this way.'[9]

Gal 3:13, 14. *Christ redeemed us from the curse of the law, having become a curse for us—for it is written, "Cursed be everyone who hangs on a tree"— [14] that in Christ Jesus the blessing of Abraham might come upon the Gentiles, that we might receive the promise of the Spirit through faith.*

These two verses are packed with deep and profound redemptive and atoning implications. We need to unpack them carefully! Paul invokes several of these principles as he begins to unfold God's scheme of redemption which he argues is received only through faith in Christ, arguing that it is through faith in

---

[9] Bruce, *op. cit.*, p. 160.

God's sacrificial work in Christ's death[10] and not through Law-keeping that God has activated his redemptive program. For Paul, God's scheme of redemption is immovably fixed in the sacrificial substitutionary death of Christ, and not the Law. Because of this, Christ was willing to become a curse for us by dying on a cross.

Paul added a new thought to his discussion of the process of God's atoning work in Christ, observing that Christ took on himself the *substitutionary curse* that should be ours because of our sin. *Christ redeemed us from the curse of the law, having become a curse for us—for it is written, 'Cursed be everyone who hangs on a tree'—* [14] *that in Christ Jesus the blessing of Abraham might come upon the Gentiles, that we might receive the promise of the Spirit through faith.*

Christ died *for us, in our place*, taking on himself the curse of being hung on a cross. Moses gave instruction to Israel regarding social and criminal behavior shortly before Israel entered the Promised Land under Joshua, Deut 21:18-23. It was to these Deuteronomic instructions, or laws, that Paul referred regarding Christ becoming a curse by dying on a tree/cross. Note Deut 21:18-23:

> [18] *If a man has a stubborn and rebellious son, who will not obey the voice of his father or the voice of his mother, and, though they chastise him, will not give heed to them,* [19] *then his father and his mother shall take hold of him and bring him out to the elders of his city at the gate of the place where he lives,* [20] *and they shall say to the elders of his city, 'This our son is stubborn and rebellious, he will not obey our voice; he is a glutton and a drunkard.'* [21] *Then all the men of the city shall stone him to death with stones; so you shall purge the evil from your midst; and all Israel shall hear, and fear.*
>
> [22] *And if a man has committed a crime punishable by death and he is put to death, and you hang him on a tree,* [23] *his body shall not remain all night upon the tree, but*

---

[10] To express this in clearer terms, through believing in Christ's death, burial, and resurrection.

you shall bury him the same day, for a hanged man is accursed by God; you shall not defile your land which the LORD your God gives you for an inheritance.[11]

I find it interesting that Paul would refer to the Deuteronomic laws of curses and blessings—curses for disobedience and loss of faith, and blessings for faith and faithfulness!

Jesus did not become a curse for personally failing to keep the dodecalogue (Deut 27:15ff), for the writer of Hebrews clearly stated at Heb 4:15 that Christ died without personal sin; *For we have not a high priest who is unable to sympathize with our weaknesses, but one who in every respect has been tempted as we are, yet without sin.* Jesus became a curse in his death by being crucified like a criminal and hung on a tree in order to redeem us from the curse. In Jewish practice hanging on a cross was the sign of a curse. Note the narrative of Joseph of Arimathea[12] who retrieved Jesus' dead body from the cross before the night set in! Jesus atoning death on a tree/cross became a shame and a curse, but he suffered that willingly, thus becoming the *hilastērion, propitiation, expiation,* or preferably *the atoning sacrifice* for our sins.

Robert Lyon and Peter Toon observe:

> If Christ is viewed as our sacrifice, he is also viewed as our representative. That is, he represented us in his death.

---

[11] In an extended article in the *Baker Encyclopedia of the Bible*, vol. 1, pp. 548ff, Hazel W. Perkin has several interesting observations. The manner of killing a person for criminal activity in Judaism was normally stoning, not hanging or crucifixion. However, as Deut 21 implies, hanging was permitted under certain conditions. Stoning was recognized as the appropriate death penalty for blasphemy of idolatry. Crucifixion or hanging/impalement on a "pole" was an Assyrian and pagan and Roman form of death penalty, with the exception demonstrated in Deut 21:22ff of hanging for extreme criminality. Under such circumstances the hanging human body had to be removed by evening and nightfall. Parental authority was so highly regarded in biblical law that a stubborn and rebellious son could be brought before the elders on the grounds of being disobedient and a glutton or a drunkard. He might then be convicted and stoned to death on the spot by the men of the city (Deut 21:18-21).
[12] Matt 27:57; John 19:38.

One of the most difficult phrases to interpret precisely is the common biblical expression "for us" ("for me," etc.). It may mean generally "for my sake" or something more specific. Does Christ represent us? More specifically, is he a substitute for us? Some texts clearly speak of him as our representative. Thus, Paul said, "We are convinced that one has died for all; therefore, all have died" (2 Cor 5:14). If "substitution" were meant, the last clause would conclude that we will not, or do not, die.[13] Hebrews speaks of Christ as our high priest before the Father, which is probably what John had in mind when he referred to Christ as our *advocate with the Father* (1 Jn 2:2).

The expression "for us" at times seems to mean much more than representation; it often carries the sense of substitution, an idea prevalent in the OT. So, "For our sake he made him to be sin who knew no sin, so that in him we might become the righteousness of God" (2 Cor 5:21). Two "ransom sayings" also portray substitution: "The Son of man came not to be ministered unto, but to minister, and to give his life a ransom for many" (Mk 10:45 KJV). He "gave himself as a ransom for all" (1 Tm 2:6). He became a "curse for us" (Gal 3:13). The unintended prophecy of Caiaphas the high priest pointed to the same reality: "It is expedient for you that one man should die for the people, and that the whole nation should not perish" (Jn 11:50).[14]

Regarding the word *cursed*, ἐπικατάρατος, *epikatáratos*[15] Bruce, citing J. Denny, *The Death of Christ*, has some insightful observations. Bruce reflects regarding Paul's conviction;

---

[13] But Paul wrote that since we are buried with Christ in baptism we will also be raised with Christ in his resurrection. Jesus himself said that if we truly believe in him then we will never die, John 11:25, 26.

[14] Lyon, Robert and Peter Toon, *Baker Encyclopedia of the Bible* vol. 1, pp. 232-233.

[15] Zodhiates, *op. cit.*, ἐπικατάρατος *epikatáratos* ...cursed. Accursed, under a curse, doomed to punishment (John 7:49; Gal. 3:10 quoted from Deut. 27:26; Sept.: Gen. 9:25; Deut. 27:15). Used as a verbal adj. from *epikataráomai*, to lay a curse on with something, one on whom the curse rests or in whom it is realized. See Gal. 3:10, 13, which corresponds with being under the curse.[15]

> ... that Christ's enduring the cross was his (Christ's) supreme act of obedience to God (cf Rom 5:19) and that in Christ God was reconciling the world to himself (2 Cor 5:19). Paul leaves the question, 'By whom was Christ cursed?' unanswered; what he does make plain is that the curse which Christ 'became' was the people's curse, as the death which he died was their death. Death 'is the experience in which the final repulsion of evil by God is decisively expressed; and Christ died. In his death everything was made His that sin had mare ours—everything in sin except its sinfulness' (J Denny, The Death of Christ, 160). So in 2 Cor 5:21 Paul speaks of Christ having been 'made sin for us'—that is, he came to stand in that relation with God which normally is the result of sin, estranged from God and the object of his wrath'... [16]

Paul closes this discussion regarding righteousness through faith in God's redemptive work in Christ who became a curse in our place in order to redeem us from the curse of sin and death. His point being that Christ became a curse on a cross for us because the Law could not redeem those who had broken the Law. All the Law could do was highlight our transgressions and indict us for sin.

He returns to his point, Gal 3:7 that we become sons of Abraham through our faith in God and Christ. At Gal 3:14 he resumes the thread of his argument stressing that our Abrahamic inheritance and reception of the Holy Spirit is realized through faith and not through the Law. *[13]Christ redeemed us from the curse of the law, having become a curse for us ...[14] that in Christ Jesus the blessing of Abraham might come upon the Gentiles, that we might receive the promise of the Spirit through faith.*

Notice first Paul's double use of the conjunction *that,* ἵνα, *hína,*[17] which carries the sense of purpose, *to the end* that we

---

[16] Bruce, *op. cit.,* pp. 165f.

[17] Zodhiates, *op. cit.,* ἵνα *hína;* conj. That, so that, for the purpose of, construed usually with a subjunctive ... often with the indication marking the end, purpose. Also, used to indicate the cause for, or on account of which anything is done. Can be translated, "to the end that," "in order that it might [or may] be."

might receive in Christ the blessings of Abraham and receive the gift of the Holy Spirit. We are reminded that Jesus taught his disciples that he would need to die and return to his Father before they could receive the counselor, the Holy Spirit. John 14:16, 26; 16:7, *Nevertheless I tell you the truth: it is to your advantage that I go away, for if I do not go away, the Counselor will not come to you; but if I go, I will send him to you ...* I find it enriching that John introduced Jesus' departing speech to his disciples with the instructions to believe in him, not to keep the Law! *Let not your hearts be troubled; believe in God, believe also in me.*[18]

Discussion Questions and Thoughts

1. What is the key thought behind this challenging pericope? Remember Paul is defending his theology of justification. How are men justified before God?
2. What is the result of attempting to be justified by Law keeping?
3. Why present Jesus' death on the cross as a curse?
4. What do we mean by substitutionary atonement?

---

[18] John 14:1

Chapter 7: Gal 3:15-18 – The Abrahamic Covenant

It is not possible to study Paul's theology of redemption without first setting it in the context of the pivotal role Abraham plays in the story of Israel and God's scheme of things, notably, redemption. Abraham is mentioned 75 times in our New Testament, and 19 times in Paul's Epistles. This is somewhat surprising since the New Testament is the story of Jesus Christ, not Abraham! That Jesus Christ should dominate the New Testament and Paul's redemptive theology should be no surprise, but the emphasis of Abraham in this story and theology does raise some interesting thoughts and emphasize the role Abraham plays in God's redemptive scheme and the overall flow of Paul's doctrine of redemption.

When Matthew began his story of Jesus, the Messiah, he began by stating that Jesus was the son of David and Abraham (Matt 1:1). An early Jewish Christian preacher began his great sermon on Jesus, which we know as the book of Hebrews, by drawing attention to Abraham, demonstrating that Jesus was even greater than Abraham. That preacher likewise spent more time and space telling of the faith of Abraham than he did on any other heroes of faith (Heb 2:16; Heb 11). The New Testament repeatedly stresses the importance of Abraham by pointing out that for the Jews YHWH was the God of Abraham (Matt 22:32), and that Abraham was the patriarchal father of the Jews (Lk 1:73).

Thus, when beginning to discuss God's redemptive program of justification, Abraham lies at the very foundation of Paul's thinking. He begins his discussion of the theology of justification in both Romans and Galatians with Abraham (Rom 4:2 and Galatians 3:6).

Abraham is in Paul's theology of justification in Galatians because in God's covenant with Abraham (Gen 12; 15; 17; *passim*) the Gentiles were included and have hope. Their hope does not lie in the story of Joseph, or even Moses, as great and significant as those stories are, it lies in the eternal purpose of God and his calling and covenant promise to Abraham.

God's covenants of promise and redemption are rooted in the story of Abraham—in his calling from the Ur of Chaldea, in Israel's God being the God of Abraham, in his being the patriarch of Israel, and in Abraham's character of faith and obedience.

In this section of Galatians, Paul argued that since Abraham was blessed on the grounds of his faith and not the Law, which had not yet been given, the inheritance of the blessings in Abraham are likewise based in faith and not in the Law.

The Text

I have included in this text both the rendering of the RSV and the ESV to demonstrate that the Greek word διαθήκη, *diathēkē* can be translated either as will or covenant. Since Paul's argument is an analogy to either Roman or Greek human jurisprudence the RSV prefers the concept *will*. We believe it is either Roman or Greek jurisprudence, and not Jewish jurisprudence since Paul was writing to Galatians. However, either will or covenant will work!

Gal 3:15-18

> RSV. *[15]To give a human example, brethren: no one annuls even a man's will, or adds to it, once it has been ratified. [16] Now the promises were made to Abraham and to his offspring. It does not say, "And to offsprings," referring to many; but, referring to one, "And to your offspring," which is Christ. [17] This is what I mean: the law, which came four hundred and thirty years afterward, does not annul a covenant previously ratified by God, so as to make the promise void. [18] For if the inheritance is by the law, it is no longer by promise; but God gave it to Abraham by a promise.*

> ESV. *[15]To give a human example, brothers: even with a man-made covenant, no one annuls it or adds to it once it has been ratified. [16] Now the promises were made to Abraham and to his offspring. It does not say, "And to offsprings," referring to many, but referring to one, "And to your offspring," who is Christ. [17]This is what I mean: the law, which came 430 years afterward, does not annul*

a covenant previously ratified by God, so as to make the promise void. ¹⁸ For if the inheritance comes by the law, it no longer comes by promise; but God gave it to Abraham by a promise.

Gal 3:15. Abraham and the rules of inheritance.

Longenecker introduces Paul's somewhat confusing argument regarding the making of promised covenants and the giving of laws with this comment:

> In Gal 3:15-18 Paul constructs an argument based on two factors: (1) that the covenant with Abraham represents God's pristine and irrevocable will, and (2) that the promise of the Abrahamic covenant has a singular recipient in mind, viz., Christ. In effect, Paul is here going behind the teaching of his opponents to remind his converts that God's promise was given long before the Mosaic law appeared and to assert that it was given not to observers of that law but to Christ (and, as he says later, to those who are Christ's own, cf. v 29). If Paul is to be charged with denigrating the law, his opponents are to be charged, he insists, with denigrating God's promise, the inheritance of that promise, Christ, and the Spirit—for these are matters associated with the Abrahamic covenant long before and apart from the law. Thus, the law has no part in their receiving the inheritance promised to Abraham.[1]

In this text, Paul introduces an attention-grabbing argument regarding God's *covenant* with Abraham and the legal aspects of wills. *To give a human example, brethren: no one annuls even a man's will* (or covenant), *or adds to it, once it has been ratified.*

Paul drew on the human everyday legal analogy of *wills*[2] which even the Jewish "legalizers" would understand! Once a

---

[1] Longenecker, *op. cit.*, pp. 125-126.
[2] The Greek word here is διαθήκη, *diathḗkē*, which can be translated either as *will* or *covenant*. Zodhiates *op. cit.*, observes that it means *to dispose in a certain order. Testament,* covenant. In Classical Greek, it always meant *the disposition which a person makes of his property in prospect of death.* Whether

will or *covenant* is activated, ratified, or is in effect, it cannot be annulled by a later will, covenant, or law.

This is a pertinent human analogy which Paul uses to remind the readers that God's covenant with Abraham was already in effect and could not be annulled even by the Law of Moses that came 430 years later. Paul's argument was that the promise to Abraham was based on a covenant which had already come into effect long before the Law was given at Sinai!

Paul's use of the *adversative* participle ὅμως, *hómōs, nevertheless, not withstanding*, is interesting. Zodhiates observes regarding the use of this adversative particle here, "Brethren, to give you a human example, *how much more then* God's covenant cannot be annulled, when in the case of a human covenant, once it is duly confirmed, no one may annul it even in the case of a later human will …"[3]

Longenecker stresses the irrevocability of the covenant made to Abraham by observing that the tense of the Greek word κεκυρωμένην, *kekurōmenēn* strengthens Paul's argument. The perfect tense behind this perfect passive participle implies action in the past whose effect is still active in the present.

> The perfect tense and mood of the participle κεκυρωμένην, from the verb κυρόω "to establish, to confirm, to ratify, or to validate," highlights the features of irrevocability (perfect tense) and unalterableness (passive mood) that Paul wants to stress in the case of the Abrahamic covenant.[4]

Thus, in this case, the legal analogy of Gal 3:15 makes the point that once a will or covenant is ratified or activated a second will, covenant, or Law cannot take its place after the covenant has been ratified, fulfilled, or in effect. God made the covenant/will with Abraham 430 years before the Law was given

---

Paul was using it according to Roman jurisprudence or Greek jurisprudence makes little difference since both systems agreed basically with this principle.

[3] Zodhiates, *op. cit.*, ὅμως, *hómōs*; adversative particle … like, similar. Nevertheless, notwithstanding, yet … however, … yet, nevertheless … yet even, how much more then? Also in Gal. 3:15 meaning "yet even a man's covenant, duly confirmed, no one annuls."

[4] Longenecker, *op. cit.*, p. 127.

at Sinai. The land inheritance and other aspects of the covenant such as religious relationship with God had already been set in motion by God and could not be annulled by a later Law. The Jews were already experiencing the principles of that covenant. They were already a Hebrew/Jewish community when the Law was given. The Law, coming so long after the covenant was ratified cannot annul the covenant which was already in effect. Abraham and his descendants had already begun to receive and benefit from God's covenant with Abraham which was in force, and continued to be so, even though a Law had been added much later. Paul's understanding of the Law was that it was not intended to nullify the covenant which had already become reality, for that was not the purpose of the law. Paul at Gal 3:19f argued that the Law was *added because of transgression*, not to nullify the covenant that was based on faith and promise. The Law was to serve as a custodian and guide to the Jewish people of the covenant.

Bruce adds an interesting comment:
> The present analogy is drawn from judicial practice; if his readers, despite all that had been said above, persist in appealing to the law, let them consider that the divine promise was embedded in a settlement which was made long before the giving of the law and which therefore cannot be annulled or even modified by the law.[5]

Paul was making two important points; *one*, the law cannot modify or change the covenant promise to Abraham; and *two*, the covenant with Abraham was based on a covenant promise, and not in the Law. Later in this letter, Paul argues that all Christians inherit the benefits of the promise to Abraham through faith in Jesus Christ, and not by Law-keeping (Gal 3:25-29).

Gal 3:16. Paul introduces an interesting hermeneutic concept using a generic singular noun, *seed, offspring*, which can refer to *one person or several persons*. This even today is a common figure of speech.

---

[5] Bruce, *op. cit.*, p. 169.

> Now the promises were made to Abraham and to his offspring. It does not say, "And to offsprings," referring to many; but, referring to one, "And to your offspring," which is Christ.

This particular promise to Abraham is interesting. The plural form descendants is found in Gen 26:1-5, God had said,

> Now there was a famine in the land, besides the former famine that was in the days of Abraham. And Isaac went to Gerar, to Abimelech king of the Philistines. ² And the LORD appeared to him, and said, "Do not go down to Egypt; dwell in the land of which I shall tell you. ³ Sojourn in this land, and I will be with you, and will bless you; for to you and to your <u>descendants</u>[6] I will give all these lands, and I will fulfil the oath which I swore to Abraham your father. ⁴ I will multiply your descendants as the stars of heaven, and will give to your descendants all these lands; and by your descendants all the nations of the earth shall bless themselves: ⁵ because Abraham obeyed my voice and kept my charge, my commandments, my statutes, and my laws.

At Gen 28:14, on another occasion God had repeated this promise to Jacob:

> And behold, the LORD stood above it and said, "I am the LORD, the God of Abraham your father and the God of Isaac; the land on which you lie I will give to you and to your <u>descendants</u>; ¹⁴ and your descendants shall be like the dust of the earth, and you shall spread abroad to the west and to the east and to the north and to the south; and by you and your descendants shall all the families of the earth bless themselves. ¹⁵ Behold, I am with you and will keep you wherever you go, and will bring you back to this land; for I will not leave you until I have done that of which I have spoken to you.

The word translated *offspring* or *seed* in both the Old Testament LXX and the New Testament, notably in Gal 3:16, is σπέρμα, *spérma*. Zodhiates observes:

---

[6] Underline emphasis on <u>descendants</u> is mine, IAF.

> In the Classical. Greek. terminology, *spérma* rarely signifies descendants collectively, and even less, posterity as a whole, but primarily only the individual, the child, offspring, son or daughter. In the Septuagint. however, *spérma* has mostly a collective meaning ... The word continues in its collective meaning in the NT (Rev. 12:17). Thus, it denotes immediate descendants, children (Matt. 22:24, 25; Mark 12:19–22; Luke 20:28). The expression "the seed of David" (John 7:42; Rom. 1:3; 2 Tim. 2:8) means progeny, posterity (see Acts 13:23). Similarly, with "the seed of Abraham" (a.t. [Luke 1:55; John 8:33, 37; Acts 3:25; 7:5, 6; 13:23; Rom. 4:13, 16, 18; 11:1; 2 Cor. 11:22; Gal. 3:19; Heb. 2:16; 11:18]). Where Christ is designated as the progeny or offspring of Abraham ... [7]

Paul picks up on the blessing made to Abraham and repeated in several other Genesis contexts regarding Abraham's offspring, and implies regarding that the *seed/offspring* who will inherit God's covenant with Abraham was *not simply* Israel collectively, but was in fact *Christ* as the messianic seed of Abraham (Gal 3:16)! However, he also quite clearly implies that Christ as the offspring is also to be understood collectively, as at Gal 3:28, 29! Here is Paul's statement at Gal 3:16:

> [16] *Now the promises were made to Abraham and to his offspring. It does not say, "And to offsprings," referring to many; but, referring to one, "And to your offspring," which is Christ.*

Longenecker explains the interesting grammatical point of the generic singular:

> "Seed" in the Abrahamic promise is a generic singular that was always understood within Judaism to refer to the posterity of Abraham as an entity, excluding only the descendants of Abraham through Ishmael ("for in Isaac shall thy seed be called") and those born of Esau ... though also those who "have forfeited their share in the world to come" by such things as denying the

---

[7] Zodhiates, *op. cit.*, σπέρμα, *spérma*.

resurrection, reading the heretical books, pronouncing the sacred name of God, and being unmerciful to others ... Jews, of course, prided themselves on being "true sons of Abraham," and therefore on being the recipients of the promises made to Abraham. The Targums, in fact, take this corporate understanding of the promise so much for granted that they uniformly and unequivocally cast the expression into the plural: "and to your sons" ... Paul, however, for whom physical descent was no guarantee of spiritual relationship (cf. Rom 9:6b–7a), and with a possible swipe at the targumic plural, argues that Christ is the "seed" in view in the Abrahamic covenant, and then goes on in v 29 to speak of those "in Christ" (or "of Christ") as also being "Abraham's seed and heirs according to the promise." ... So, it seems that Paul is here invoking a corporate solidarity understanding of the promise to Abraham wherein the Messiah, as the true descendant of Abraham and the true representative of the nation, is seen as the true "seed" of Abraham—as are, of course, also the Messiah's own, as v 29 insists.[8]

Gal 3:17, 18. The covenant predates the Law and is loftier than the Law.

This is what I mean: the law, which came four hundred and thirty years afterward, does not annul a covenant previously ratified by God, so as to make the promise void. [18] For if the inheritance is by the law, it is no longer by promise; but God gave it to Abraham by a promise.

How we are to determine the "430 years" has generated several options. Longenecker offers the solution that is held by many:

> The most perplexing feature of v 17 is the statement that the law appeared in history "430 years" after God's covenant with Abraham. The exact figure, of course, whether 430 years or 400 years, is of no great importance for Paul's argument, though, of course, the impact would

---

[8] Longenecker, *ibid.*, pp. 131, 132.

be slightly increased with the larger number. Yet it has often seemed strange to many that in working extensively from the Genesis accounts, Paul should speak of 430 years from Abraham to Moses, which is the figure given in Exod 12:40 for Israel's captivity in Egypt, whereas Gen 15:13 has 400 years for that same period of enslavement.

The rabbis found the difference between Gen 15:13 ("400 years") and Exod 12:40 ("430 years") somewhat perplexing as well ...Usually they solved the problem by taking 430 years as the time between God's covenant with Abraham and Moses' reception of the law and 400 years as the period Israel spent in Egypt ... It seems, therefore, that this was the traditional way in Paul's day of treating the discrepancy between Gen 15:13 and Exod 12:40 and of understanding the respective time spans. And so Paul here is probably not relying on Exod 12:40 versus Gen 15:13, but only repeating the traditionally accepted number of years for the time span between the Abrahamic covenant and the Mosaic law.[9]

However we decide to address the issue of 430 years or 400 years, at this text we have 430 as indication of the considerable time difference between the covenant of Abraham and the giving of the Law. Paul's point is that the Abrahamic covenant is not, in fact, cannot be annulled or abrogated by the giving of the Law. The covenant is based on a faith principle, not a Law principle.

Discussion Questions and Thoughts
1. What are we to make of this discussion of laws, covenants, promises, and Paul's concern for the Galatians?
2. How does this pericope and lesson fit into Paul's discussion with the Galatians?

---

[9] Longenecker, *op. cit.*, p. 133.

Chapter 8: Gal 3:19-4:7 – The Proper Function of the Law

This pericope and its theology have deep implications for our understanding of Christ, the Old Testament Law, and our overall understanding of justification. If the Jews were so inextricably attached to the Law of Moses, how were they to understand the role that Jesus' ministry, grace, faith, and the Law played in justification? If they did not understand the purpose of the Law, grace and faith in Jesus would be meaningless! In both Galatians and Romans, Paul definitively addressed the fact that the Jews had a misunderstanding of the role of the Law and consequently misapplied the real purpose of the Law.

We might add that without a heathy attitude and respect for the real purpose of the Law, neither the Jew nor the Gentile would understand the relationship of the Law to grace, forgiveness, and righteousness.

Paul was always careful in his attitude toward theology and parenesis! He consequently was meticulous in bedding his practical ethical parenetic advice on sound doctrine and theology. Thus, in Paul's theology both grace and sin, and grace and the Law, are held in dynamic tension. The point is that one cannot fully understand grace separated from Law, or Law separated from grace, and this was the steady current of Paul's theology.

In Paul's epistle to the Romans in which he explained his great doctrine of justification by grace through faith in Jesus Christ, he first clearly defined the lost nature of humanity—*What then? Are we Jews any better off? No, not at all; for I have already charged that all men, both Jews and Greeks, are under the power of sin, ^{10} as it is written: "None is righteous, no, not one; ^{11} no one understands, no one seeks for God. ^{12} All have turned aside, together they have gone wrong; no one does good, not even one.*[1]

Thus, even before he articulated the doctrine of grace through faith in Jesus Christ which defined the primary theology of Romans and the Christian faith, he clearly established the fact

---

[1] Rom 3:9-12.

that all men are under the power of sin, and that the consequence of sin is death. Romans 1-3 establish that a necessary foundation to justification by grace through faith is a clear conviction of sin and death. Romans 3-8 then sets grace, mercy, and faith in Jesus on the proper knowledge of sin and death. Understanding the relationship of grace and Law are necessary precursors to understanding Paul's view of righteousness and justification.

What was true in Romans is likewise true in Galatians! Understanding the relationship of grace and Law were precursors to understanding justification and a proper relationship with God. Hence, in this pericope Paul began to address the purpose of the Law.

The Text

Gal 3:19-29. *Why then the law? It was added because of transgressions, till the offspring should come to whom the promise had been made; and it was ordained by angels through an intermediary. [20] Now an intermediary implies more than one; but God is one.*

[21] Is the law then against the promises of God? Certainly not; for if a law had been given which could make alive, then righteousness would indeed be by the law. [22] But the scripture consigned all things to sin, that what was promised to faith in Jesus Christ might be given to those who believe.

[23] Now before faith came, we were confined under the law, kept under restraint until faith should be revealed. [24] So that the law was our custodian until Christ came, that we might be justified by faith. [25] But now that faith has come, we are no longer under a custodian; [26] for in Christ Jesus you are all sons of God, through faith. [27] For as many of you as were baptized into Christ have put on Christ. [28] There is neither Jew nor Greek, there is neither slave nor free, there is neither male nor female; for you are all one in Christ Jesus. [29] And if you are Christ's, then you are Abraham's offspring, heirs according to promise.

Gal 4:1-7. *I mean that the heir, as long as he is a child, is no better than a slave, though he is the owner of all the estate; [2] but he is under guardians and trustees until the date set by the father. [3] So with us; when we were children, we were slaves to the elemental spirits of the universe. [4] But when the time had fully come, God sent forth his Son, born of woman, born under the law, [5] to redeem those who were under the law, so that we might receive adoption as sons. [6] And because you are sons, God has sent the Spirit of his Son into our hearts, crying, "Abba! Father!" [7] So through God you are no longer a slave but a son, and if a son then an heir.*

Gal 3:19, 20. [19] *Why then the law? It was added because of transgressions, till the offspring should come to whom the promise had been made; and it was ordained by angels through an intermediary.* [20] *Now an intermediary implies more than one; but God is one.*

Paul introduced a line of thought that would not sit well with his Jewish opponents, but which was critical to his gospel. The Law was intended to last only until the offspring of Abraham came! This was a mind-bending claim which certainly needed elaboration, and which Paul immediately provided! His claim that *"It was added because of transgressions"* set his answer in motion! The Law was never intended to justify or save anyone!

Rom 3:20: *For no human being will be justified in his sight by works of the law, since through the law comes knowledge of sin.*

Rom 7:7: *What then shall we say? That the law is sin? By no means! Yet, if it had not been for the law, I should not have known sin. I should not have known what it is to covet if the law had not said, "You shall not covet."*

2 Cor 3:6: *... our competence is from God, [6] who has made us competent to be ministers of a new covenant, not in a written code but in the Spirit; for the written code kills, but the Spirit gives life.*

1 Tim 1:9: *Now we know that the law is good, if any one uses it lawfully, [9] understanding this, that the law is not laid down for the just but for the lawless and disobedient, for the ungodly and sinners, for the unholy and profane, for* *murderers of fathers and murderers of mothers, for manslayers, ¹⁰ immoral persons, sodomites, kidnapers, liars, perjurers, and whatever else is contrary to sound doctrine ...*

Paul continued by explaining that it never was God's intention to establish the Law permanently; it was intended to serve *till the offspring should come to whom the promise had been made*. The preposition ἄχρι, *áchri; till, can serve as an adverb of time*. With a relative pronoun ... οὗ, *hoú*, it has the nature of a conjunction, *until*.²

In a succinct observation which takes the temporal ἄχρι, *áchri* seriously, Longenecker adds:

> The whole clause beginning with the temporal conjunction ἄχρι "until" (ἄχρις before a vowel) sets the *terminus ad quem (the point of completion*, IAF) for the law, just as προσετέθη set its *terminus a quo (the starting point, IAF)*. Thus, the Mosaic law, for Paul, was intended by God to be in effect for God's people only up until the coming of Christ. Or stated more positively and comprehensively, as Burton does: "Thus the covenant of promise is presented to the mind as of permanent validity, both beginning before and continuing through the period of the law and afterwards, the law on the other hand as temporary, added to the permanent covenant for a period limited in both directions" (*Galatians*, 189).³

Paul has already discussed the generic singular expression *offspring*, σπέρμα *spérma, seed,* at Gal 3:16, now he resumes the discussion of that offspring being Christ, the *terminus* of the Law, *till the offspring should come to whom the promise had been made*. The concept of promise obviously refers to God's covenant promise to Abraham. Christ is that end to which the Law has been working, preparing His people for the final fulfillment of the promise. The point is that *the promise had been made* with Christ in mind! The use of the perfect form of the verb, ἐπαγγέλλομαι, *epaggellomai, promise* indicates the

---

² Zodhiates, *op. cit.*, Bauer, Arndt and Gingrich, *op. cit.*, "an improper preposition with the genitive of time *until*, 2 Macc 14:15, ...*until the day when*."

³ Longenecker, *op. cit.*, p.139; Burton, E. W. *A Critical and Exegetical Commentary on the Epistle to the Galatians*, Edinburgh: T. & T. Clark, 1921.

permanence and continuation of the promise, whereas the Law was only temporary. Longenecker observes, "The perfect tense of the deponent verb ἐπαγγέλλομαι ("promise") signals a past action with present results, thereby suggesting that the promise is still in effect."[4]

Paul introduces an interesting thought with his observation that the Law *was ordained by angels through an intermediary.* *[20] Now an intermediary implies more than one; but God is one.* The concept of the Law being *ordained* by angels, although not being mentioned in the Old Testament, was a well-established principle in Jewish thought. Stephen, as recorded in Acts 7:51-53, said:

> *You stiff-necked people, uncircumcised in heart and ears, you always resist the Holy Spirit. As your fathers did, so do you. [52] Which of the prophets did not your fathers persecute? And they killed those who announced beforehand the coming of the Righteous One, whom you have now betrayed and murdered, [53] you who received the law as delivered by angels and did not keep it.*

Likewise, the preacher/writer of Hebrews was aware of this tradition of angelic involvement in the giving of the Law, Heb 2:1, 2:

> *Therefore, we must pay the closer attention to what we have heard, lest we drift away from it. [2] For if the message declared by angels was valid and every transgression or disobedience received a just retribution, [3] how shall we escape if we neglect such a great salvation?*

The inclusion of the statement "*Now an intermediary implies more than one; but God is one,*" has intrigued scholars for centuries as they seek a reason for including it! The point seems that although in passing on the Law to Moses God used intermediaries, in his covenant with Abraham God acted *unilaterally*, indicating the *superiority* of the promise over the Law.[5] This comment in no way deprecates the Law, only

---

[4] Longenecker, *op. cit.*, p. 139.
[5] Cf. Bruce, *op. cit.*, p. 178, Longenecker, *op cit*, p. 142.

emphasizes the unique and grander nature of God's promise to Abraham.

Gal 3:21, 22. The Law does not conflict with the promise.

In the next few paragraphs, Paul argues that the Law does not work contrary to the promise but serves the purpose of the promise by drawing people to the promised Christ/Messiah.

> *Is the law then against the promises of God? Certainly not; for if a law had been given which could make alive, then righteousness would indeed be by the law. [22] But the scripture consigned all things to sin, that what was promised to faith in Jesus Christ might be given to those who believe.*

First, Paul resorts to the emphatic μὴ γένοιτο, *mē genoito, certainly not*, not in any manner! *Second*, he argues that if it were possible for one to be declared righteous by a law then righteousness would indeed be by the Law, but as Paul elsewhere argues, righteousness is not based in the Law principle, but in the faith principle (Cf. Rom 3:20; Rom 5:20; Rom 7 *passim*; Rom 8:1, 2). *Third*, the role of "the scripture,"[6] the Law, consigns all men to sin since the Law indicts men for sin. *Fourth*, the whole purpose of the Law was to bring all men to Christ and the righteousness that is by faith in Christ.

There is considerable discussion regarding what Paul meant by ἡ γραφὴ, hē graphē, *the scripture*. Longenecker observes:

> The use of ἡ γραφή ("the Scripture") as the subject of the sentence, rather than ὁ νόμος as in the first sentence, has raised all sorts of questions as to what exactly Paul had in mind. Is ἡ γραφή to be identified with ὁ νόμος ... or to be differentiated from ὁ νόμος ...? And if it is to be differentiated, does it refer to Scripture generically ... to Scripture as a metonomy for God himself ... Or, as Lightfoot and Burton have argued, does Paul here have in mind a particular passage of Scripture that he has cited earlier, either Ps 143:2, possibly alluded to in 2:16, or Deut 27:26, quoted in 3:10 ... Paul's normal use of the singular γραφή ... and the presence of the article ἡ ...

---

[6] Zodhiates, *op. cit.*, ἡ γραφὴ, hē graphē, the writings, or the scripture.

suggest that he had a particular passage in mind, probably the more immediate antecedent of 3:10, i.e. Deut 27:26—a passage he learned from his rabbinic training but one also probably vividly impressed on him ... That he had in mind Deut 27:26 rather than Ps 143:2 is made more probable by the fact that the function of the law is under discussion, and so a passage from the Pentateuch would be most appropriate. [7]

We conclude that whichever alternative meaning one arrives at, it was meant by Paul to be a reference to final authority in matters of defining sin. Scripture is the final word on sin! Cf. Rom 3:9ff, 7:7.

Gal 3:23-3:29. The superiority of faith over Law.
[23]Now before faith came, we were confined under the law, kept under restraint until faith should be revealed. [24] So that the law was our custodian until Christ came, that we might be justified by faith. [25] But now that faith has come, we are no longer under a custodian; [26] for in Christ Jesus you are all sons of God, through faith. [27] For as many of you as were baptized into Christ have put on Christ. [28] There is neither Jew nor Greek, there is neither slave nor free, there is neither male nor female; for you are all one in Christ Jesus. [29] And if you are Christ's, then you are Abraham's offspring, heirs according to promise.

This pericope is in many ways the high point, perhaps even the pivotal point, in Paul's epistle to the Galatians! It is loaded with critical points in his argument against the false teachers who would bind the Law, particularly circumcision on the Galatian Gentile believers as the mark of a true relationship with God.

As we begin to unpack this powerful text we need to comment on the introductory expressive particle *"now,"* in Greek, δέ, *dé*. It often introduces some new thought *contrary* to what has been suggested by the others regarding circumcision as the covenant marker. *Now,* δέ, *dé* can be emphatic when introducing

---

[7] Longenecker, *op. cit.*, p, 144; Bruce, op. cit., p. 180.

such new points.[8] The new thought develops, and refutes, the discussion of the Law and circumcision as a sign of covenant relationship, introducing the contrary thought of faith, which as Paul has already argued, with Abraham as his proof, predates the Law by 430 years. The new thought that Paul introduces into his argument is that the Law served Israel *only until* the faith of Christ came.

Gal 3:23. *Now before faith came, we were confined under the law, kept under restraint until faith should be revealed...*

Before Christ and the gospel of Christ *became a reality*, Israel was confined in its relationship with God and its religious behavior by the Law. Because of their calling and heritage in Abraham, they were already in a covenant relationship with God. The Law had been introduced to guide Israel in this covenant relationship with God. Paul argued in his several epistles that even though Israel was under the Law, their covenant relationship was maintained by their faithfulness to God. Here in Galatians, Paul emphasized this point by adding that Israel was *kept under restraint* by the Law. Now that Christ and faith in Christ had come, the restraining purpose of the Law had been lifted. Now Christ, rather than the Law, has become the restraining influence in Christian behavior.

In an arresting text, 2 Cor 5:14-20, Paul makes the point that Christians are controlled by a new and different principle than the written code that kills[9];

> *For the love of Christ controls us, because we are convinced that one has died for all; therefore all have died.* ¹⁵ *And he died for all, that those who live might live no longer for themselves but for him who for their sake died and was raised.*
>
> ¹⁶ *From now on, therefore, we regard no one from a human point of view; even though we once regarded Christ*

---

[8] Zodhiates, *op. cit.*, δέ *dé*; a particle standing after one or two words in a clause ...but more frequently denoting transition or conversion, and serving to introduce something else, whether opposed to what precedes or simply continuative or explanatory ... sometimes emphatic.
[9] 2 Cor 3:6.

from a human point of view, we regard him thus no longer. *[17] Therefore, if anyone is in Christ, he is a new creation; the old has passed away, behold, the new has come. [18] All this is from God, who through Christ reconciled us to himself and gave us the ministry of reconciliation; [19] that is, in Christ God was reconciling the world to himself, not counting their trespasses against them, and entrusting to us the message of reconciliation. [20] So we are ambassadors for Christ, God making his appeal through us.*

A prominent feature of Paul's theology, reflected in Rom 6:1-4, was that *Christians in Christ have been raised with Christ as a new creation*, Rom 6:1-4:

What shall we say then? Are we to continue in sin that grace may abound? [2] By no means! How can we who died to sin still live in it? [3] Do you not know that all of us who have been baptized into Christ Jesus were baptized into his death? [4] We were buried therefore with him by baptism into death, so that as Christ was raised from the dead by the glory of the Father, we too might walk in newness of life.

Paul's point spelled out repeatedly in his correspondence was that the Law would kill one, cf. 2 Cor 3:6, and that it was not the purpose of the Law to save but to clarify the real nature and danger of sin. His point, which he picks up in Galatians, and in particular in the pericope we are examining, was that the purpose of the Law was to lead one to Christ and to life in the Spirit which brings real righteousness.

Gal 3:24-26. *So that the law was our custodian until Christ came, that we might be justified by faith. [25] But now that faith has come, we are no longer under a custodian; [26] for in Christ Jesus you are all sons of God, through faith.* Paul introduced an additional concept, that of the Law serving as the *custodian* of the Jews. The readers would have clearly understood the word παιδαγωγός, *paidagōgós*, pedagogue, which Zodhiates describes as "an instructor or teacher of children, a schoolmaster, a pedagogue (1 Cor. 4:15; Gal. 3:24, 25). Originally, it referred to

114

the slave who conducted the boys from home to the school. Then it became a teacher or an educator."[10]

Paul developed his point, already discussed, that now that faith had come, Christians no longer need a custodian/teacher to lead them to Christ and righteousness.

The clincher to his argument, and a high point in Galatians, was that in Christ, through faith, Christians—Jew and Gentile—are sons of God and descendants of the promises to Abraham. The thought is so profound that I repeat it for emphasis. *For in Christ Jesus you are all sons of God, through faith.* This is what Galatians is all about!

Longenecker observes regarding the custodian/guardian purpose of the Law:

> "…but now that this faith has come, we are no longer under a supervising guardian." Here Paul delivers the *coup de grâce* to the Judaizers' argument for Gentile Christians to live a lifestyle governed by the Mosaic law. For with the coming of the Christian gospel … as effected by Christ, the law no longer has validity as a παιδαγωγός (*pedagogue*) regulating the life of faith. One may, of course, as a Jew continue to live a Jewish nomistic lifestyle for cultural, national, or pragmatic reasons. To be a Jewish believer in Jesus did not mean turning one's back on one's own culture or nation. Yet no longer could it be argued that circumcision, Jewish dietary laws, following distinctly Jewish ethical precepts, or any other matter having to do with a Jewish lifestyle were requisite for the life of faith. Certainly not for Gentile Christians in any sense, though Paul and the Jerusalem apostles for cultural, national, and/or pragmatic reasons allowed Jewish believers in Jesus to live a Jewish lifestyle, but not as required spiritually.[11]

Gal 3:27-29. [27] For as many of you as were *baptized into Christ have put on Christ.* [28] There *is neither Jew nor Greek*, there is

---

[10] Zodhiates, *op. cit.*
[11] Longenecker, *op. cit.*, p149.

neither slave nor free, there is neither male nor female; for *you are all one in Christ Jesus.* ²⁹ *And if you are Christ's, then you are Abraham's offspring, heirs according to promise.*

Although baptism is not mentioned in Galatians outside of Gal 3:27, its role in the theology and practical message of Galatians and Paul's theology of justification and righteousness is profound! As articulated in this text, baptism examines the relationship of both the *result* or *goal* of faith or trusting in the death and resurrection of Christ, and the means of becoming *integrated with* and *entering* into Christ and the covenant promise and blessings of God to Abraham and his descendants.

Several prominent New Testament theologians and commentators have stressed the importance of baptism in Paul's overall theology. Two of these, G. R. Beasley-Murray in his book *Baptism in the New Testament*, and Everett Ferguson, *Baptism in the Early Church* have enriched our knowledge and understanding of baptism in both Galatians and the New Testament liturgy and practice.

Beasley-Murray succinctly observes regarding this significant text:

> The drift of the passage is clear. It forms the climax of the chapter in which Paul labours to refute the claim of the Judaisers that men become 'sons of Abraham' only through conforming to the law; on the contrary urges Paul, Abraham's heirs are the 'men of faith'. And the time of faith is present! In the period when law held the sway, men were held in custody, as a child is subject to the domination of his pedagogue; now that the time of faith has come through the preaching of the good news, all who exercise faith attain to Sonship through Christ, with whom they were united in baptism and in whom we are Abraham's seed and heirs of the promise ... If faith is to be taken seriously, so is baptism ... Rendtorff ... asserts "The experience of baptism is the experience of faith ..." It would be equally permissible to affirm. "The grace that is for faith is experienced in baptism." Baptism is the baptism of faith and grace, so that in it faith

receives what grace gives ... that in baptism faith receives the Christ in whom the adoption is effected.[12]

Ferguson, in his *magnus opus* on Baptism asserts regarding baptism at Gal 3:27:

> The distinctive of Christian baptism is its relationship to Christ. The baptized believer is now "Christ's" (3:29), the genitive case indicating either possession or belonging to the group derived from Christ ... whether the idea of "into" in εἰς is to be pressed, the preposition at least expresses that Christian baptism is directed toward Christ ... Baptism places one into Christ, so that one is now clothed with Christ having put him on as one puts on clothing."[13]

One can appropriately say *that baptism as the product of grace and faith establishes a new relationship with Christ.* The believer is baptized into Christ, into a new relationship with Christ, and as such into the inheritance of the covenant promise to the seed of Abraham.

Gal 3:28. Paul advances his argument on the Jew-Gentile relationship/fellowship by stating unambiguously that in Christ *there is neither Jew nor Greek*, there is neither *slave nor free*, there is neither *male nor female*; for *you are all one in Christ Jesus*. He is not saying that *in Christ ethnic, cultural*, and *gender differences* are *cancelled*. He is stating that in Christ the Christian still remains a Jew or Gentile, a slave or a free person, a male or a female, but in Christ all share an equal right to Abraham and the covenant blessings, to Christ, and to a real relationship with God without regard for the Law, ethnic, cultural, and gender distinctions. The critical issue is faith in God's redemptive promises and blessings that are found and experienced by faith and baptism into Christ where there are no ethnic, cultural, or gender priority rights. In baptism stemming from faith in Christ all Christians are children of God, and seed

---

[12] G. R. Beasley-Murray, *Baptism in the New Testament*, Grand Rapids: Wm. B. Eerdmans, 1962, pp. 146ff.

[13] Everett Ferguson, *Baptism in the Early Church*, Grand Rapids: Wm. B. Eerdmans, 2009, p. 148.

of Abraham with equal rights to the blessings of the Abrahamic covenant.

Paul was not addressing ethnic, cultural, or gender *roles* or *distinctive privileges* associated with being either a Jew or Gentile, a slave of freedman, or a male or female. He was only concerned with equal rights to the blessings and inheritance of God's covenant promises to Abraham.

Gal 3:29. *And if you are Christ's, then you are Abraham's offspring, heirs according to promise.*

The small conjunction "*if*" at the beginning of this verse (the protasis) introduces a strong statement of affirmation and is better translated "*and since*[14] *you are Christ's, then you are Abraham's offspring ...*" Longenecker completes the vigorous *since* statement with the point:

> Here Paul states his conclusion (note the εἰ ... ἄρα, "if ... then," construction), which, simply stated, is that (the) relationship with Christ (Χριστοῦ) relates Gentile Christians directly to Abraham and God's covenantal promise. [15]

Gal 4:1-3. Christians are no longer slaves to the rudimentary principles of the *stoicheía* world.

> *¹I mean that the heir, as long as he is a child, is no better than a slave, though he is the owner of all the estate; ² but he is under guardians and trustees until the date set by the father. ³ So with us; when we were children, we were slaves to the elemental spirits of the universe.*

Understanding the first expression of slave-heirs is not difficult. Whether he had reference to Roman or Greek inheritance laws is immaterial; the Galatians would have known what he had in mind.

---

[14] "The sentence is a first-class conditional sentence, which assumes the truth of what is stated in the protasis." Longenecker, *op. cit.*, p. 159.
[15] Longenecker, *ibid.*, p. 158.

However, what Paul meant by the expression *so with* **us***; when* **we** *were children,* **we** *were slaves to* the elemental spirits of the universe is challenging!

Exactly who does Paul have in mind with the first-person plural, **us/we**. Furthermore, what does he mean by *the elemental spirits of the universe*?

First, the phrase καὶ ἡμεῖς, *kai hēmeis, even we*, is emphatic, making a clear strong statement. But to whom does the *we* refer to, Jews, Jewish Christians, or Gentile Christians? Longenecker and Bruce believe that "here, we believe, the first-person plural of 4:3, as well as that of 4:5, ought to be understood as referring primarily to Jewish believers ..."[16]

Clarifying the use of the first-person *we* will help determine what Paul meant by *the elemental spirits of the universe*. If we are to work with this text in the context of Jewish or Jewish Christian concerns, then this refines somewhat what the term *elementary spirits* might refer. We will adopt the view as per Bruce and Longenecker that in this context of Gal 4:3 and 5 it refers to the Law of Moses, seen as the rudimentary principle of

---

[16] Bruce, *op. cit.*, p. 193; Longenecker, *op. cit.*, p. 164. "Paul's use of the first-person plural "we" in a letter addressed to Gentile Christians and where the second-person plural "you" predominates is a phenomenon that has appeared a number of times already (cf. 2:15-16; 3:13-14, 23-25). And as in those earlier occurrences, so in 4:3-5 the use of the first-person plural seems to carry greater significance than usually credited. Almost all commentators today take the first-person plural here to refer inclusively to all Christians, whether Jewish or Gentile ... Occasionally someone argues, based on Paul's evident concern for his Gentile converts, that "we" in Galatians means "Gentiles" with whom Paul identifies spiritually ... It may be that "we" is used here inclusively for both Jewish and Gentile believers. It is important to note, however, that in the three earlier passages where the first-person plural occurs, it either ... specifically refers to those who are Jewish (so 2:15-16, "we who are Jews by birth," and 3:23-25, "we ... under the law"), or ... can be read as a portion stemming from early Jewish Christianity ... Likewise, here, we believe, the first-person plural of 4:3, as well as that of 4:5, ought to be understood as referring primarily to Jewish believers: in v 3 as Paul's application of his illustration of the Jewish experience under the custodianship of the law ... and in vv 4-5 as Paul's quotation of an early Jewish Christian confessional portion, with vv 6-7, then, applying the thrust of the confession cited in vv 4-5 to his Gentile converts' situation and therefore reverting back to his usual second person plural "you."

Jewish faith. Later at Gal 5:1 Paul will in a slightly different context refer to the *stoicheía* as including the pagan rudimentary principles along with the Jewish rudimentary principles of the Law. Turning away from Christ and turning back to the Jewish and Pagan *stoicheía* would be turning away from the freedom in Christ in favor of slavery.

The Greek expression τὰ στοιχεῖα, *ta stoicheía, elemental spirits* is interesting since in the Greek the word *spirits* does not appear, but is derived or inferred from the original Greek meaning of *stoicheía*. However, we must ask, what is the meaning of the Greek word *stoicheía*? Zodhiates and others observe that the word is best understood as the *rudimentary elements, principles, or features* of something; hence in this context, *the rudimentary principles of Judaism, that is the Law of Moses.*[17] We should remember that for the Jew the Law was considered the rudimentary principle under which the world operated and would be judged. Bruce adds "For the present stage of Paul's argument it suffices to observe that the law ranks as one of the stoicheia."[18]

Gal 4:4-7. Christians are no longer slaves but are God's adopted sons who cry out in gratitude, adoration, and worship *Abba Father*.

> *But when the time had fully come, God sent forth his Son, born of woman, born under the law, ⁵ to redeem those who were under the law, so that **we** might receive*

---

[17] Zodhiates, *op. cit.*, στοιχεῖον *stoicheíon*; ... Always in the pl., *tá stoicheía*, the basic parts, rudiments, elements, or components of something. Among the ancient Greek philosophers, it designated the four basic and essential elements of which the universe consisted, namely, earth, water, air, and fire. In 2 Pet. 3:10, 12 the word carries this meaning. Figuratively it refers to the elements or first principles of the Christian doctrine (Heb. 5:12). Paul calls the ceremonial ordinances of the Mosaic Law worldly elements (Gal. 4:3; Col. 2:8, 20). In Gal. 4:9 he calls them weak and poor elements when contrasted with the great realities to which they were designed to lead. These elements contain the rudiments of the knowledge of Christ. The Law, as a school–master, was to bring the Jews to this knowledge (Gal. 3:24). Cf also Bauer Arndt and Gingrich, *op. cit.*, pp. 768f.

[18] Bruce, *op. cit.*, p. 194.

adoption as sons. ⁶ *And because **you** are sons, God has sent the Spirit of his Son into our hearts, crying, "Abba! Father!"* ⁷ *So through God you are no longer a slave but a son, and if a son then an heir.*

In keeping with his view that God had ever since Abraham been working his plan of redemption, Paul draws attention to the fact that when God was ready, *when the time had fully come*, he sent his Son in human form, *born of a woman*, and fully Jewish, *born under the law*, to redeem those under the law.

This is not the place to explore the profound significance of the eternal Sonship of Jesus, or the eternal nature of the Trinity. Both are fundamental theological principles of the Christian faith.

But like Paul, for now, we accept them as fundamental theological principles and move on to his discussion of God's scheme of redemption, promised in his covenant with Abraham, and fulfilled in the giving of his son, to explain that this scheme of redemption, triggered by the incarnation of Jesus and his subsequent passion, are *inclusive of both Jew and Gentiles*.

It is interesting that Paul inserts the expression *when the time had fully come* into the incarnational purpose of God, indicating that Jesus' death was not an accident, but was fully within God's purpose.

Longenecker observes that the structure and framing of Gal 4:4-5 is both interesting and complex:

> Structurally, vv 4-5 are complex. They begin with a temporal clause, "when the fullness of time came." Then there appears what many have taken to be a "sending formula," which seems to crop out also elsewhere in Paul and the Johannine writings (cf. Rom 8:3-4; John 3:16-17; 1 John 4:9 and 10): "God sent his Son ... to redeem." ... Within this apparently carefully crafted formulation is a chiastic construction, as J. B. Lightfoot (*Galatians*, 168) long ago noted:
>
> A   God sent his Son,
>   B   born under the law,
>   B´ to redeem those under the law,

A′ that we might receive our full rights as sons.[19]

The idea expressed in the clause "when the fullness of time came"—i.e., that the coming of Christ was fixed in the purpose of God—was common in early Jewish Christianity. It was part of Jesus' consciousness (cf. Mark 1:15; Luke 1:21), appears in the Church's early preaching (cf. Acts 2:16ff.; 3:18), and is particularly prominent in the Gospels of Matthew (cf., e.g., the evangelist's use of πληρόω, "fulfill," at 1:22; 2:15, 17, 23; 3:15; 4:14; 5:17; 8:17; 12:17; 13:35; 21:4; 27:9, ten of these being his distinctive introductory "fulfillment formulae") and John (cf., e.g., the evangelist's seven editorial quotations: 2:17; 12:15, 38, 40; 19:24, 36, 37).[20]

The thought of *God having a plan whose time had fully come* is well in keeping with Paul's claim that God had chosen him before the foundation of the world or his birth, Eph 1:3-11; Gal 1:15.

Gal 4:5. Paul returns to the interesting and challenging interplay of we/you, introduced at Gal 4:3 where it is concluded by several— Bruce, Longenecker, Cole, and others—that the **we/you** referred in Gal 4:3 refers to Jews and Jewish Christians.

Longenecker notes the linguistic difficulty found in Paul's use of the first and second-person use of the pronouns, **we/you** which we find in this pericope, Gal 4:3, 5:

There is, of course, the linguistic problem of the change from the first-person plural "we" (vv 3-5) to the second-person plural "you" (vv 6-7) mentioned earlier (see Comment at vv 3 and 5).[21]

Here in Gal 4:5 Paul introduces an interesting structure with two *hína* clauses we know of as *conditional* or *purpose* clauses; the concept is built off the Greek conjunction ἵνα, *hína, that, so that*.[22] Translated, the two *hína* clauses are in parallel form as

---

[19] Longenecker, *op. cit.*, p.166.
[20] Longenecker, *ibid.*, p. 170.
[21] Longenecker, *ibid.*, p.173.
[22] Zodhiates, *op. cit.*, ἵνα, *hína*, that, so that, for the purpose of ... often with the indicative, marking the end, purpose. Also, used to indicate the cause for,

indicated below. He came in human form, sent by God at a specific point in time, *in order to redeem* those under the Law, and so that we might *receive the adoption of sonship*.

> *(hína) in order to redeem **those** who were under the law* (the Jews)
> *(hína) so that **we** might receive adoption as sons* (the Gentiles).

Bruce adds a brief discussion that helps work through the **us/we**, first-person pronouns, and the **those-you/we** second-person pronouns, which has challenged scholars over the past two centuries.

> Even if Paul begins this section (3-7) by thinking in particular of Jewish Christians (*even we*), who lived more directly (*under law*), it is plain now that the beneficiaries of Christ's redeeming work (as in 3:13f) include gentiles as well as Jews. The oscillation between "we" ... v. 5 ... "you" v. 6... and "thou" v. 7 attests the inclusive emphasis of Paul's wording and argument ...[23]

It appears that Paul is stressing that what **we** (Jewish Christians who had been under the Law) had received, that is redemption and sonship, **you** (the Gentiles) have now also received in parallel fashion and form with the Jewish Christians.

Longenecker draws attention to the parallel nature present in the **we/you** statement of Gal 4:5a and 5b; pointing out that what the Jewish Christians received is in parallel with what the Gentile Christians now receive. For clarity purposes, I have inserted JC, *Jewish Christians,* and GC, *Gentile Christians* in Longenecker's observation;

> ... those under the law" (**we**, JC) of v 5a and "we" (now including the GC) of v 5b are to be seen in parallel fashion ... with the result that what is said about God's activity in these two cases should also be taken as roughly parallel. The statements, then, are probably to be interpreted as complementary facets of what Jewish

---

or on account of which anything is done. Can be translated, "to the end that," "in order that it might [or may] be."

[23] Bruce, *op. cit.*, pp. 196f. For simplicity, I have translated the Greek words cited by Bruce into English. Cf. also Longenecker, *op. cit.*, p. 172.

believers in Jesus had experienced (*which now in Christ the Gentile Christians receive*, IAF): (that is IAF) (1) redemption from both the law's condemnation (cf. 3:13) and the law's supervision (cf. 3:23-25), and (2) reception of a new relationship with God, which involved primarily the enjoyment of full sonship rights.[24]

It is difficult to read and follow the quote from Longenecker, so let me open it up! Paul is arguing that what the Jewish believers had received, that is redemption and adoption without the Law, the Gentile believers had also now received without the Law, that is, redemption and adoption. *In both cases the redemption and adoption were the result of faith in Christ and the presence and working of the Holy Spirit, and not the Law of Moses.*

Gal 4:6. Gentile Christians, now adopted as God's sons, cry by the Spirit "Abba Father."

Paul returns to a point made at Gal 3, both Jew and Gentile Christians have received the Holy Spirit by faith and not the Law. It is this same Holy Spirit who is responsible for their adoption, both Jew and Gentiles in Christ, as sons or children of God. Now in Christ both Jewish and Gentile Christians empowered by the same Holy Spirit cry *Abba Father*!

Longenecker observes that there has been considerable debate over the theological order of sonship and the gift of the Holy Spirit:

> The argument as to whether the proper order is first sonship and then the gift of the Spirit, or first the reception of the Spirit and then sonship ... If, however, we take 4:4-5 to be a confessional portion drawn from the early church that Paul quotes for his own purposes ... with vv 6-7 being Paul's application of that confession for the purposes at hand, much of the perceived awkwardness ... we suggest, is dissipated or at least explainable. Certainly the change from "we" to "you" is understandable on this basis, and probably also the change in soteriological order from (1)

---

[24] Longenecker, *op. cit.*, p.172.

the reception of the Spirit to sonship, as in 3:2-5, 14b and 26, to (2) sonship as the basis for receiving the Spirit, as here in 4:6.

For Paul, it seems, sonship and receiving the Spirit are so intimately related that one can speak of them in either order ... So in 3:2-5 Paul begins ... by reminding his converts of their experiences as recipients of the Spirit in order then to lead them on to the climax of his argument as to their status as "sons of God" (3:26), with the conclusion being that they are therefore "Abraham's seed" and heirs of the promise given to Abraham (3:29).[25]

There is some debate regarding the origin of Paul's use of the Aramaic term *Abba*. Cole observes, appropriately, that it is a mistake to interpret and "over-sentimentalize" *Abba* as "Daddy."[26] In keeping with Cole's comment regarding over-sentimentalizing Abba, Bruce adds that although *Abba* is not used in reference to God in the Old Testament, it was often used in post-biblical Aramaic and Hebrew circles. Bruce argues that Jesus was unique in using *Abba* in reference to God. In doing this Jesus was indicating his *sense of the nearness of the loving God and his implicit trust in him.*[27]

Longenecker observes:

> The content of the cry or acclamation epitomizes the believer's new relationship with God: "Father." The use of both Ἀββᾶ (the Greek transliteration of the Aramaic ... *'abbā*, which is the emphatic form of the Hebrew and Aramaic ... *āb*) and πατήρ ("Father") reflects the bilingual character of the early church. Its retention in Christian thought evidently reflects Jesus' own filial use of the term ... Many have assumed as well that the acclamation "Father" stems from a liturgical use of the invocation "Our Father" in the Lord's Prayer ... That may be so, though probably the relationship ... stemmed primarily from Jesus' own consciousness and usage, with

---

[25] Longenecker, *ibid.*, p. 173.
[26] Cole, *op. cit.*, p. 117.
[27] Bruce, *op. cit.*, p. 199.

the early Christians' remembrance of Jesus' usage giving expression to their new realization of a more intimate relationship with God "in Christ" ... As those "in Christ," believers experience a more intimate and truly filial relationship with God the Father, one that displaces the legal relationship that existed earlier for God's own. Now God's own, as inspired by the Spirit, address God directly as "Father."[28]

As Longenecker has pointed out it is possible that due to the bilingual nature of his readers in both Gal 4:6 and Rom 8:15 that Paul doubled up on "father" in the use of *αββα ὁ πατήρ, abba ho patēr, Abba the Father*, to emphasize the special nature of the Christian's relationship with God, using the Aramaic *Abba* for the Jewish readers, and the Greek *patēr* for the Greek speaking Gentiles.[29]

Paul's use of the nominative/vocative *ho, the*, before pater indicates a vocative use of the noun, *patēr*, as in an invocation, for instance in the Lord's Prayer of Matt 6:9, addressing God as Πάτερ ἡμῶν, *Patēr, humōn, our Father*.

Gal 4:7. Paul closes his thought with the comment *So through God you are no longer a slave but a son, and if a son then an heir.* Since they had received the Holy Spirit and adoption through faith in Christ, and not through the Law they are no longer under the slavery of the Law. They are free! A point to which Paul returns at Gal 5:1, *[1] For freedom Christ has set us free; stand fast therefore, and do not submit again to a yoke of slavery.*

Discussion Questions and Thoughts
1. In your own words, define the role the Law played in God's eternal purpose.
2. What does the word pedagogue mean and how does Paul use it in Gal 3:24?

---

[28] Longenecker, *op. cit.*, p. 174–175.
[29] Cf. also Bruce, *op. cit.*, p. 199

3. What was the power behind the redemption and adoption of the Jewish and Galatian Christians?
4. What might the elemental spirits of Gal 4:3 refer to?

Chapter 9: Gal 4:8-31 – The Danger of the Galatians' Impending Return to Bondage

Paul was acutely aware of the spiritual danger in the direction the Galatians were headed if they continued to accept the false doctrine regarding the Law and circumcision that the Judaizers were teaching the Galatians. If they continued in that direction all of the promises God had made to Abraham for both the Jews and Gentiles would be negated. The spiritual redemption and freedom from sin they had in Christ would be lost to bondage, slavery under the Law which he has strenuously argued against both while present with them, and in the opening chapters of this Galatian letter. Again, he expresses his amazement and frustration over the ease in which they were adopting the false teaching.

The Text

> [8] *Formerly, when you did not know God, you were in bondage to beings that by nature are no gods;* [9] *but now that you have come to know God, or rather to be known by God, how can you turn back again to the weak and beggarly elemental spirits, whose slaves you want to be once more?* [10] *You observe days, and months, and seasons, and years!* [11] *I am afraid I have labored over you in vain.*
>
> [12] *Brethren, I beseech you, become as I am, for I also have become as you are. You did me no wrong;* [13] *you know it was because of a bodily ailment that I preached the gospel to you at first;* [14] *and though my condition was a trial to you, you did not scorn or despise me, but received me as an angel of God, as Christ Jesus.* [15] *What has become of the satisfaction you felt? For I bear you witness that, if possible, you would have plucked out your eyes and given them to me.* [16] *Have I then become your enemy by telling you the truth?* [17] *They make much of you, but for no good purpose; they want to shut you out, that you may make much of them.* [18] *For a good purpose it is always good to be made much of, and not only when I am*

present with you. [19] My little children, with whom I am again in travail until Christ be formed in you! [20] I could wish to be present with you now and to change my tone, for I am perplexed about you.

[21] Tell me, you who desire to be under law, do you not hear the law? [22] For it is written that Abraham had two sons, one by a slave and one by a free woman. [23] But the son of the slave was born according to the flesh, the son of the free woman through promise. [24] Now this is an allegory: these women are two covenants. One is from Mount Sinai, bearing children for slavery; she is Hagar. [25] Now Hagar is Mount Sinai in Arabia; she corresponds to the present Jerusalem, for she is in slavery with her children. [26] But the Jerusalem above is free, and she is our mother. [27] For it is written,

> *"Rejoice, O barren one who does not bear;*
> *break forth and shout, you who are not in travail;*
> *for the children of the desolate one are many more*
> *than the children of her that is married."*

[28] Now we, brethren, like Isaac, are children of promise. [29] But as at that time he who was born according to the flesh persecuted him who was born according to the Spirit, so it is now. [30] But what does the scripture say? "Cast out the slave and her son; for the son of the slave shall not inherit with the son of the free woman." [31] So, brethren, we are not children of the slave but of the free woman.

Gal 4:8-11. Paul stressed no turning back to elemental principles.
[8] Formerly, when you did not know God, you were in bondage to beings that by nature are no gods; [9] but now that you have come to know God, or rather to be known by God, how can you turn back again to the weak and beggarly elemental spirits, whose slaves you want to be once more? [10] You observe days, and months, and seasons, and years! [11] I am afraid I have labored over you in vain.

Paul introduces a technical concept of turning back at vs. 9. Longenecker adds that this refers to a religious *conversion*, in this case a *re-version, apostacy*:

> "How can you turn back?" is a rhetorical question that puts before the Galatian Christians a dilemma: Knowing God the Father in the intimacy established by Christ and the Spirit, how is it possible for them to want any other relationship? The use of πῶς in such questions suggests "how is it possible that" ... The verb ἐπιστρέφω ("turn around," "turn back") is a technical term for either religious conversion (cf. 1 Thess 1:9; also Luke 1:16; Acts 3:19; 9:35; 11:21; 14:15; 15:19; 26:18, 20; passim) or religious apostasy (cf. 2 Peter 2:21-22). Its use here in the present tense indicates that the Galatians' action of apostatizing was then in progress (cf. v 10; also Comment at 1:6 and 5:2-4).[1]

At Gal 4:8, 9 Paul reminds the Galatian Gentiles that there was a time when they did not know God, or more importantly, when God did not know them! To *know God* or to *be known by God* implies a close relationship with God.[2] They were strangers to God! Paul expresses the same point regarding Gentiles at Eph 2:11:

> *Therefore remember that at one time you Gentiles in the flesh, called the uncircumcision by what is called the circumcision, which is made in the flesh by hands—*
> *[12] remember that you were at that time separated from Christ, alienated from the commonwealth of Israel, and strangers to the covenants of promise, having no hope and without God in the world. [13] But now in Christ Jesus you who once were far off have been brought near in the blood of Christ.*

---

[1] Longenecker, *op. cit.*, p. 180.
[2] Cole, *op. cit.*, p. 118; Bruce, *op. cit.*, p. 208; Longenecker notes that to know God in the religious sense is to have and enjoy an intimate experience and relationship with God, *op. cit.*, p. 180.

Again, Paul refers to the elemental spirits which he had introduced at Gal 4:3 where he used the word *stoicheia*,[3] the *beggarly elemental spirits* of both the universe and Judaism, hence in this case the elementary principles of Judaism, the Law. Longenecker observes regarding these *stoicheia* elementary spirits:

> The object of the Galatians' attention had become Torah observance, which Paul here calls "the weak and miserable basic principles"—carrying on the epithet τὰ στοιχεῖα ("basic principles") used for the Mosaic law in v 3 and adding the highly uncomplimentary adjectives ἀσθενῆ ("weak," "powerless," "feeble") and πτωχά ("poor," "beggarly," "miserable," "impotent"). The use of πάλιν ("again," "once more") that appears here and in the appended relative clause points up the fact that Paul lumped the pre-Christian religious experiences of both Jews and Gentiles under the same epithet, that of being τὰ στοιχεῖα or "basic principles." For though qualitatively quite different, both have been superseded by the relationship of being "in Christ."[4]

Paul argues that this is a serious matter, for the Galatians would be returning to slavery, which in any sense in the Roman world of first century CE would be a decided negative. Paul's definition of the elementary principles is a return to holding to the Jewish holy days as a religious observation which for a Gentile would not make sense. He observes that returning to

---

[3] Zodhiates, *op. cit.*, στοιχεῖον *stoicheíon* ... Always in the pl., *tá stoicheía*, the basic parts, rudiments, elements, or components of something. Among the ancient Greek philosophers, it designated the four basic and essential elements of which the universe consisted, namely, earth, water, air, and fire. In 2 Pet. 3:10, 12 the word carries this meaning. Figuratively it refers to the elements or first principles of the Christian doctrine (Heb. 5:12). Paul calls the ceremonial ordinances of the Mosaic Law worldly elements (Gal. 4:3; Col. 2:8, 20). In Gal. 4:9 he calls them weak and poor elements when contrasted with the great realities to which they were designed to lead. These elements contain the rudiments of the knowledge of Christ. The Law, as a school–master, was to bring the Jews to this knowledge (Gal. 3:24).

[4] Longenecker, *op. cit.*, pp. 180–181; Bruce, *op. cit.*, p. 203f for an extensive discussion of *stoicheia*.

such elementary principles would mean that his ministry and preaching to them was all in vain! *You observe days, and months, and seasons, and years!* *¹¹ I am afraid I have labored over you in vain.*

Gal 4:12-20. Paul asks a penetrating question, "Have I become your enemy by telling you the truth?" The text reads:

> *¹² Brethren, I beseech you, become as I am, for I also have become as you are. You did me no wrong; ¹³ you know it was because of a bodily ailment that I preached the gospel to you at first; ¹⁴ and though my condition was a trial to you, you did not scorn or despise me, but received me as an angel of God, as Christ Jesus. ¹⁵ What has become of the satisfaction you felt? For I bear you witness that, if possible, you would have plucked out your eyes and given them to me. ¹⁶ Have I then become your enemy by telling you the truth? ¹⁷ They make much of you, but for no good purpose; they want to shut you out, that you may make much of them. ¹⁸ For a good purpose it is always good to be made much of, and not only when I am present with you. ¹⁹ My little children, with whom I am again in travail until Christ be formed in you! ²⁰ I could wish to be present with you now and to change my tone, for I am perplexed about you.*

Gal 4:12, 13. Paul adopts a new approach, a sentimental personal appeal. *¹² Brethren, I beseech you, become as I am, for I also have become as you are.* We might translate this as "Brethren, follow my example! Although I am a Jew, in Christ I became a 'Gentile' by giving up circumcision and the Law as markers of a relationship with God!"

Paul then referred to an intensely personal situation he experienced in the region of Galatia; a physical "bodily ailment." Defining the real nature of that problem has challenged scholars and commentators for centuries. What was that physical ailment, or was it really a physical ailment? Bruce traces several proposals made by scholars in more recent years, concluding that possibly it might be better to leave the question undefined other than to accept that something occurred to Paul while he was in Galatia that the Galatians freely accepted and through which they treated him kindly.

Longenecker argues clearly for the "illness" being a physical sickness of some undefined form.[5] However, it must have been serious in some way for it could have caused the Galatians to turn against him, which they did not. Their relationship was firm enough that they supported him through his illness. Longenecker suggests that it may have been seen by some as an illness caused by some demon attack, which Paul rejected. Regarding this statement *though my condition was a trial to you, you did not scorn or despise me,* Longenecker further observes:

> Evidently, Paul's illness would have been reason enough for the Galatians to have rejected him when he was first with them. Illness would probably have been interpreted by them as demonic in nature (cf. 2 Cor 12:7, where Paul calls his "thorn in the flesh" an ἄγγελος Εατανᾶ, "messenger of Satan"), and so they could easily have been tempted to dismiss both Paul and his message because of his illness. Thus while the grammar is awkward, perhaps because of the idiomatic nature of what we have in the first part of v 14, a sense translation would be something like: "Though my illness was a temptation for you [to reject me]."[6]

Proposals regarding Paul's illness have ranged from malaria, ophthalmia or some other affliction of the eyes, an evil spell, epilepsy, or the result of the many hardships and beatings Paul had endured at the hands of the Jews during his ministry.[7]

Paul's comment that the Galatians *if possible ... would have plucked out your eyes and given them to me ...* has been interpreted by some as ample evidence for an ophthalmic eye disease, but in view of Paul's tendency to speak metaphorically, even in this pericope, this weakens this argument.

---

[5] Longenecker, *op. cit.*, p. 191.
[6] Longenecker, *ibid.*
[7] Bruce, *op. cit.*, pp 208 ff; Cole, *op. cit.*, pp 122 ff.

Gal 4:14. Angels in Jewish tradition.

Paul observes that the Galatians had been serious when they accepted him and his message as though he were an angel, even as Jesus Christ himself! At Gal 3:19 Paul had alluded to the view held among Jews that angels were divine messengers even in regard to the giving of the Law at Sinai. Longenecker observes regarding Paul's comment, *but, you received me as an <u>angel</u> of God, as Christ Jesus*:

> The adversative ἀλλά ("instead," "rather") sets up a strong contrast between how the Galatians could have received Paul and how they actually did. The particle ὡς ("as," "as if") appears twice to introduce two exaggerated comparisons that compare the Galatians' earlier reception of Paul to the reception they would have given "an angel of God" or even "Christ Jesus" himself. ἄγγελος is commonly used in the NT to mean "messenger" ... Paul, however, usually uses ἀπόστολος for messenger ... with ἄγγελος elsewhere in Galatians and Paul's other writings signifying an extraterrestrial, superhuman being (cf. 1:8; 3:19; also 1 Cor 4:9; 13:1; perhaps 2 Cor 12:7). And that is how it should be taken here ... Yet Paul is not saying here that he believed himself to be either "an angel of God" or "Christ Jesus" himself. The exaggerated comparisons are used to praise the Galatians with regard to their earlier response to Paul and his evangelistic ministry, and not to extol Paul himself.[8]

Gal 4:15-20. Reflecting on how well the Galatians had earlier received and accepted him, one can see why Paul was so astonished and disturbed by how they were now so easily accepting the Judaizers from Jerusalem and their rejection of his message.

> *What has become of the satisfaction you felt? For I bear you witness that, if possible, you would have plucked out your eyes and given them to me.* [16] *Have I then become your enemy by telling you the truth?* [17] *They make much of*

---

[8] Longenecker, *op. cit.*, p. 192.

you, but for no good purpose; they want to shut you out, that you may make much of them. [18] For a good purpose it is always good to be made much of, and not only when I am present with you. [19] My little children, with whom I am again in travail until Christ be formed in you! [20] I could wish to be present with you now and to change my tone, for I am perplexed about you.

Paul suggested a possible reason for the opposition of the Judaizers; they wanted to destroy Paul and his message so that they could become their leaders, *that you may make much of them!*

Gal 4:21-31. Bondage to the Law (Hagar) contrasted with the Freedom (Sarah and Isaac).

Paul drew on a familiar Jewish allegory: Hagar and Sarah! His convoluted and extremely complex analogy is difficult to follow but is interesting because Paul uses a midrashic hermeneutic to demonstrate a hidden message wrapped up in the well-known story of Abraham, Sarah, Hagar, Isaac, and Ishmael. Most Jews and Christians would have been familiar with the narrative of Genesis 16. God had made a promise to Abraham and Sarah, but Sarah was barren, so Sarah gave Hagar, her slave woman to Abraham to bear a child for him. The son, Ishmael, was not the seed or son promised by God based on faith, but the son of the flesh! Hagar and Ishmael were rejected in favor of Sarah and Isaac who bore Israel, the children of the promise.

The text: Gal 4:21-31

[21] Tell me, you who desire to be under law, do you not hear the law? [22] For it is written that Abraham had two sons, one by a slave and one by a free woman. [23] But the son of the slave was born according to the flesh, the son of the free woman through promise. [24] Now this is an allegory: these women are two covenants. One is from Mount Sinai, bearing children for slavery; she is Hagar. [25] Now Hagar is Mount Sinai in Arabia; she corresponds to the present Jerusalem, for she is in slavery with her children. [26] But the Jerusalem above is free, and she is our mother. [27] For it is written,

> *"Rejoice, O barren one who does not bear;
> break forth and shout, you who are not in travail;
> for the children of the desolate one are many more
> than the children of her that is married."*
> ²⁸ *Now we, brethren, like Isaac, are children of promise.*
> ²⁹ *But as at that time he who was born according to the flesh persecuted him who was born according to the Spirit, so it is now.* ³⁰ *But what does the scripture say? "Cast out the slave and her son; for the son of the slave shall not inherit with the son of the free woman."* ³¹ *So, brethren, we are not children of the slave but of the free woman."*

Paul broadens our understanding of the law, referring back to the Abraham narrative as part of the law. We should remember that the Jewish understanding of law was *torah*, instruction, which originally included all of the Pentateuch. If the Galatian readers knew the law they should have understood the promise to Abraham and the Sarah/Hagar and Isaac/Ishmael narrative.

As mentioned above, Paul builds an intricate analogy to the freedom all have in Christ and the slavery the Jews experienced under the Law. He had already explained in the previous chapter that the Law was the custodian intended to control Israel until faith in Christ became a reality. Christ who was born of a woman after the seed of Abraham and Sarah the free woman, had come to redeem those in slavery under the Law and Hagar.

Longenecker suggests an interesting structural frame for Gal 4: 25, 26, forming two halves of a chiasm:

> A Hagar
>   B Mt. Sinai
>   C slavery
>   D the present city of Jerusalem
>   D´ the Jerusalem that is above
>   C´ freedom
>   B´ (Mt. Zion)
> A´ (Sarah) our mother.[9]

---

[9] Longenecker, op. cit., p. 213.

Thus, Paul presents his complicated Sarah/Hagar analogy, framing Sarah as the freedom in Christ and the new Jerusalem which comes from above. This draws on the Jewish eschatological expectation of a new dwelling place with God in heaven. Sarah and Isaac were symbolic of promise and faith and the New Jerusalem. Hagar was symbolic of the present Jerusalem of Law keeping which was characteristic of the slavery of Hagar, Ishmael.

In his citation of Isa 54:1, Longenecker draws on an accepted form of Jewish hermeneutic, that developed by the Jewish sage and teacher, Hillel (ca. 80 BCE – 10CE). Paul would be very familiar with this hermeneutic, having been trained under Gamaliel (1st century CE), a grandson of the great Hillel, and himself one of the prominent sages of Judaism.

> According to the second of the seven middôt or interpretive principles ascribed to Rabbi Hillel, when the same word occurs in two separate passages, then the considerations of the one can be applied to the other (*gĕzêrâ sāwâ*, or interpretation by verbal analogy). Here the fact that Sarah was barren (cf. στεῖρα in Gen 11:30 LXX) allows Paul to connect Sarah with Isa 54:1, which also contains the word "barren" (cf. στεῖρα in Isa 54:1 LXX). Thus the "barren one" is also the city of Jerusalem, who, though barren, is the wife of the Lord (54:5-8) and should rejoice because she will be rebuilt by the Lord (54:11-12; cf. Tob 13:16-18) and because her sons will be taught by the Lord (54:13).[10]

The barren city of Isa 54:1, in the theology of Isaiah, was to be rebuilt by trusting in God's deliverance. It is thus the eschatological city of faith and promise, represented by Sarah, the barren wife of Abraham, but essentially the wife of promise. The other city, the present city of Jerusalem, emblematic of Hagar is thus representative of slavery. The present Jerusalem was to Paul and all Jews the seat of the Law, and thus for Paul the seat of slavery![11]

---

[10] Longenecker, *ibid.*, p. 215.
[11] Cf Bruce, *op. cit.*, pp. 222 ff.

Gal 4:28. Paul expounds on the force of his Sarah/Hagar analogy.

He begins with the expression, *Now we, brethren* ... The word *now*, δέ, *de*, is a conjunction used to present *a logical contrast* to the previous thought, in this case the Hagar story of slavery. In other words, in contrast to the Hagar slavery situation, *we, brethren* are like Isaac, children of promise and the free woman.

> The postpositive particle δέ functions here as a consequential connective ("so"). The personal pronoun ὑμεῖς ("you") is not only well supported externally (see *Note* g) but also required by the thrust of Paul's argument. For against the Judaizers' claim, Gentiles "in Christ"—apart from any Jewish nomistic lifestyle—are true sons and daughters of Abraham's freeborn wife Sarah and true children of the heavenly Jerusalem through God's promise made to Abraham. They are represented by Isaac, not Ishmael. Therefore they are "brothers" with all who come to God by faith through Christ, both Jews and Gentiles (on Paul's use of ἀδελφοί in Galatians for Gentile believers, see Comment at 1:11; also 3:15; 4:12, 31; 5:11, 13; 6:1, 18).[12]

The discussion of the textual variant in Gal 4:28 with the choice of Ὑμεῖς, *humeís, you*, a second-personal plural pronoun referenced by Longenecker above is interesting. Several very good manuscripts have here *hēmeis* in place of *humeís*. The RSV prefers the second-person plural pronoun *hēmeis we*. The ESV prefers the second-person plural pronoun *humeís you*. In the use of *we* Paul might have been including himself along with the Galatians. In the use of *you* he might have been speaking of the Galatians. There is little theological difference in the choice, for both Paul and the Galatians are children of Isaac and promise, not of Ishmael and slavery.

---

[12] Longenecker, *op. cit.*, p. 216.

Gal 4:29. Paul lays down an obvious conclusion; the flesh is opposed to the Spirit!

²⁹ But as at that time (Isaac and Ishmael) *he who was born according to the flesh* (Ishmael) *persecuted him who was born according to the Spirit (Isaac), so it is now*. The flesh (the present Jerusalem and Judaism) was given to persecuting the Spirit (the new Jerusalem from above, the children of promise in Christ).

Gal 4:30. Paul asks; *"what does Scripture say?"* and gives a stern answer. *Cast out the slave and her son* (the Judaizers); *for the son of the slave shall not inherit with the son of the free woman* (those in Christ).

Gal 4:31. The conclusion to the problem!
So, brethren, we (those Christians, Jew and Gentile in Christ) *are not children of the slave but of the free woman.*

This statement of being children of the free woman leads Paul into his discussion of freedom in Christ in chapter 5.

Discussion Questions and Thoughts
1. Where did Paul get his story of Hagar/Sarah and Ishmael/Isaac? What was the context of that original discussion?
2. Who are the children of the promise in Paul's narrative?
3. What was Paul's purpose of presenting this fascinating analogy?

Chapter 10: Gal 5:1-15 – Christian Freedom and the Law

At Gal 3:2 Paul asked the Galatians how they had received the Spirit, "Did you receive the Spirit by works of the law, or by hearing with faith? ³ Are you so foolish? Having begun with the Spirit, are you now ending with the flesh?" His point was that they had enjoyed the presence and miraculous manifestations of the Spirit in their lives, and that they had received the indwelling Spirit through *hearing with faith*, or *believing what they had heard*, that is hearing and believing the gospel of Jesus Christ and his death and resurrection. It was not through hearing and keeping the Law that the Spirit had been poured out and given to them and had empowered them. We remember that Luke recorded in Acts 10 and 11 that it was when Cornelius had with faith heard and obeyed the gospel preached by Peter that Spirit had been poured out on Cornelius and his household. Later, Peter referred the Jewish Christians in Jerusalem to what had occurred, the Holy Spirit had been poured out on Cornelius and his household. He reminded them that in the beginning of the Church in Jerusalem as recorded in Acts 2, the gospel preached by Peter had been heard with faith resulting in the baptism of the Jewish believers and their consequent reception of the Holy Spirit, Acts 2:38.

Paul's point in Gal 3 and 4 was that it was not through believing in the Law of Moses that they had received the indwelling of the Holy Spirit, it was through faithful hearing and obedience to the gospel that they had received the Spirit.

In Gal 5 Paul builds on this foundation and contrasts the flesh, which he associates with the Law whose purpose it had been to point out the sins of the flesh, and the Spirit which he associates with the life of faith lived under Christ. He begins Gal 5:1 with the point that in Christ Christians are freed from the life-threatening Law (cf. 2 Cor 3:6) and are alive in Christ through the Spirit (again, cf. 2 Cor 3:6 where Paul states that it is the Spirit and not the written code that gives life).

So, in Gal 5 Paul builds on the contrast of life lead by the flesh resulting in death (life lived under the Law), and life lived in Christ free from the Law, and led by the Spirit.

The Text

[1] For freedom Christ has set us free; stand fast therefore, and do not submit again to a yoke of slavery.
[2] Now I, Paul, say to you that if you receive circumcision, Christ will be of no advantage to you. [3] I testify again to every man who receives circumcision that he is bound to keep the whole law. [4] You are severed from Christ, you who would be justified by the law; you have fallen away from grace. [5] For through the Spirit, by faith, we wait for the hope of righteousness. [6] For in Christ Jesus neither circumcision nor uncircumcision is of any avail, but faith working through love. [7] You were running well; who hindered you from obeying the truth? [8] This persuasion is not from him who calls you. [9] A little leaven leavens the whole lump. [10] I have confidence in the Lord that you will take no other view than mine; and he who is troubling you will bear his judgment, whoever he is. [11] But if I, brethren, still preach circumcision, why am I still persecuted? In that case, the stumbling block of the cross has been removed. [12] I wish those who unsettle you would mutilate themselves!

[13] For you were called to freedom, brethren; only do not use your freedom as an opportunity for the flesh, but through love be servants of one another. [14] For the whole law is fulfilled in one word, "You shall love your neighbor as yourself." [15] But if you bite and devour one another take heed that you are not consumed by one another.

In Chapter 5 Paul opens what scholars call the parenesis of Galatians, that is the practical exhortation that follows the major doctrinal or theological section of the book, Gal 1-4.

Gal 5:1. Freedom from the Law in the Spirit.

Paul opens the chapter by connecting it with the free woman, Sarah, with the statement that is crucial to his argument: *For freedom Christ has set us free; stand fast therefore, and do not submit again to a yoke of slavery.*

We need to notice here, in context, that Paul is not discussing absolute freedom, but only the freedom from *the yoke of slavery*, namely the Law. It is the freedom associated with the well-known social issue of the day, manumission. Longenecker observes that because of Adolf Deissmann's great work, freedom has been seen as a religious freedom, not simply a social freedom:

> "Since" Deissmann's discovery that τῇ ἐλευθερίᾳ was used in the "sacral manumission procedures" ... to signal destiny or purpose (cf. *Light from the Ancient East*, esp. 326–28), commentators have been more prepared to speak of τῇ ἐλευθερίᾳ here as being a "dative of goal, destiny, or purpose" and so parallel in meaning to ἐπ' ἐλευθερίᾳ of Gal 5:13 ... C. F. D. Moule ... comments: "Gal. 5:1 τῇ ἐλευθερίᾳ ... ἠλευθέρωσεν ... seems to be an *emphatic* use ... understood in this way, Gal 5:1a is a ringing declaration of the indicative (goal or purpose, IAF) of the gospel: "For freedom Christ set us free!"[1]

Paul's comments on freedom in Christ are introduced by the controlling verbal clause of Gal 5:1, *stand fast, therefore*, στήκετε οὖν, στήκετε. Zodhiates observes that *στήκετε, stand,* derives *"from* στήκω, *stēkō,* ...to stand firm in faith and duty, to be constant, to persevere ... meaning steadfast in the faith and profession of Christ ..."[2]

Στήκετε, stand firm furthermore, is a *present active hortatory imperative verb*, obviously *intense* in its exhortation and instruction, and being in the present tense, requiring *constant steadfast standing* firmly in the freedom they enjoy.

Zodhiates observes regarding the dative use of *freedom* as the goal or purpose of the work of the Spirit:

---

[1] Longenecker, *op. cit.*, p. 224.
[2] Zodhiates, *op. cit.*

Freedom is presented as a signal blessing of the economy of grace, which, in contrast with the OT economy, is represented as including independence from religious regulations and legal restrictions (1 Cor. 10:29; 2 Cor. 3:17; Gal. 2:4; 2 Pet. 2:19). Freedom from the yoke of the Mosaic Law (Gal. 5:1, 13); from the yoke of observances in general (1 Pet. 2:16); from the dominion of sinful appetites and passions (James 1:25; 2:12); from a state of calamity and death (Rom. 8:21). In contrast with the present subjection of the creature to the bondage of corruption, freedom represents the future state of the children of God (Rom. 8:20, 21). "The perfect law of liberty" or freedom in James 1:25 is the freedom of generosity, especially in James 2:12 when the Judge shows His generosity in proportion to the mercifulness of the believers on earth.[3]

Considered with the above thoughts in mind, Paul is denoting that the purpose of the gospel of Christ and the work of the Holy Spirit was *to set all Christians, both Jew and Gentile, free from the yoke of slavery.*

We need next to examine the Greek term ζυγός, *zugós* which was used in ancient times in several ways, either literally or figuratively. In the literal sense, it did not have a negative meaning but was used to define the instrument for equaling or balancing two things, as in a balance or scale in which two pans or containers were held in balance by a "beam" the *zugós*, that balanced them. The *zugós* or yoke connecting two oxen helped equalize the burden they had to bear or pull. In this sense *zugós* means balancing or sharing a load.

However, in a figurative or negative connotation a *zugós* or yoke spoke of a burden that had to be born, such as a physical weight or burden, or the burden or weight of slavery.

The following quote from Longenecker, which is almost paralleled by Bruce, discusses the two meanings in which the ζυγός, *zugós yoke* was used.

---

[3] Zodhiates, *op. cit.*

The word ζυγός ("yoke") was current in an honorable sense for Torah study and for various kinds of governmental, social, and family responsibilities, as in *Abot* 3.5: "R. Nehunya ben. HaKanah [*Ca., AD* 70–130] said: 'He who takes upon himself the yoke of the Law, from him shall be taken away the yoke of the kingdom and the yoke of worldly care; but he who throws off the yoke of the Law, upon him shall be laid the yoke of the kingdom and the yoke of worldly care.' Also used in an honorable way are such expressions as "the yoke of the kingdom of heaven" and "the yoke of the commandments" (cf. *m. Ber.* 2.2), "wisdom's yoke" (cf. Sir 51:26), and, of course, Jesus' invitation to "take my yoke upon you and learn from me ... for my yoke is easy and my burden is light" (Matt 11:29–30). But "yoke" was also used figuratively in antiquity for any disagreeable burden that was unwillingly tolerated, like slavery (cf. Sophocles, *Ajax* 944; Herodotus 7.8.3; Plato, *Leg.* 6.770E; Demosthenes 18.289; Gen 27:40 LXX; 1 Tim 6:1). And paralleling Paul's use here in 5:1b is the statement attributed to Peter in Acts 15:10: "Now then, why do you try to test God by putting on the necks of the [Gentile] disciples a yoke that neither we nor our fathers have been able to bear?"[4]

It seems apparent that Paul was using the term *yoke* in a figurative sense implying the *impossible burden of keeping the Law* in a satisfactory manner as implied by Peter in Acts 15:10. *Now therefore why do you make trial of God by putting a yoke upon the neck of the disciples which neither our fathers nor we have been able to bear?* [11] *But we believe that we shall be saved through the grace of the Lord Jesus, just as they will.*

Karl Rengstorf in Kittel's *Theological Dictionary*, in a lengthy article on ζυγός, *zugós*, has the following comments:

> The combination of ζυγός and δουλεία can also describe bondage in the moral and spiritual sense. In Gl. 5:1 Paul warns the Galatians, who have been released by

---

[4] Longenecker, *op. cit.*, pp. 224-225; Bruce *op. cit.*, pp. 226 f.

the Gospel from slavery to the → στοιχεῖα τοῦ κόσμου (cf. 4:8ff.), not to rob themselves of this divinely effected and established freedom by subjecting themselves to the Jewish Law, for in so doing they will again be reduced to the position of the δοῦλος who lives under the ζυγός: μὴ πάλιν ζυγῷ δουλείας ἐνέχεσθε. The essential point is that the νόμος is here on the same level as the στοιχεῖα τοῦ κόσμου. Both rob man of his freedom, and therefore both Jews and Gentiles need Christ, who alone can lead them to freedom, i.e., to a relationship to God which corresponds, not to that of a slave to his master, but to that of a child to its father (→ υἱοθεσία).[5]

There will always be some uncertainty regarding whether Paul meant that the Gentile Galatians had been under the same rudimentary principles of the Law before their conversion to Christianity. At this point in Paul's mind the Gentiles certainly were as pagans under the *stoicheía* or rudimentary spirits *of their pagan world*. Longenecker, citing Rengstorf, handles this dilemma well:

> The use of the word πάλιν ("again") does not mean that before becoming believers in Christ the Galatians had been under the "yoke" of the Jewish law. Rather, in Paul's words, they had been under τὰ στοιχεῖα τοῦ κόσμου ("the basic principles of the world"), which for them meant paganism. Yet in Paul's view, from the perspective of being "in Christ," Judaism and paganism could be lumped together under the rubric "the basic principles of the world" … and so a leaving of Christian principles for either one or the other was a renunciation of freedom and a return "again" to slavery. "The essential point," to quote Karl Rengstorf, "is that the νόμος is here on the same level as the στοιχεῖα τοῦ κόσμου. <u>Both rob man of his freedom</u>" ("ζυγός," *TDNT* 2:899).[6]

---

[5] Karl Heinrich Rengstorf, ζυγός, *zugós*, *Kittel's Theological Dictionary of the New Testament*, vol. 2, p. 899.
[6] Longenecker, *op. cit.*, p. 225.

In Paul's argument, the yoke of slavery referenced in Gal 5:1 is therefore best understood as the unbearable burden of keeping the Law of Moses, or the unsatisfactory and purposeless principles of paganism with their idolatrous ideologies that would form a barrier to hearing the gospel message.

Gal 5:2-6. The misuse of circumcision as a sign of a right relationship with God.

> *Now I, Paul, say to you that if you receive circumcision, Christ will be of no advantage to you. ³ I testify again to every man who receives circumcision that he is bound to keep the whole law. ⁴ You are severed from Christ, you who would be justified by the law; you have fallen away from grace. ⁵ For through the Spirit, by faith, we wait for the hope of righteousness. ⁶ For in Christ Jesus neither circumcision nor uncircumcision is of any avail, but faith working through love.*

Paul again becomes resolutely direct! He gets right to the center of the issue of the Judaizers, circumcision as a marker of righteousness and a right relationship with God. He picks up this theme again at Gal 6:12:

> *It is those who want to make a good showing in the flesh that would compel you to be circumcised, and only in order that they may not be persecuted for the cross of Christ. ¹³ For even those who receive circumcision do not themselves keep the law, but they desire to have you circumcised that they may glory in your flesh. ¹⁴ But far be it from me to glory except in the cross of our Lord Jesus Christ, by which the world has been crucified to me, and I to the world. ¹⁵ For neither circumcision counts for anything, nor uncircumcision, but a new creation.*

Paul argues that circumcision will only sever them from the grace in Christ! Paul's opening statement of Gal 5:2 is direct. He opens with an interjection, a particle of exclamation and calling attention to something he is about to claim. It could be translated "behold, look carefully at, pay attention to" what I am about to say. Our English translations are not as expressive as the Greek. *"Now I,"* does not do justice to Paul's concern! The Greek reads Ἴδε ἐγὼ, *ide egō*, which is better read as *now mark my words! I, Paul, tell you that if you let yourselves be circumcised, Christ will be of no use to you at all.*[7] Circumcision negates Christ! It flies in the face of the Gospel of Christ which they had originally accepted.

Paul returns to a point he had previously stated, "If you would adopt circumcision then you must keep the whole Law, which you obviously have not been able to do!"

His next point is devastating! ... *if you accept circumcision then you are severed from Christ and have fallen away from grace!* Paul reminded them that they had received the Spirit, freedom, and righteousness (a right relationship with God), by grace though faith in Jesus Christ, and not through Law-keeping.

In Christ, neither circumcision nor uncircumcision means anything; all that matters in a right relationship with God is *faith working through love.*

Up to this point Paul has not mentioned the word *love*, ἀγάπη, *agápē*, although it was a major feature in his moral teaching. *Agápē* love is an outward seeking love that seeks the best for others. For those who would argue that since Paul was discarding the Law with its moral implications he argues that it is love working through faith that defines the Christian, not simply a love defined by a legal system. Longenecker cites Burton on this point:

> Paul realizes he needs to emphasize more directly the ethical dynamic inherent in the relationship of being "in Christ Jesus." So as Burton expresses it: "Anticipating the objection that freedom from law leaves the life without moral dynamic, he answers in a brief phrase that faith begets love and through it becomes operative in conduct" (*Galatians*, 280).[8]

Gal 5:7-12. The Galatians had given in to the Judaizers.

[7] You were running well; who hindered you from obeying the truth? [8] This persuasion is not from him who calls you.

---

[7] Longenecker, *ibid.*, p. 225. Zodhiates adds, ἴδε *ide* ... calling attention to what may be seen or heard or mentally apprehended in any way. Lo, behold, observe. A particle of exclamation and calling attention to something.

[8] Longenecker, *op cit.*, pp. 229-230.

> *⁹ A little leaven leavens the whole lump. ¹⁰ I have confidence in the Lord that you will take no other view than mine; and he who is troubling you will bear his judgment, whoever he is. ¹¹ But if I, brethren, still preach circumcision, why am I still persecuted? In that case, the stumbling block of the cross has been removed. ¹² I wish those who unsettle you would mutilate themselves!*

That Paul felt that the Galatians had given up on him and his gospel message should not surprise anyone, for Paul had been indicating this ever since Gal 1:8, 9. In this pericope he warns them that they were in process of giving up on Christ and his atoning death on the cross.

Again, Paul highlights the heart of the problem: circumcision. He had from the beginning of his ministry in Galatia preached faith in the death and resurrection of Christ as the means of a right relationship with God and keeping the Law as two opposing theological alternatives; faith in Christ offering freedom and a right relationship with God, and the futility of Law as a means of providing a right relationship with God. In this text, he identifies the chief locus of contention: *circumcision*. His message stressed that his persecution by the Jews proved that he was preaching against the Law or circumcision as a marker or proof of a right relationship, or righteousness with God. If he were still preaching circumcision then *the stumbling block of the cross for the Jews would have been removed.* For Judaism, the cross had according to the Law been interpreted as a curse, so why preach a curse if the Law of circumcision was still operative. The logic of Paul's argument should have been clear to the Galatians. If they were still holding on to circumcision then they had given up on the cross!

Paul's argument with the Corinthians at 1 Cor 1:17-2:2 emphasizes his stress on preaching the message of the cross over any other doctrine, Christian or otherwise! His point was that the Corinthians were making the argument of who baptized them the center of their identity with God. He obviously was not opposed to baptism, but the Corinthian arguments over who baptized them was not teaching the central feature of the Christian faith, namely, the cross of Christ.

¹⁷ For Christ did not send me to baptize but to preach the gospel, and not with eloquent wisdom, lest the cross of Christ be emptied of its power.

¹⁸ For the word of the cross is folly to those who are perishing, but to us who are being saved it is the power of God. ¹⁹ For it is written,

*"I will destroy the wisdom of the wise,
and the cleverness of the clever I will thwart."*

²⁰ Where is the wise man? Where is the scribe? Where is the debater of this age? Has not God made foolish the wisdom of the world? ²¹ For since, in the wisdom of God, the world did not know God through wisdom, it pleased God through the folly of what we preach to save those who believe. ²² For Jews demand signs and Greeks seek wisdom, ²³ but we preach Christ crucified, a stumbling block to Jews and folly to Gentiles, ²⁴ but to those who are called, both Jews and Greeks, Christ the power of God and the wisdom of God ...
^{2:1} When I came to you, brethren, I did not come proclaiming to you the testimony of God in lofty words or wisdom. ² For I decided to know nothing among you except Jesus Christ and him crucified.[9]

Gal 5:13-15. The limitation of Christian freedom.

¹³ For you were called to freedom, brethren; only do not use your freedom as an opportunity for the flesh, but through love be servants of one another. ¹⁴ For the whole law is fulfilled in one word, "You shall love your neighbor as yourself." ¹⁵ But if you bite and devour one another take heed that you are not consumed by one another.

Too often, people fail to realize that what Paul says about freedom at Gal 5:13 is as important as what he said at Gal 5:1. The major problem is overlooking the context of freedom in Galatians and notably at Gal 5:1. Paul's argument must be seen in the context of the Law as a vehicle for righteousness where Paul has argued that attempting to follow the Law to earn

---

[9] 1 Cor 1:17-2:2.

righteousness leads one only into slavery. The Law was not intended to lead one to righteousness. Its purpose was to retain one under strict control as a pedagogue or custodian (Gal 3:23, 24), and not to bring one to righteousness. Paul stated that the scriptures, obviously referring to the Law, merely consigned on to sin. By that he meant that scripture, or the Law, clarified the nature and consequences of sin, and served only to indict one under sin, and not deliver one from sin. The redemption and forgiveness that can only be obtained by God's grace through faith in Jesus Christ could not be provided by the Law, for that was not the purpose of the Law. Within that context, freedom can only mean freedom from the indictment of the Law. In Christ believers are free from the constraint and condemnation of the Law. In Gal 5:1, Paul was not arguing for an absolute freedom from any other principles; only freedom from the condemnation and requirements of the Law regarding a right relationship with God.

Longenecker expresses the thrust of this pericope well:

> Whereas previously Paul had argued for Christian freedom against Jewish nomism, here he redirects his thought to argue for Christian freedom against supposedly "Christian" self-centered libertinism. For just as freedom in Christ must never become regulated by law, so it must never become an occasion for "the flesh." Rather than laws or license, the realities that characterize Christian freedom are "love," "serving one another," and "the Spirit." In fact, these three emphases of love, serving one another, and the Spirit appear throughout the exhortations of 5:13–6:10 ...[10]

There is considerable discussion as to what Paul meant by the flesh, σάρξ, *sárx, which literally refers to the* flesh of a living creature in distinction from that of a dead one ... meat ...one of the constituent parts of the body.[11] Metaphorically, it is used in Scripture in reference to the human sinful side of man. "It has often been noted that σάρξ used ethically has to do with

---

[10] Longenecker, *ibid.*, p. 236.
[11] Zodhiates, *op. cit.*, σάρξ *sárx*.

humanity's fallen, corrupt, or sinful nature, as distinguished from human nature as originally created by God."[12] Paul encouraged the Galatians in their freedom to not give in to their human nature which is too often motivated by their sinful nature.

However, as Paul stressed at Gal 5:13, freedom does not negate other religious and moral obligations, such as how Christians treat others, whether Christian others or Gentile others! His observation regarding using freedom as an opportunity for fleshly desires, which desires he will discuss at Gal 5:19, is sharpened by his stress on Christians being *servants* to others *out of love*. Implying being a servant certainly sets a limitation on absolute freedom. The word we translate as *servant* here is in Greek "δουλεύω, *douleúō*, derived from δοῦλος *doúlos*, being a servant *under obligation to others or some principle.*"[13] In the sense used by Paul here it speaks of an obligation to love others. Christian service requires an obligation to love others just as God and Christ have loved us.

As Paul had stressed, commitment to Christ carried with it ethical obligations. On that both Paul and the Judaizers agreed. The difference between them, however, was in the manner in which that obligation is to be fulfilled. For the Judaizers, that obligation is to be understood in terms of subjection to the Mosaic law as the expressed will of God, with the prescriptions of Torah giving guidance for ethical living. For Paul, the obligation of the Christian is love that expresses itself in service to others, with that obligation being grounded in and guided by the Christian's new existence in "the Spirit."[14]

Paul explains that the ethical obligation of Christian freedom is balanced by love, or by acting out of love for others. *Love*, from ἀγάπη, *agápē*, is not simply an emotional feeling for others,

---

[12] Longenecker, *op. cit.*, p. 239
[13] Zodhiates, op. cit., δουλεύω *douleúō* ... from *doúlos* δοῦλος *doúlos* ... A slave, one who is in a permanent relation of servitude to another, his will being altogether consumed in the will of the other (Matt. 8:9; 20:27; 24:45, 46). Generally one serving, bound to serve, in bondage ... a slave ... Used in the absolute sense, it means to be deprived of freedom (Gal. 4:25); to be under the law (see Gal. 4:21); serve in bondage ...
[14] Cf. Longenecker, *op. cit.*, p. 241.

although there should always be a sense of emotion in our concern for others. *Agápē*, however, involves an intentional, *rational, clearly thought out attitude of concern for others*. Possibly the best definition of love as it is used by Paul is the example of God who so loved the world that he gave his only Son to die to redeem the lost world (John 3:16).

Because of their freedom in Christ, Christians consciously and intentionally consider others in the exercise of their freedom. Freedom does not negate Christian concern for the faith and spiritual concerns of others. In another context, a few years later Paul addressed such concern for other Christians whose faith may not be as strong as it should be. Romans 14 and 15 are a wonderful pattern of Christian concern for others.

> *As for the man who is weak in faith, welcome him, but not for disputes over opinions. [2] One believes he may eat anything, while the weak man eats only vegetables. [3] Let not him who eats despise him who abstains, and let not him who abstains pass judgment on him who eats; for God has welcomed him. [4] Who are you to pass judgment on the servant of another? It is before his own master that he stands or falls. And he will be upheld, for the Master is able to make him stand ... So do not let your good be spoken of as evil. [17] For the kingdom of God is not food and drink but righteousness and peace and joy in the Holy Spirit; [18] he who thus serves Christ is acceptable to God and approved by men. [19] Let us then pursue what makes for peace and for mutual upbuilding ...* [Rom 15:1]*We who are strong ought to bear with the failings of the weak, and not to please ourselves; [2] let each of us please his neighbor for his good, to edify him. [3] For Christ did not please himself; but, as it is written, "The reproaches of those who reproached thee fell on me." [4] For whatever was written in former days was written for our instruction, that by steadfastness and by the encouragement of the scriptures we might have hope. [5] May the God of steadfastness and encouragement grant you to live in such harmony with one another, in accord*

> with Christ Jesus, *⁶ that together you may with one voice glorify the God and Father of our Lord Jesus Christ.*
> *⁷ Welcome one another, therefore, as Christ has welcomed you, for the glory of God.*

Gal 5:14. Love fulfills the Law.
> *For the whole law is fulfilled in one word, "You shall love your neighbor as yourself."*

Scholars have for centuries addressed this expression of the love fulfilling the Law. The discussion obviously derives from Jesus' discussion of Lev 19:18 with the Sadducees and Pharisees at Matt 22:15ff over the doctrine of the resurrection which the Sadducees rejected and the Pharisees accepted. When the Pharisees saw that Jesus had silenced the Sadducees, one of the Pharisees, a lawyer, a legal expert in the Law of Moses attempted to test Jesus with this question: *"Teacher, which is the great commandment in the law?"*[15] Jesus' answer formed the background to Paul's comment at Gal 5:14;

> *You shall love the Lord your God with all your heart, and with all your soul, and with all your mind. ³⁸ This is the great and first commandment. ³⁹ And a second is like it, You shall love your neighbor as yourself. ⁴⁰ On these two commandments depend all the law and the prophets.*[16]

Careful examination of the ten Commandments of Ex 20 will demonstrate that the first four address reverence and love for God; the final six address love for one another.

Jesus was defining the nucleus of the Law; *loving God and loving your neighbor*! In other words, love is the key to the heart of the ten Commandments and the Law.

That Paul had on several occasions argued that keeping the Law was not a sign of entry into a right relationship with God some scholars find in Gal 5:14 and Paul's commandment a contradiction of thought or inconsistency. However, there is a clear difference in Law keeping as a condition *of entering a right relationship* with God, and keeping the heart of the Law, loving

---

[15] Mat 22:36.
[16] Mat 22:37-40.

God and one's neighbor, *as the result* of being in a right relationship with God.

Longenecker observes:

> So with respect to Paul's statement here, Galatians 5:14 is not itself a command to fulfill the law but a statement that, when one loves one's neighbor, the whole law is fully satisfied in the process ... The focus of Paul's statement in Gal 5:14, as also in Rom 13:8–10, is not on law but on love. So it is love... that motivates the ethical life of a Christian, with the results of that love ethic fulfilling the real purport of the Mosaic law.[17]

Longenecker cites Hans Dieter Betz and Stephen Westerholm in support of this:

> Hans Dieter Betz proposed that one must see Paul in v 14 "carefully distinguishing between the 'doing' and the 'fulfilling' of the Torah—the 'doing' of the Jewish Torah is not required for Christians, but the 'fulfilling' is" (*Galatians*, 275). And Stephen Westerholm has taken up Betz's thesis here, developing it more fully ... Rather, as Westerholm cogently argues (following Betz), Paul in his own mind drew a deliberate distinction between "doing" the Mosaic law (as in 3:10, 12; 5:3; cf. Rom 10:5) and "fulfilling" the Mosaic law (as here; cf. Rom 8:4; 13:8, 10), never saying that Christians "do" the law (ibid., 233–35). As Westerholm points out ... For Paul it is important to say that Christians "fulfill" the whole law, and thus to claim that their conduct ... fully satisfies the "real" purport of the law in its entirety ...[18]

The freedom Christians enjoy by being in Christ through faith in Christ results in balancing that freedom with a genuine love and concern for others. As Longenecker and others have so clearly demonstrated, the difference here is *between getting into a right relationship with "God, which cannot be achieved by keeping the Law, and expressing the freedom Christians have in fulfilling the heart of the law in love for one another."*

---

[17] Longenecker, *op. cit.*, p. 243.
[18] Longenecker, *ibid.* p. 242.

At Gal 6:2 Paul returned to the discussion of love, instruction to the Galatians to *Bear one another's burdens, and so fulfill the law of Christ*. Paul picked up on Jesus' instruction to the Lawyer at Matt 22:39 by speaking here of the Law of Christ. Bruce adds, "Paul is in complete accord with Jesus; the real demand of the Law is love, in which all of the other commandments are summed up."[19]

Gal 5:15. Reflecting on the apparent conflict introduced by the Judaizers from Jerusalem, Paul observed, "But if you bite and devour one another take heed that you are not consumed by one another." Bruce notices that the attitude reflected in this verse suggested the behavior of a pack of wild animals who attack and eat one another!

The cause of this violent attitude of the Galatians reflects more on the nature of the internecine behavior present among the Galatian Christians, possibly aggravated by the Judaizers' false teaching. However, Longenecker and others suggest that this abrasive characteristic may also be a reflection on the cultural character of the Galatians:

> Perhaps their fighting stemmed from differing attitudes toward the Judaizers' activities among them. More likely, however, it was an expression of their own indigenous and loveless libertine attitudes. So in a comment similar to that of 5:12 Paul here sarcastically denounces the libertine tendencies present among his Galatian converts just as he earlier castigated the Judaizers in their midst.[20]

Discussion Questions and Thoughts
1. Why did Paul feel it essential to enlarge on his discussion of freedom from the Law?
2. Freedom from the Law was a more theological point; what was the nature of his discussion on freedom in Gal 5:12-15?

---

[19] Bruce, *ibid.*, p. 242.
[20] Longenecker, *op. cit.*, p. 244.

3. Discuss the concept of love being the fulfillment of the Law.
4. How does Paul's rejection of the Law in earlier discussions in Galatians balance with his discussion of love in this pericope?

Chapter 11: Gal 5:16-26 – Responsible Freedom in Practice

Paul had argued that the freedom Christians enjoy in Christ is the result of Jesus' death and resurrection (the gospel) and the working of the Holy Spirit. Law-keeping had no part in the freedom Christ offered, faith in Christ was the only emancipating power in the freedom in Christ. Paul had also stressed at Gal 5:1-15 that Christian freedom was not an absolute freedom but one in which love for others was a guiding and controlling dynamic.

In this pericope, Gal 5:16-26, Paul argues that Christian freedom must also be an expression of a Spirit filled life in which the Christian is led by the influence and guidance of the indwelling Holy Spirit. We will learn in this pericope that the indwelling Holy Spirit coalesces with the indwelling word of Christ to guide and strengthen the faith and practice of Christians.

At Colossians 3:1-17, in a passage almost parallel to Gal 5:16ff, Paul reminded the Colossian Christians who had died with Christ in baptism and been raised with Christ, that love, the peace of Christ, and the word of Christ work in harmony to clothe Christians with the fruits of the Spirit:

> *¹If then you have been raised with Christ, seek the things that are above, where Christ is, seated at the right hand of God. ² Set your minds on things that are above, not on things that are on earth. ³ For you have died, and your life is hid with Christ in God. ⁴ When Christ who is our life appears, then you also will appear with him in glory.*
>
> *⁵ Put to death therefore what is earthly in you: fornication, impurity, passion, evil desire, and covetousness, which is idolatry. ⁶ On account of these the wrath of God is coming. ⁷ In these you once walked, when you lived in them. ⁸ But now put them all away: anger, wrath, malice, slander, and foul talk from your mouth. ⁹ Do not lie to one another, seeing that you have put off the old nature with its practices ¹⁰ and have put on the new nature, which is being renewed in knowledge after the image of its creator. ¹¹ Here there cannot be Greek*

> *and Jew, circumcised and uncircumcised, barbarian, Scythian, slave, free man, but Christ is all, and in all.*
> *[12] Put on then, as God's chosen ones, holy and beloved, compassion, kindness, lowliness, meekness, and patience, [13] forbearing one another and, if one has a complaint against another, forgiving each other; as the Lord has forgiven you, so you also must forgive. [14] And above all these put on love, which binds everything together in perfect harmony. [15] And let the peace of Christ rule in your hearts, to which indeed you were called in the one body. And be thankful. [16] Let the word of Christ dwell in you richly, teach and admonish one another in all wisdom, and sing psalms and hymns and spiritual songs with thankfulness in your hearts to God. [17] And whatever you do, in word or deed, do everything in the name of the Lord Jesus, giving thanks to God the Father through him.*

We should note that the contexts of Galatians and Colossians are somewhat different, but the dynamic working in each is similar and complementary. In Galatians, it is the indwelling Holy Spirit that provides the works of the Spirit, but in Colossians it is the indwelling peace and word of Christ that enables Christians to be Christ-like, and therefore manifest the same works of the Spirit as delineated in Gal 5:16ff.

Notice at 2 Thess 2:13-15, the same combination of Holy Spirit, the truth, the gospel, and the "taught Apostolic word" work together to save and sanctify the Christian:

> *But we are bound to give thanks to God always for you, brethren beloved by the Lord, because God chose you from the beginning to be saved, through sanctification by the Spirit and belief in the truth. [14] To this he called you through our gospel, so that you may obtain the glory of our Lord Jesus Christ. [15] So then, brethren, stand firm and hold to the traditions which you were taught by us, either by word of mouth or by letter.*

The Text: Gal 5:16-26

> *But I say, walk by the Spirit, and do not gratify the desires of the flesh. [17] For the desires of the flesh are against the Spirit, and the desires of the Spirit are against*

the flesh; for these are opposed to each other, to prevent you from doing what you would. [18] *But if you are led by the Spirit you are not under the law.* [19] *Now the works of the flesh are plain: fornication, impurity, licentiousness,* [20] *idolatry, sorcery, enmity, strife, jealousy, anger, selfishness, dissension, party spirit,* [21] *envy, drunkenness, carousing, and the like. I warn you, as I warned you before, that those who do such things shall not inherit the kingdom of God.* [22] *But the fruit of the Spirit is love, joy, peace, patience, kindness, goodness, faithfulness,* [23] *gentleness, self-control; against such there is no law.* [24] *And those who belong to Christ Jesus have crucified the flesh with its passions and desires.*

[25] *If we live by the Spirit, let us also walk by the Spirit.* [26] *Let us have no self-conceit, no provoking of one another, no envy of one another.*

Paul's contrasting of virtues and vice listed here may reflect Platonic, Hellenistic, and Jewish traditions. Longenecker proposes that although there would be clear Hellenistic concerns manifest in Paul's listing, the Jewish "Two Way" tradition probably weighed heavily on Paul's thinking:

> It seems beyond dispute that the catalogue form of virtues and vices had its origin in Greek ethical teaching. Of late, however, while acknowledging the Hellenistic provenance of the catalogue genre, it has been argued that a closer parallel to Gal 5:16-23 is to be found in the "Two Ways" tradition that was taken over by the early Christians from a thoroughly Jewish model ... The "Two Ways" tradition combined with catalogues of virtues and vices is represented at Qumran by 1QS 3.25-4.11, where, in the context of a discussion of "the spirits of truth and of perversity" set by God within every man, there are lists of virtues and vices associated with the activities of these two spirits—though, it need also be noted, there are other lists of virtues and vices in 1QS that are not in a "Two Ways" or "two spirits" context ... And the theme of "Two Ways" was explicitly developed in such second-century Christian writings as *Did.* 1-5, *Barn.* 18-20, and *Hermas*

Mandates 6.2.1-7. All of this, it has been proposed, suggests that while catalogues of virtues and vices were common in the Hellenistic world, Gal 5:19-23 is probably more accurately to be seen against the background of a Jewish "Two Ways" ethical tradition that was taken over by the early Christians.[1]

Some, (Lightfoot, *Galatians*, p. 210, and Burton, *Galatians*, p. 304) have suggested a four-fold category in the listing which does make sense:
(1) three sins of sensuality (i.e., sexual immorality, impurity, debauchery);
(2) two associated with heathen religions (i.e., idolatry and witchcraft);
(3) eight having to do with conflict among people (i.e., hatred, discord, jealousy, fits of rage, selfish ambition, dissensions, factions, envy); and
(4) two that have to do with drunkenness and its natural consequences (i.e., drunkenness and orgies).[2]

Gal 5:16. *But I say, walk by the Spirit, and do not gratify the desires of the flesh.*

This pericope with vs. 25 forms an *inclusio* focusing on the contrast of a life lived in the Spirit and the life lived in the flesh!

The thought is introduced by the Greek expression Λέγω δέ, *lego de*, with de, a logical contrasting conjunction emphasizing the word, *lego, I say*. In contrast to *biting* and *devouring* one another, which he had stressed would be the result of the Judaizers' emphasis on circumcision according to the Law, Paul stresses the desired action of a life lived in the Spirit. The sayings formula, λέγω δέ ("so I say"), connects Paul's emphasis on the life to be lived in the Spirit rather than in the Law. As a literary convention, it contrasts a life lived in love and in the spirit with the life lived under the Law and the flesh.[3]

We might translate Paul's argument in Gal 5:16 as *So in contrast to a life lived in dispute, devouring one another, let me*

---

[1] Longenecker, *ibid.*, p. 251.
[2] Longenecker, *ibid.*, p. 253.
[3] Longenecker, *ibid.*, p. 244

give you a better way of living; live in love with one another guided by the works of the spirit which are ...

Gal 5:17. *For the desires of the flesh are against the Spirit, and the desires of the Spirit are against the flesh; for these are opposed to each other, to prevent you from doing what you would.* Again, Paul accentuates the point that the life in the Spirit is opposed to, or against, the life of the flesh. His repetition of this thought in such close proximity mirrors his close repetition at Gal 1:8, 9 of the dangers of those teaching a different gospel; they will be accursed. He wanted the Galatians to understand the seriousness of his point! Paul later in his epistle to the Romans explains how in our fleshly mindset we struggle to do what we know is good, that is, live by the Spirit. This reflects our human nature. But by living in and with the Spirit we have the power to resist the works of the flesh.

Gal 5:18. *But if you are led by the Spirit you are not under the law.*

Again, Paul introduces his next point with the logical contrast conjunction, δέ *dé, but.* In contrast to those who might struggle with the works of the flesh, Paul stresses that those who are led by the Spirit are not under the Law or controlled by the Law. They are controlled or empowered by the indwelling Spirit. Again, Paul resorts to a first-class conditional clause εἰ ... ἄγεσθε, *ei ... agesthe, since you are being led by the Spirit.* He uses the continuous present tense to emphasize the *continuing action of being led by the Spirit.* Since they are constantly being led by the Spirit they are not under the condemnation of the flesh and the Law.

Gal 5:19-21. Paul describes the works or life of the flesh.
> *Now the works of the flesh are plain: fornication, impurity, licentiousness, [20] idolatry, sorcery, enmity, strife, jealousy, anger, selfishness, dissension, party spirit, [21] envy, drunkenness, carousing, and the like. I warn you, as I warned you before, that those who do such things shall not inherit the kingdom of God.*

The overriding thought of these verses is that should the Galatians be caught up in these works, they would not inherit the kingdom of God or the promises to Abraham. They would end up without God and any hope. Cf. Eph 2:11ff:

> *Therefore remember that at one time you Gentiles in the flesh, called the uncircumcision by what is called the circumcision, which is made in the flesh by hands—*
> *[12] remember that you were at that time separated from Christ, alienated from the commonwealth of Israel, and strangers to the covenants of promise, having no hope and without God in the world.*

The following listing of vices defines or enlarges on each of these works of the flesh. Most of them would easily be recognized as common in the Gentile lifestyle, but even the moderate Jew would recognize these as having been found in the Jewish community:[4]

> **Fornication** – πορνεία, *porneía*, to commit fornication or any sexual sin. Fornication, lewdness, or any sexual sin.
> **Impurity** - ἀκαθαρσία, *akatharsía*; unclean or filth in a natural or physical sense ... moral uncleanness, lewdness, incontinence in general.
> **Licentiousness** - ἀσέλγεια, *asélgeia* ... licentious, brutal, lasciviousness, license, debauchery, sexual excess, absence of restraint, insatiable desire for pleasure.
> **Idolatry** - εἰδωλολατρία, *eidōlolatria*, the worship or reverence of idols, that which characterizes the heathen.
> **Sorcery** – φαρμακεία, *pharmakeía* ... derived from *phármakon*, a drug which in the Greek writers was used both for a curative or medicinal drug, and also as a poisonous one. *Pharmakeía* means the occult, sorcery, witchcraft, illicit pharmaceuticals, trance, magical incantation with drugs.
> **Enmity** - ἔχθρα, *échthra* .... noun from *echthrós* ... enemy, thus enmity, hatred, hostility.
> **Strife** - ἔρις, *éris*; ... Strife, contention, wrangling ... Metaphorically, it means love of strife.

---

[4] For word definitions cf. Zodhiates, *op. cit.*, and Kittel, *op. cit.*

Jealousy - ζῆλος, *zélos* from *zéō* ... to be hot, fervent. Zeal, used in a good sense ... and more often in an evil sense, meaning envy, jealousy, anger ... fiery wrath.
Anger – θυμός, *thumós* ... to move impetuously ... a violent motion or passion of the mind, anger, wrath, indignation.
Selfishness - ἐριθεία, *eritheía*; ... used in a bad sense of those who seek only their own. Contention, strife, rivalry. It represents a motive of self–interest, mercenary interest ... It also meant canvassing for public office, scheming.
Dissension – διχοστασία, *dichostasía*; ... separately ... dissension... a separate faction, division, separation.
Party spirit - αἵρεσις, *haíresis*; ... to choose, select, heresy, a form of religious worship, discipline, or opinion with a negative connotation. Envy – φθόνος, *phthónos*; ... envy, jealousy, pain felt and malignity conceived at the sight of excellence or happiness ... bursts of envy ... is incapable of good and always is used with an evil meaning.
Drunkenness – μέθη, *méthē* ... drunkenness.
Carousing - κῶμος, *kōmos* ... feasting used in the plural. In the NT such feasting and carousing results in riotous conduct ... festivities in honor of several gods, especially Bacchus, the god of wine, hence feastings and drunkenness with impurity and obscenity of the grossest kind. Therefore, it always presupposes a festive company and drunken revelers.
And like things.

Gal 5:21b. Paul repeats his warnings of judgment.

> *I warn you, as I warned you before, that those who do such things shall not inherit the kingdom of God.*

Paul sums up the list of vices with a stern warning. The phrase καθὼς προεῖπον, "even as I warned you before," points back to what Paul had previously told his converts either in the immediate context of his letter (possibly, Gal 1:90) or in his moral teaching before and following their baptism. The purpose being that they might realize the seriousness of allowing their freedom in Christ to degenerate into "an opportunity for the flesh" (cf. 5:13b) which would have serious consequences.

Gal 5:22, 23. The fruits of the Spirit.

²² But the fruit of the Spirit is love, joy, peace, patience, kindness, goodness, faithfulness, ²³ gentleness, self-control; against such there is no law.

It is informative to recognize that Paul speaks of the *works* of the flesh but the *fruits* of the Spirit! It is obvious that Paul intentionally set the *works* of the flesh in contrast to the fruit of the Spirit. At least four reasons have been proposed by scholars to explain this, but it may be that Paul saw the works of the flesh as those works which had a human or fleshly origin or motivation, but in contrast he saw the fruits of the Spirit as being found in the spiritual side of man motivated and empowered by the Holy Spirit.

His choice of the adversative or contrastive particle conjunction δέ, *de, now, but, in contrast to* ... certainly highlights the difference between the impelling influence of the works of the flesh and the fruits of the Spirit. In keeping with his teaching that love should be the controlling influence in the Christian's exercise of freedom, he introduces his list of Christian virtues with love.[5]

> ***Love*** - ἀγάπη, *agápē*, outward directed concern and love for others.
> ***Joy*** – χαρά, *chará*; ... to rejoice, joy, rejoicing, gladness.
> ***Peace*** - εἰρήνη, *eirḗnē*... Particularly in a single sense, the opposite of war and dissension ... Among individuals, peace, harmony ... Metaphorically peace of mind, tranquility, arising from reconciliation with God and a sense of a divine favor ...
> ***Patience*** – μακροθυμία, *makrothumía*; ... to be long–suffering, forbearing, self–restraint before proceeding to action. The quality of a person who is able to avenge himself yet refrains from doing so.

---

[5] Zodhiates, *ibid.*, Kittel, *ibid.*

Kindness – χρηστότης, *chrēstótēs* ... useful, profitable, kind, useful. It often occurs with philanthropy... forbearance ... and is the opposite of ... severity or cutting something too short and quickly.
Goodness - ἀγαθωσύνη, *agathōsúnē* ... benevolent active goodness ... virtuous ... gentleness, kindness, of a mellowing of character. It is character or energized by active good.
Faithfulness – πίστις, *pístis* ... to be persuaded ... trusted, faithful ... meaning firm persuasion, conviction, belief in the truth, veracity, reality or faithfulness ...
Gentleness – πραΰτης, *praútēs*; ... meek, gentle ... in one's relations to one's fellow man ... it is an inwrought grace of the soul.
Self-control - ἐγκράτεια, *egkráteia*...temperate, self–controlled, sober clear thinking, not self-indulgent.

Gal 23b, 24. There is no law that controls or produces Christian virtues. They are the product of the Spirit.

Bringing his list of vices and virtues to conclusion Paul adds *against such there is no law.* [24] *And those who belong to Christ Jesus have crucified the flesh with its passions and desires.*

Once more Paul alludes to the transformation that takes place in faith in Christ and baptism (Rom 6:1-11; Col 2:11-13).

Gal 5:25, 26. Living in the Spirit.

... If we live by the Spirit, let us also walk by the Spirit. [26] *Let us have no self-conceit, no provoking of one another, no envy of one another.*

The strength of a first-class conditional sentence, introduced by Εἰ ζῶμεν, *Ei zōmen*, strengthens Paul's point. The Greek expression *"ei zōmen"* is emphatic and is better understood as *since we live* by the Spirit we should walk by the Spirit. The Greek verb I have translated here as we should is a present subjunctive verb explaining how Christians led by the Spirit should walk. The apodosis statement Greek πνεύματι καὶ στοιχῶμεν, *pneumatic kai stoichōmen* following the protasis,[6] *since* (the first part of a clause) is better translated as *"in the spirit indeed we should walk,"* or *indeed we should keep in step* with the leadership of the Spirit.

Longenecker has commented meaningfully on Paul's significant statement at Gal 5:25 as follows:

> The apodosis of the statement, "let us keep in step with the Spirit," lays emphasis on the obligation of Christian living as being neither to legal prescriptions (nomism) nor to the dictates of the flesh (libertinism) but to the Spirit, who both directs and enables and who is fully sufficient both for bringing to birth a believer's new life "in Christ" and for effecting a truly Christian lifestyle. The verb στοιχέω has as its basic meaning the idea of "stand in a row" ... and so came to connote "be in line with" or "agree with." Its use elsewhere by Paul, however, suggests "walking in the footsteps" of another (cf. Rom 4:12) or "living in accordance with a standard" (cf. Gal 6:16; Phil 3:16; also Acts 21:24). So here by exhorting his converts to "be in line" or "keep in step" with the Spirit, Paul is asking those who claim to live by the Spirit to evidence that fact by a lifestyle controlled by the Spirit. That he exhorts believers to do what it is the work of the Spirit to produce (cf. vv 22–23) is typical of Paul's understanding of Christian ethics, for Paul never views the ethical activity of the believer apart from the Spirit's work nor the Spirit's ethical direction and enablement apart from the believer's active expression of his or her faith.[7]

Paul concludes this magnificent pericope on life in the Spirit with the strong moral point, relevant to the Galatian context of disagreement and conflict, *"Let us have no self-conceit, no*

---

[6] Protasis and apodosis are terms used in conditional clauses. The protasis is the statement expressing or introducing the condition in a conditional sentence (e.g., *if* you asked me I *would* agree). Often the protasis is contrasted with an apodosis, the main (consequent) clause of a conditional sentence. Cf. Oxford English Dictionary.

[7] Longenecker, *ibid*, pp. 265-266.

provoking of one another, no envy of one another." We could translate that meaningfully as *out of our love for one another we should have no self-conceit and no provoking of one another ...*

Discussion Questions and Thoughts
1. What is the central thrust of Gal 5:16-24?
2. How is Christian freedom controlled; by Law or some other force or influence?
3. What should the impelling influence be in Christian freedom?
4. What should the guiding influence be in the Christian walk?
5. Against what is there no law?

Chapter 12: Gal 6:1-10 – Exhortations and Warnings

Paul had in the previous chapter described the difference between living in the flesh and living in the Spirit. He had listed a number of vices and virtues, warning against, and defining the consequences of a life lived according to the flesh. In chapter 6 he picks up on the closing thoughts of chapter 5 in which he had encouraged the Christians in Galatia to be led and to walk in step with the spirit, both their own spirit and their spirit guided by the indwelling Holy Spirit.

We should notice again how he begins this pericope, *Brethren...* never forgetting that the Galatian Christians, Jewish and Gentile, were brothers and sisters in Christ and in the family of God.

The Text

> *Brethren, if a man is overtaken in any trespass, you who are spiritual should restore him in a spirit of gentleness. Look to yourself, lest you too be tempted. ² Bear one another's burdens, and so fulfil the law of Christ. ³ For if any one thinks he is something, when he is nothing, he deceives himself. ⁴ But let each one test his own work, and then his reason to boast will be in himself alone and not in his neighbor. ⁵ For each man will have to bear his own load.*
>
> *⁶ Let him who is taught the word share all good things with him who teaches.*
>
> *⁷ Do not be deceived; God is not mocked, for whatever a man sows, that he will also reap. ⁸ For he who sows to his own flesh will from the flesh reap corruption; but he who sows to the Spirit will from the Spirit reap eternal life. ⁹ And let us not grow weary in well-doing, for in due season we shall reap, if we do not lose heart. ¹⁰ So then, as we have opportunity, let us do good to all men, and especially to those who are of the household of faith.*

Gal 6:1. Brotherly love extended to one another.

> *Brethren, if a man is overtaken in any trespass, you who are spiritual should restore him in a spirit of gentleness. Look to yourself, lest you too be tempted.*

The vocative "Brethren" is interesting for a couple of reasons! *First*, Paul was reminding the Galatians that together in Christ they were all Children and "sons of God" according to the promise to *Abraham, Gal 3:25, 26; But now that faith has come, we are no longer under a custodian; ^{26} for in Christ Jesus you are all sons of God, through faith.* I am reminded of a fine theological and ecclesiological study by Dr. J. D. Thomas, *"We Be Brethren,"* Abilene: Biblical Research Press, 1958. It was written at a time when Churches of Christ were struggling to determine their identity with a tendency to divide repeatedly over doctrinal disputes. Thomas, in line with the Apostle Paul, wrote to remind Christians that unnecessary doctrinal divisions tended only to negate the gospel of Christ whose intention it was to unite Christians in Christ, and not divide into sectarian groups.

Second, the vocative case of "Brethren" at the opening of the pericope was intended to get the reader's attention regarding the seriousness of the situation in the Galatian churches.

Third, that Paul uses the term 11 times in 6 chapters, that is once in every 13.5 verses, serves as a corrective to their tendency to divide over religious and ethnic lines, and remind them of their divinely intended unity in Christ.

Paul's deliberate statement regarding *any trespass*, *"if a man is overtaken in any trespass,"* stresses the point that repentance and forgiveness, rooted in faith in Christ and fellowship with God and Christ, must be a primary ingredient to any form of unity and church effectiveness in spreading the gospel of Christ to all nations. Christians participate in the process of repentance, forgiveness, and reconciliation with God through their love and concern for one another. For some, a Christian spirit of love and forgiveness is fundamental to encouraging one another to avail themselves of God's grace.

Note Paul's closing point in this thought, *you who are spiritual should restore him in a spirit of gentleness.* Paul's use of the expression, *"you who are spiritual"* is meaningful, connecting those who are spiritual with those who are led by, and follow the Spirit, Gal 5:16-24, emphasizing love, gentleness, kindness, goodness, and self-control!

Although Jews living under the Law and its system of annual atonement enjoyed cleansing from the defilement of sin, this was based on the annual atonement sacrifice and personal repentance. This could not be compared with the *constant* blessing of the unbroken atonement in Christ and living in the Spirit. Paul called on those who were spiritual to ensure that this ever-present blessing was a daily experience for those in Christ, even those who were *overtaken in any trespass*. Encouraging, mentoring, and restoring those who were weak and had fallen, who had trespassed into the world of the flesh and sin, was a sign of being led by the spirit, in other words, of those who were spiritual.

The word *trespass*, παράπτωμα, *paráptōma*; refers to those who fall by the wayside, who are at fault, who lapse, are in error, who make a mistake, who are caught up in wrongdoing.[1] Interesting, the Greek word *paráptōma* for *trespass* is set in parallel to *walking by the Spirit*! To trespass is going in a different direction, or in the opposite direction, to walking in the Spirit, or in the Johannine expression, *walking in the light*, cf. 1 John 1:7 below.

True brethren, those led by the Spirit, are those who serve in the "priestly" role of restoring the imprudent in a spirit of gentleness and love. It may be best in context of Galatians to see in those who trespass the image or spirit of the Judaizers, and in the *true brethren* those who are encouraged to bear the burdens of others, those who are led by the Spirit.

The Apostle John in his Epistle to the Christians in Asia wrote many years later, stressing the point that *those who walk in the light* are the ones who *have fellowship with one another and with Christ*. John's application of Paul's term of *walking in the Spirit* and *in faith with God and Christ*, as "*walking in the light.*" In the spiritual blessing of *fellowship* with one another and with God, Christians are *constantly* cleansed *from every sin*.

---

[1] Zodhiates, *op. cit.*

> *This is the message we have heard from him and proclaim to you, that God is light and in him is no darkness at all. ⁶ If we say we have fellowship with him while we walk in darkness, we lie and do not live according to the truth; ⁷ but if we walk in the light, as he is in the light, we have fellowship with one another, and the blood of Jesus his Son cleanses us from all sin.*[2]

Paul's admonition to the Galatians was that those in the Spirit who were walking in the light should be sensitive to those who are overtaken in *any* trespass, or who have fallen aside, and should minister to them in love and gentleness, assisting them to overcome their weakness and lapse from the truth of the gospel, in their error, and mistaken ways.

However, they *should look to themselves*, to their own faithfulness, *lest they too be tempted* by the wiles of the Judaizers and compromise their commitment to the truth of the gospel.

Gal 6:2. In a spirit of true fellowship Christians should *"Bear one another's burdens, and so fulfil the law of Christ."* The concept of *burdens* here raises several possibilities! Zodhiates observes that the Greek for *burdens* is:

> βάρος, *báros*; a burdensome weight in reference to pressure, a burden, a load ... it could be used to designate precepts which are burdensome to observe; to indicate sinful conduct and its consequences resulting in trouble and sorrow.[3]

The context here in Galatians seems to refer to the weight of the challenging arguments imposed by the Judaizers which might seem rational since they are seemingly based in the religious Law, so as such bear a serious responsibility. The challenge of the Judaizers must have placed a burden on the young churches established by Paul. "How do we stay faithful to God in the face of serious opposition from Jerusalem?" Paul warns that the task of working through these challenges was serious, even a burden! The Galatian Christians must stand firm and faithful to the

---

[2] 1 John 1:5-7.
[3] Zodhiates, *ibid*.

gospel, for the consequences of departing from the truth of the gospel were serious. Obviously, several, and from the need to write an Epistle to the churches, possibly even many, were having to make weighty decisions, both spiritual and regarding fellowship.

It was evident that their predicament must involve love, the law of Christ or Christian fellowship, *so fulfilling the law of Christ*.

Longenecker, Barnes, Cole[4], and others observe, in the words of Cole, that this discussion is *arresting*! For convenience, I have included part of Longenecker's discussion which reflects Bruce's views:

> Central to the believers' new existence "in Christ" is the concept of mutuality. Such a concept is highlighted here in v 2 by the emphatic position of ἀλλήλων ("one another") at the beginning of the sentence. The noun βάρος means literally "weight," but is used in the NT figuratively for an "oppressive burden" ... Here τὰ βάρη has primary reference to "the burdens of temptation" spoken of in v 1, though probably also has in mind more generally oppressive ... burdens of any kind (cf. Rom 15:1 and 1 Cor 12:26, though without the noun βάρος). It is doubtful, however, that Paul is using βάρος with any idea of "financial support for Jerusalem," as some have posited ...
>
> To understand what Paul meant by "the law of Christ" here, much depends on how we understand the purpose and focus of 5:13–6:10. For if we view 5:13–6:10 as a continuation of Paul's arguments and exhortations against the Judaizing threat, then "the law of Christ" must have relevance to what the Judaizers were proposing. One can then, in fact, wonder why this expression does not appear earlier in the Galatian letter. Likewise, if we take 5:13–6:10 to reflect the polemics of Paul's antinomistic stance, then νόμος here may very well be used in

---

[4] Longenecker, *op. cit.*, pp. 274ff; Bruce, *op. cit.*, pp. 260ff; Cole *op. cit.*, p. 172.

contradistinction to the Judaizers' usage. If, however, 5:13–6:10 be seen more in terms of the libertine issues that were also present in the churches of Galatia, then "the law of Christ" may be taken as an expression stemming from Paul's own ethical vocabulary that is used here to check libertine tendencies among his Galatian converts.

Taking this latter approach, and abbreviating a lengthy discussion quite considerably, I propose that ὁ νόμος τοῦ Χριστοῦ here … stands in Paul's thought for those "prescriptive principles stemming from the heart of the gospel (usually embodied in the example and teachings of … Jesus), which are meant to be applied to specific situations by the direction and enablement of the Holy Spirit, being always motivated and conditioned by love" … Paul is not setting forth Jesus as a new Moses. Nor does he view Jesus' teachings as ethical prescriptions to be carried out in rabbinic fashion. Nonetheless, just as the designation of his readers as οἱ πνευματικοί ("who are spiritual") probably reflects Paul's own understanding of his converts' status "in Christ" and is not used either ironically or polemically … so ὁ νόμος τοῦ Χριστοῦ should probably be seen as expressing an important feature of Paul's own ethical understanding and not taken in an ad hominem or polemical fashion. The expression does not appear earlier in Paul's antinomistic arguments or exhortations, evidently because it did not arise from or have direct relevance to those concerns. Here in countering his converts' libertine tendencies, however, it highlights what Paul sees to be an appropriate check to such tendencies. For when there is mutual concern among believers to "bear one another's oppressive burdens"—which, of course, is the exact opposite of libertine attitudes based on a desire to live solely for one's own self—the whole intent of Jesus' example and teaching comes to fulfillment within the church.[5]

---

[5] Longenecker, *op. cit.*, pp. 274–276.

Gal 6:3. This temptation to compromise and to be judgmental was contextually very real for the Galatians. *For if anyone thinks he is something, when he is nothing, he deceives himself.* Championing the truth tempts Christians to fall into the trap of pride and an attitude of judgment. Love for one another is the key to walking in the Spirit in regard to how we relate to others whose views we decline. *For if anyone thinks he is something, when he is nothing, he deceives himself.*[6]

I reference here a personal spiritual struggle I have experienced when deciding whether I could not conscientiously continue to worship in a congregation that sang accompanied by an instrument in Sunday formal worship. I was, and am, biblically convinced that singing in the New Testament church in the worship assembly was and should be *acapella*, non-instrumental. It was a personally deeply challenging decision. I personally believed they were wrong, but did not want to get into a judgmental mindset. I have always desired to leave the judgment business to God and Christ. I love the people in the congregation deeply, but for my conscience I needed to separate from them and their practice, but I needed to do so in a non-judgmental manner. How does one do this without seeming to be judgmental; only with great spiritual struggle and with personal difficulty. I decided not to say anything negative about my brethren, but only to adopt a positive attitude and approach. I explained that I needed to worship with a congregation that was more in line with New Testament traditional practice than secular in thinking. The members are still my brothers in Christ even though I do not worship with them at present, and do not judge them!

Perhaps you can find in my struggle a pattern of how we relate to brothers in Christ with whom we do not agree, even in doctrinal issues. Paul on other occasions teaches a withdrawal of fellowship from those whose life is immoral and who divide the body of Christ (I Cor 5:1ff; and 2 Thess 3:14; Tit 3:9ff), but in regard to the Galatian churches he promotes no such practice at this time.

---

[6] Gal 6:3.

Gal 6:4, 5. *But let each one test his own work, and then his reason to boast will be in himself alone and not in his neighbor. ⁵ For each man will have to bear his own load.* The construction of the adversative conjunction dé in τὸ δὲ ἔργον, to dé érgon, is interesting since it introduces a point clearly in distinction to what has gone before, being conceited and self-indulgent. Christians must be careful not to overlook their own weakness and burdens or spiritual loads. Paul introduces a synonym for burden/ βάρος, báros, namely φορτίον, phortíon ... a diminutive in form but not in sense ... the burden of one's own responsibilities and failures (Gal. 6:5 ...).[7]

Temptation to boast of our own "maturity" is ever present. Each Christian must test and examine their own situation and recognize their own weakness and fallibility, for we all have our own spiritual burdens and weaknesses. We do not boast in our self-perceived maturity in comparison with our neighbor. Before we judge others, we should first examine ourselves and our motives.

Gal 6:6. *Let him who is taught the word share all good things with him who teaches.* Some commentators question the relationship of this verse to the moral and ethical instruction in Galatians,[8] and observe that it is somewhat different from his own personal practices where he personally declined financial support from others.[9] Nevertheless, there is a slight connection in that the Galatians needed to learn to provide financial assistance to those who were designated as teachers or prophets, possibly even those appointed as elders.

Longenecker and Bruce conclude that there was apparently a formal teaching process in play in the Galatian churches and that Paul is instructing the churches to financially support the teachers. Longenecker observes:

> For whereas elsewhere in his letters Paul asserts the right of those who preach and teach to claim support (cf. 1

---

[7] Zodhiates, βάρος, báros, *op. cit.*
[8] Longenecker, *op. cit.*, p. 278.
[9] Cf. Bruce, *op. cit.*, p. 263.

Cor 9:3–14; 1 Tim 5:18, citing both Scripture and the words of Jesus), here he speaks of the duty of those who are taught to make material provision for their teachers. And whereas in his own practice he personally renounced his rights to such material provision (cf. 1 Cor 9:15–18; 1 Thess 2:9; also Acts 20:33–35) … here he commands his Galatian converts to "share all good things" with their teachers … that is, those teachers who teach in accord with Paul's doctrine (cf. 6:16), not the judaizing teachers.[10]

Dominating Gal 1:6 is the imperatival verb κοινωνείτω, *koinōneitō* from κοινωνέω, *koinōnéō*, *to share*, serving as a present imperative in a hortatory command: "Let him share with his instructor."

Paul is careful to exclude the Judaizers from this ministry of financial support by stating that it is those who *teach the word*, namely the gospel of Christ who are to be supported.

Gal 6:7-10. Sow to the spirit and you will reap from the Spirit.

Paul sums up his moral instruction and comments on the life in the Spirit with a command to take every opportunity to do right, especially to those in the household of faith. God knows where the Christian's heart is and is not deceived by false intentions such as seen in the Judaizers who Paul has charged with leading the saints astray for personal advantage, Gal 4:17; 6:11, 12.

> *Do not be deceived; God is not mocked, for whatever a man sows, that he will also reap.* ^{8} *For he who sows to his own flesh will from the flesh reap corruption; but he who sows to the Spirit will from the Spirit reap eternal life.* ^{9} *And let us not grow weary in well-doing, for in due season we shall reap, if we do not lose heart.* ^{10} *So then, as we have opportunity, let us do good to all men, and especially to those who are of the household of faith.*

Paul cites a proverbial statement that would be readily recognized by those living in an agrarian culture, you reap what you sow! Sow to the flesh (the Law) and you will reap from the

---
[10] Longenecker, *ibid.*, pp. 278-279.

flesh (the Law) corruption, condemnation and judgment. Sow to the Spirit and you will reap the fruits of the Spirit, and eternal life. Eternal here implying the kind of life God lives, real life.

Gal 6:9. Do not tire of doing good. *And let us not grow weary in well-doing, for in due season we shall reap, if we do not lose heart.* Sometimes, the maturation of the sowing does not appear overnight, it takes time for good seed to yield good fruit. Be patient with our good deeds, they will produce results.

Gal 6:10. *So then, as we have opportunity, let us do good to all men, and especially to those who are of the household of faith.*

Paul recognizes that it will not always be possible due to circumstances to do good; patience is necessary! However, Christians should always be on the alert to opportunities to do good. We have a Latin term which has been taken over into our English vocabulary, *Carpe diem, seize the day or opportunity*!

The last part of the instruction, *especially to those who are of the household of faith* implies that Christians should seek also the good of the non-Christian, but without question this should imply *especially* serving the family of God, the Jew and the Gentiles, since both are in the household of the faith and heirs of Abraham, which has been Paul's emphasis throughout the Epistle!

Discussion Questions and Thoughts
1. What principle led into the moral exhortations of this pericope? Cf. Gal 5:25, 26.
2. What significant way can we be of help to our Christian brothers? Cf. Gal 6:1?
3. What kind of burdens does Paul have in mind in this exhortation?
4. What spirit should prevail as we seek to help others with their spiritual struggles? Cf. Gal 6:3, 4.
5. If we sow to the Law, what will we reap?
6. How can we sow to the Spirit? Cf. the fruits of the Spirit and our attitude in helping others.

Chapter 13: Gal 6:11-18 – Conclusion: Liberty and the Cross

In the conclusion to his epistle, as was to become normal in his literary style, Paul got straight to the heart of the issue, *circumcision*! The problem was typical of the difficulty Jews had in accepting Gentiles into the faith, whether it be the faith of Judaism or the faith of Christianity. Accepting something as simple as faith in a Messiah rather than the more substantial and corporeal sign of circumcision as a marker of identity certainly did not sound like righteousness according to the Law in the Jews' understanding of righteousness.

The following discussion of the conclusion of Galatians by Longenecker is extremely important not only to understanding Galatians, but also for interpreting Paul's epistolary style.

> The conclusions of Paul's letters have generally been treated in a rather cursory manner, largely because of (1) the natural tendency of commentators to focus on the weightier matters found in the thanksgivings and bodies of Paul's letters, and (2) the supposition that the salutations and subscriptions that open and close a Pauline letter are primarily conventional in nature and serve only to establish or maintain contact with the readers. The conclusion of Galatians, however, has been the object of more scholarly attention than the subscriptions of Paul's other letters. This appears to be so primarily because of its greater length and its more obvious relevance to the body of its letter. J. B. Lightfoot, for example, long ago observed that 6:11-18 functions by way of "summing up the main lessons of the epistle in terse eager disjointed sentences" (*Galatians* [1896], 220); and Adolf Deissmann early insisted regarding Paul's letters in general and Galatians in particular: "More attention ought to be paid the concluding words of the letters generally; they are of the highest importance if we are ever to understand the Apostle. The conclusion to the Galatians is certainly a very remarkable one" (*Bible Studies*, 347-48; cf. also the comments of G. Milligan, *Documents*, 21-28). Since

Lightfoot, Deissmann, Milligan, and others drew attention to it, scholars have generally viewed Paul's conclusion in Galatians as summing up the contents of the body of the letter—though, it need be noted, their views have usually been based simply on a comparison of topics and without any analysis of epistolary or rhetorical forms.

Of late, Hans Dieter Betz has highlighted the fact that 6:11-18 is not only a summation of Paul's letter but is also "most important for the interpretation of Galatians. It contains the interpretive clues to the understanding of Paul's major concerns in the letter as a whole and should be employed as the hermeneutical key to the intentions of the Apostle" (*Galatians*, 313) ... But if Galatians cannot be understood entirely in terms of Greco-Roman forensic rhetoric, but also exhibits, as we have proposed, Jewish ways of arguing (esp. in 3:8-4:7) and Greco-Roman deliberative rhetorical features (esp. in 4:12-6:10), one may legitimately question whether 6:11-18 is properly to be seen in terms of the forensic rhetorical category *peroratio* ... Betz's insistence on the importance of 6:11-18 for the interpretation of Galatians is highly laudatory, even though the rationale for such a claim can be better supported on an epistolary rather than a rhetorical basis.

The conclusions of Paul's letters function like the thanksgivings of his letters, though in reverse: they provide important clues for understanding the issues previously discussed in the bodies of their respective letters. For as the thanksgivings foreshadow and point ahead to the major concerns to be addressed in their respective bodies, the subscriptions serve to highlight and summarize the main points that have been dealt with in those bodies. Galatians, of course, is the primary example of a Pauline letter without a thanksgiving section (probably also 2 Corinthians, though uncertainties regarding how that letter was composed tend to confuse any certain epistolary analysis). But the Galatian θαυμάζω ("I am astonished") subsection of 1:6-10 that begins the long rebuke section of 1:6-4:11 takes its place in setting out the occasion for writing and the issues at stake. And it is to that subsection of 1:6-10 that the conclusion of 6:11-18 can be compared when attempting to identify the major concerns of Paul in writing his Galatian letter, and so to seek interpretive keys for understanding what is discussed in the major portion of the body of that letter.[1]

The Text: Gal 6:11-18

See with what large letters I am writing to you with my own hand. [12] It is those who want to make a good showing in the flesh that would compel you to be circumcised, and only in order that they may not be persecuted for the cross of Christ. [13] For even those who receive circumcision do not themselves keep the law, but they desire to have you circumcised that they may glory in your flesh. [14] But far be it from me to glory except in the cross of our Lord Jesus Christ, by which the world has been crucified to me, and I to the world. [15] For neither circumcision counts for anything, nor uncircumcision, but a new creation. [16] Peace and mercy be upon all who walk by this rule, upon the Israel of God. [17] Henceforth let no man trouble me; for I bear on my body the marks of Jesus.

[18] The grace of our Lord Jesus Christ be with your spirit, brethren. Amen.

Gal 6:11. Paul personally signs the letter.
See with what large letters I am writing to you with my own hand.

It was not usual for Paul to "sign" his letters. It was a common practice for persons of position to have a scribe, or the Latin term *amanuensis*, to transcribe the *"actual writer's"* dictated letter in clear and good form. Paul had previously in his salutation introduced himself in the formal epistolary form. What he was doing in this verse was personalizing the letter and its contents in a more direct manner.

---

[1] Adapted from Longenecker, *ibid.*, pp. 286-287.

His first word, ἴδετε, *idete*, is an aorist Imperative verb from of ὁπάω, *horaō, to see*. To grasp the intended meaning, we might translate this more appropriately as "*Behold!*" It was intended by Paul to draw attention of the fact that he was adding his personal approval of the importance of the message. Of side interest was that Paul apparently did not have a good script style!

Gal 6:12. Paul intentionally identifies the source of the Galatian problem.
> *It is those who want to make a good showing in the flesh that would compel you to be circumcised, and only in order that they may not be persecuted for the cross of Christ.*

The central issue was clearly the intention of the Judaizers from Jerusalem to encourage the Gentile Christians in Galatia to be circumcised and thus identify with Jerusalem and the Law. For Paul, this was not simply a personal issue, distancing the Galatians from himself. The problem was distancing the Galatians from the gospel of Christ, the death burial and resurrection of Jesus, as the power of their new relationship with God and Christ. It also tended to separate the Galatian Christians from Christ and the brotherhood of Christians. The Judaizers were more interested in bringing the Galatian Christians into the brotherhood of Judaism and Jerusalem. Furthermore, an appeal was that circumcision would shield the Galatian Christians from the persecution related to the cross of Christ.

Gal 6:13. There was also a deeper reason for teaching circumcision.
> *For even those who receive circumcision do not themselves keep the law, but they desire to have you circumcised that they may glory in your flesh.*

The Judaizers were seeking personal approval and glory! Winning the Galatians away from Paul's message would obviously seem like a victory over Paul! But, Paul points to their hypocrisy; while preaching circumcision and the Law the Judaizers were not keeping the Law as the Law required!

The Judaizers were not interested in bringing glory to Christ who had died in their behalf and had suffered the humiliation and curse of the cross. They desired to glory in their position and message of circumcision, a sign of the flesh not of the Spirit.

Gal 6:14. Paul's glory was far different from theirs, it was not personal but focused on Jesus.

> *But far be it from me to glory except in the cross of our Lord Jesus Christ, by which the world has been crucified to me, and I to the world.*

The tone of Paul's reacting to personal glory is introduced by his introduction to this verse with the Greek, δὲ μὴ γένοιτο, *de mē genoito*, a strong negation of any possibility of glorying in anything else other than the cross of Christ. In the fourteen occurrences in Paul's letters of δὲ μὴ γένοιτο, *de mē genoito*, it expresses an abhorrence to a statement just made, or to an inference that could be falsely drawn from the apostle's teaching; cf. 2:17; 3:21; Rom 3:4, 6, 31; 6:2, 15; 7:7, 13; 9:14; 11:1, 11; 1 Cor 6:15.

Although Paul, even at this early stage of his ministry, could present a long and impressive list of achievements, his glory is not found in his personal achievements, only in the glory and working of Christ on the cross.

It is obvious from his comments on several occasions that Paul's humility was grounded in the depth of his gratitude for God's and Christ's grace. Note 1 Cor 15:9, 10:

> *For I am the least of the apostles, unfit to be called an apostle, because I persecuted the church of God. ¹⁰ But by the grace of God I am what I am, and his grace toward me was not in vain. On the contrary, I worked harder than any of them, though it was not I, but the grace of God which is with me.*

Regarding Paul's personal achievements Longenecker observes:

> In two autobiographical passages elsewhere in his letters, Paul enumerates a number of things in his life that could be the cause for boasting if viewed from a merely human perspective: in 2 Cor 11:21b–29 he attempts to demonstrate the futility of his converts' boasting about their spiritual attainments by setting out a list of his own

attainments, evidently to outclass and shame them, but then he concludes with the statement, "If I must boast, I will boast of the things that show my weakness" (11:30); in Phil 3:4-6 he attempts to counter any Judaizer's claimed pedigree by citing his own Jewish pedigree, but concludes with statements regarding his far greater desire to "know Christ" and to experience in his own life all that is his because he is associated with Christ (3:7-14).

Becoming one of Christ's people, whether that is expressed as being "of Christ" (Χριστοῦ, cf. Comment at 3:29) or "in Christ" (ἐν Χριστῷ Ἰησοῦ, cf. Comment at 3:26-28), effects a radical change in one's perspective. As Paul says in 2 Cor 5:16, "So from now on we regard no one from a merely human perspective (κατὰ σάρκα, "according to the flesh"); even if we once regarded Christ from a merely human perspective (κατὰ σάρκα, "according to the flesh"), we regard him now in this manner no longer." Thus, with regard to boasting, Paul expresses the fervent wish that he may never exult in matters having to do with "the flesh"—that is, merely human attainments, with particular application here to counting converts and success in ministry—but only in that which has to do with the cross of Christ.[2]

In fact, when Paul speaks of the personal experiences and achievements in Galatians, and elsewhere, his focus is entirely on "the cross" and "Christ crucified," see 1:4; 2:20; 3:1, 13, as well as here at 6:12 and 14. But this reflection was true in his other epistles as well; cf. 1 Cor 1:17-18, 23; 2:2; 5:7b; 8:11; 11:24-26.[3]

The key to Paul's self-denial was that he had died to the world and all that the world had to offer. He speaks of the cross of Christ *by which the world has been crucified to me, and I to the world.*[4] By being united with Christ in baptism Paul understood that he had died to the Law, to sin, and to the appeal of the flesh. At Col 2 and 3 Paul laid out a clear statement

---

[2] Longenecker, op. cit., pp. 293-294.
[3] Cf. Bruce, *op. cit.*, pp. 270 ff; Longenecker, *ibid.*, pp. 294f.
[4] Gal 6:14b.

regarding how the cross of Jesus, and being baptized into Christ, should change the believer's life. You get the idea that the person who wrote Galatians was also the person who would later write Col 2:8-3:17!

> [8] *See to it that no one makes a prey of you by philosophy and empty deceit, according to human tradition, according to the elemental spirits of the universe, and not according to Christ.* [9] *For in him the whole fulness of deity dwells bodily,* [10] *and you have come to fulness of life in him, who is the head of all rule and authority.* [11] *In him also you were circumcised with a circumcision made without hands, by putting off the body of flesh in the circumcision of Christ;* [12] *and <u>you were buried with him in baptism, in which you were also raised with him through faith in the working of God, who raised him from the dead</u>.* [13] *And you, who were dead in trespasses and the uncircumcision of your flesh, God made alive together with him, having forgiven us all our trespasses,* [14] *having canceled the bond which stood against us with its legal demands; this he set aside, nailing it to the cross.* [15] *He disarmed the principalities and powers and made a public example of them, triumphing over them in him ...*
>
> 20 *<u>If with Christ you died to the elemental spirits of the universe, why do you live as if you still belonged to the world</u>? Why do you submit to regulations,* [21] *"Do not handle, Do not taste, Do not touch"* [22] *(referring to things which all perish as they are used), according to human precepts and doctrines?* [23] *These have indeed an appearance of wisdom in promoting rigor of devotion and self-abasement and severity to the body, but they are of no value in checking the indulgence of the flesh.*
>
> *Chapter 3*
> [1] *<u>If then you have been raised with Christ</u>, seek the things that are above, where Christ is, seated at the right hand of God.* [2] *Set your minds on things that are above, not on things that are on earth.* [3] *For you have died, and your life is hid with Christ in God.* [4] *When Christ who is*

our life appears, then you also will appear with him in glory.
⁵ Put to death therefore what is earthly in you: fornication, impurity, passion, evil desire, and covetousness, which is idolatry. ⁶ On account of these the wrath of God is coming. ⁷ In these you once walked, when you lived in them. ⁸ But now put them all away: anger, wrath, malice, slander, and foul talk from your mouth. ⁹ Do not lie to one another, seeing that you have put off the old nature with its practices ¹⁰ and have put on the new nature, which is being renewed in knowledge after the image of its creator. ¹¹ Here there cannot be Greek and Jew, circumcised and uncircumcised, barbarian, Scythian, slave, free man, but Christ is all, and in all.
¹² Put on then, as God's chosen ones, holy and beloved, compassion, kindness, lowliness, meekness, and patience, ¹³ forbearing one another and, if one has a complaint against another, forgiving each other; as the Lord has forgiven you, so you also must forgive. ¹⁴ And above all these put on love, which binds everything together in perfect harmony. ¹⁵ And let the peace of Christ rule in your hearts, to which indeed you were called in the one body. And be thankful. ¹⁶ Let the word of Christ dwell in you richly, teach and admonish one another in all wisdom, and sing psalms and hymns and spiritual songs with thankfulness in your hearts to God. ¹⁷ And whatever you do, in word or deed, do everything in the name of the Lord Jesus, giving thanks to God the Father through him.

Gal 6:15. Paul gets right back to the root of the problem, binding circumcision and the Law as a marker of a relationship with God.
For neither circumcision counts for anything, nor uncircumcision, but a new creation.
Paul introduces a new triumphant thought into his argument, one which he makes in several other contexts. Baptism involves a death to the old life lived under the Law or paganism, and a new birth in Christ, *a new creation*, *a new beginning*. Note the similar point Paul made to the Corinthians at 2 Cor 5:17-19:

> *Therefore, if any one is in Christ<u>, he is a new creation</u>; the old has passed away, behold, the new has come. ¹⁸ All this is from God, who through Christ reconciled us to himself and gave us the ministry of reconciliation; ¹⁹ that is, in Christ God was reconciling the world to himself, not counting their trespasses against them, and entrusting to us the message of reconciliation.*

His encouragement to the Colossians was along the same line at Col 3:10:

> *Do not lie to one another, seeing that you have put off the old nature with its practices ¹⁰ and <u>have put on the new nature, which is being renewed in knowledge after the image of its creator</u>. ¹¹ Here there cannot be Greek and Jew, circumcised and uncircumcised, barbarian, Scythian, slave, free man, but Christ is all, and in all.*

At Eph 4:22 Paul expresses the same thought in a concise statement,

> *Put off your old nature which belongs to your former manner of life and is corrupt through deceitful lusts, ²³ and be renewed in the spirit of your minds, ²⁴ and <u>put on the new nature</u>, created after the likeness of God in true righteousness and holiness.*

Gal 6:16. *Peace and mercy be upon all who walk by this rule, upon the Israel of God. ¹⁷ Henceforth let no man trouble me; for I bear on my body the marks of Jesus.*

The expression grace and peace, with the occasional mention of mercy, became meaningful thoughts for Paul in his epistolary greetings to the churches. Here, in keeping with the context of his epistle, with Judaizers unsettling the believers in the Galatian churches, Paul reminds them of the true nature of the Christian faith and lifestyle, *peace* and *mercy*.

Peace, εἰρήνη, *eirēnē*, a spirit of tranquility, peace, and spiritual harmony,[5] would reflect a fundamental concern of

---

[5] Zodhiates, *op. cit.*, εἰρήνη *eirēnē*; particularly in a single sense, the opposite of war and dissension (Luke 14:32; Acts 12:20; Rev. 6:4). Among individuals, peace, harmony (Matt. 10:34; Luke 12:51; Acts 7:26; Rom. 14:19). In Heb. 7:2, "King of peace," means a peaceful king. Metaphorically peace of mind,

Judaism often reflected in their prayerful greetings, *shalom*! Even the Judaizers would understand the need for *shalom*!

Mercy, ἔλεος, *éleos*,[6] *compassion*, is best understood as seen in the mercy of God who loves the lost and is willing to forgive transgressions. It is hard to disconnect the thought of compassion and mercy from love and the fruits of the Spirit (Gal 5:22).

Paul introduces an interesting thought, especially following the emphasis on freedom and the slavery of the Law! Peace upon *all who walk by this rule, upon the Israel of God*. What does he mean by *this rule*? The word order in the Greek is interesting. Literally translated this clause would be *and on all the ones who according to this canon, system of living, peace and mercy*! The word used by Paul and translated *rule* is κανών, *kanṓn, a measuring rod, rule, norm, principle, or standard*.[7] Paul's intention was that all should live by the principle of faith in Christ, the fruits of the Spirit, and loving one another, and not by the principle of circumcision and the Law.

In the context of Galatians and its theology and message, the term the *Israel of God* cannot refer to the Jews who had been converted, as is proposed by some, but must include *all Christians, both Jew and Gentile*. It refers to all those who have in Christ inherited the promised blessings of Abraham, and who now are recognized as the true Israel or people of God. There is now in the Israel of God neither Jew nor Gentile, they are all one, united in Christ. The Judaizers, and those who live in the old Jerusalem, are no longer the Israel of God!

---

tranquility, arising from reconciliation with God and a sense of a divine favor (Rom. 5:1; 15:13; Phil. 4:7 [cf. Is. 53:5]).

[6] Zodhiates, *op. cit.*, ἔλεος *éleos*. Mercy, compassion. Mercy, compassion, active pity (Matt. 23:23; Titus 3:5; Heb. 4:16; Sept.: Is. 60:10). With the sense of goodness in general, especially piety ... special and immediate regard to the misery which is the consequence of sin.

[7] Zodhiates, *ibid.*, κανών *kanṓn*, Friberg, Timothy, *et al.*, *op. cit.*

Gal 6:17. *Henceforth let no man trouble me; for I bear on my body the marks of Jesus.* This is a strange expression, but it expresses Paul's frustration of those who would question his authenticity. He had paid the human price of freedom in Christ with his own body.

Paul warned that opposing the Judaizers and the Jewish leaders in Jerusalem would come with a price, not always easy, possibly even the price of imprisonment and severe beatings! Paul reminded the Galatians that he had already paid that price so could not be threatened by the Judaizers or Jerusalem! His comment "for I bear on my body the marks of Jesus" was meaningful and known by the Galatians.

At Col 1:24-29 Paul makes an astonishing statement:

> [24] *Now I rejoice in my sufferings for your sake, <u>and in my flesh I complete what is lacking in Christ's afflictions for the sake of his body, that is, the church</u>,* [25] *of which I became a minister according to the divine office which was given to me for you, to make the word of God fully known,* [26] *the mystery hidden for ages and generations but now made manifest to his saints.* [27] *To them God chose to make known how great among the Gentiles are the riches of the glory of this mystery, which is Christ in you, the hope of glory.* [28] *Him we proclaim, warning every man and teaching every man in all wisdom, that we may present every man mature in Christ.* [29] *For this I toil, striving with all the energy which he mightily inspires within me.*

Paul's point was that as members of the church, the body of Christ (Col 1:18), we all share in Christ's suffering. In fact, as Isaiah had warned Israel, the true Israel of God must be God's suffering servant, both the Messiah and his people.

In his defense of his ministry in 2 Corinthians Paul repeatedly mentions the price he willingly paid for his new life in Christ. Note 2 Cor 11:21-28:

> *But whatever any one dares to boast of—I am speaking as a fool—I also dare to boast of that.* [22] *Are they Hebrews? So am I. Are they Israelites? So am I. Are they descendants of Abraham? So am I.* [23] *Are they*

servants of Christ? I am a better one—I am talking like a madman—with far greater labors, far more imprisonments, with countless beatings, and often near death. ^{24} Five times I have received at the hands of the Jews the forty lashes less one. ^{25} Three times I have been beaten with rods; once I was stoned. Three times I have been shipwrecked; a night and a day I have been adrift at sea; ^{26} on frequent journeys, in danger from rivers, danger from robbers, danger from my own people, danger from Gentiles, danger in the city, danger in the wilderness, danger at sea, danger from false brethren; ^{27} in toil and hardship, through many a sleepless night, in hunger and thirst, often without food, in cold and exposure. ^{28} And, apart from other things, there is the daily pressure upon me of my anxiety for all the churches.

Previously in his second epistle to the Corinthians Paul had made moving references to the price and rewards of discipleship of Christ:

For as we share abundantly in Christ's sufferings, so through Christ we share abundantly in comfort too. ^{6} If we are afflicted, it is for your comfort and salvation; and if we are comforted, it is for your comfort, which you experience when you patiently endure the same sufferings that we suffer. ^{7} Our hope for you is unshaken; for we know that as you share in our sufferings, you will also share in our comfort. ^{8}

But we have this treasure in earthen vessels, to show that the transcendent power belongs to God and not to us.

^{8} We are afflicted in every way, but not crushed; perplexed, but not driven to despair; ^{9} persecuted, but not forsaken; struck down, but not destroyed; ^{10} always carrying in the body the death of Jesus, so that the life of Jesus may also be manifested in our bodies. ^{11} For while we live we are always being given up to death for Jesus'

---

^{8} 2 Cor 1:5-7.

sake, so that the life of Jesus may be manifested in our mortal flesh. ^{12} So death is at work in us, but life in you. [9]

Gal 6:18. The Benediction. *The grace of our Lord Jesus Christ be with your spirit, brethren. Amen.*

Longenecker's closing comments to Paul's concluding comments on grace in his benedictory prayer are meaningful:

> While the word χάρις ("grace") appears regularly in the Pauline opening salutations and closing benedictions, its appearance in Galatians is particularly meaningful. Thus set between the theological salutation of 1:3 that speaks of grace "from God our Father and the Lord Jesus Christ" and the benediction here at 6:18 that speaks of "the grace of our/the Lord Jesus Christ," Paul refers explicitly to the Galatians being called "by the grace of Christ" (1:6), to his being called "by his [God's] grace" (1:15), to the Jerusalem apostles' recognition that "the grace" had been given him by God (2:9), and, using the verbal form of the word, to the fact that God "graciously gave" the inheritance to Abraham through a promise and not on the basis of the law (3:18). In fact, throughout Galatians grace and law are set out as opposite poles, certainly with regard to being accounted righteous before God (2:15-16, 21; 3:1-18), but also with regard to living a proper Christian lifestyle (2:17-21; 3:19-4:11). So in closing his Galatian letter, Paul concludes on that note of grace. It may even have been, particularly if Galatians is Paul's earliest extant pastoral letter, that it was this note all of Paul's concluding benedictions. [10]

Discussion Questions and Thoughts
1. Summarize in your own words the theology of Galatians.
2. What was the gospel Paul was so concerned to defend and maintain?
3. What was the role of the Law of Moses?

---

[9] 2 Cor 4:7-12.
[10] Longenecker, *op. cit*, pp. 300-301.

4. How according to the gospel Paul preached was one declared righteous in the sight of God?
5. What is the significance of Paul referring to the Galatians as brethren at least 11 times in Galatians?
6. What do we gain from this lesson regarding the main concern Paul had for the Galatians?
7. What was the error Paul highlighted in this lesson?

Addendum 1: Paul's Doctrine of Righteousness

Introduction

In this study, we will examine Paul's doctrine of righteousness. Our primary purpose will be to examine two opposing views of righteousness; imputed righteousness and personal righteousness. We will also explore the difference between legal rectitude in keeping the Law; the personal righteousness received by God's grace; the faithfulness of Jesus Christ; faith in Jesus Christ and his death, burial, and resurrection; personal forgiveness; and being personally declared not guilty by God.

Imputed righteousness[1]

I understand this as our not being *personally righteous but receiving the righteousness of Christ imputed* to us based on faith.

This view is common among Christians who are keenly aware of their humanness or sinfulness. Its roots lie first in Roman Catholic thinking which was then sharpened by Martin Luther and Reformed Theology. This righteousness is not the believer's own righteousness; rather *it is Christ's righteousness 'imputed'* to the believer.

Our examination of this view is that it is not rooted in a study of the biblical text, but is grounded in Roman catholic and Reformed theology, and the proposed depravity of the individual inherited from Adam.

---

[1] *Theopedia: An Encyclopedia of Christianity*, Imputed righteousness is a theological concept directly related to the doctrine of Justification. It is particularly prevalent in the Reformed tradition. "Justification is that step in salvation in which God declares the believer righteous. Protestant theology has emphasized that this includes the *imputation* of Christ's righteousness (crediting it to the believer's "account"), whereas Roman Catholic theology emphasizes that God justifies in accord with an *infused* righteousness merited by Christ and maintained by the believer's good works," (Elwell Evangelical Dictionary). Imputed righteousness ... is not the believer's own righteousness, rather it is Christ's own righteousness 'imputed' to the believer. Cf. also Alan Richardson, ed., "Righteousness," *A Dictionary of Christian Theology*, SCM Press, 1969.

Personal righteousness

We understand this as *the Christian being declared righteous* by God based on God's forgiveness. We see this as an alternative to imputed righteousness. It is a righteousness in which the Christian is righteous in his/her own right.

This view is based on Paul's doctrine of atonement, redemption, and reconciliation as set out primarily in Rom 3:21-26, and reflected in his pastoral writings to the churches in his ministry.

It is grounded in God's atoning grace, the death burial and resurrection of Jesus, in the faith one has in Jesus Christ in which the Christian is *forgiven and declared not guilty* by God.

This righteousness relates to the Christian having been born again into the family of God and thus being in a right relationship with God through faith in Jesus.

In this study, we will explore several texts in an effort to understand Paul's doctrine of righteousness.

Moral or Ethical Righteousness in Accordance with Keeping or Conforming to some Legal System

We will ask whether the righteousness spoken of by Paul is an ethical or moral righteousness according to keeping a legal system, or a righteousness based in God's forgiveness of the sinner and consequently in his declaring the sinner not guilty of their sin.

Moral and ethical righteousness, hence *imputed righteousness* leads to the view of imputed righteousness and resides in the recognition that the Christian never will live above sin and needs to receive Christ's righteousness *imputed* to the Christian through faith in Jesus.

It is our view that this is not the kind of righteousness Paul speaks of in his epistles.

We will explore Paul's negative views on being declared righteous by keeping the Law of Moses which inevitably leads to a false view of moral and ethical righteousness. A Pauline theological view of righteousness is based on faith in Jesus Christ and divine forgiveness and justification, and not on keeping laws of any kind.

We will demonstrate that Paul never viewed or taught that a person, Jew or Gentile, could be declared righteous by keeping the Law, and that even in Abraham, born 430 years before the Law was given, God had declared men righteous based on faith and not Law keeping.

A legitimate question would be to ask since we cannot earn righteousness by living moral lives, how then if we are still sinners can we be righteous in God's sight?

One answer to this is that we might "inherit" Christ's righteousness, and have his righteousness *transferred* to us as an *imputed* righteousness, as was held by some Reformed theologians such as by Martin Luther in his reaction to a Catholic works-oriented theology.

In this study, we will reject imputed righteousness as not being either biblical or Pauline.

We will work off the presupposition that personal righteousness results from our not being perfect but being *forgiven and declared not guilty by God*.

We will also be stressing that this righteousness is grounded in the fact, as stressed by Paul in his Epistle to the Romans, that God is himself *a righteous God* who *justifies* all men, Jews and Gentiles alike, by the same principle of faith in Jesus Christ, and not by their ability to keep the Law of Moses.

An Introductory Text – Phil 3:8-11

Note Paul's personal argument and statement:

Indeed, I count everything as loss because of the surpassing worth of knowing Christ Jesus my Lord. For his sake I have suffered the loss of all things, and count them as refuse, <u>in order that I may gain Christ [9] and be found in him, not having a righteousness of my own, based on law, but that which is through faith in Christ, the righteousness from God that depends on faith</u>; [10] that I may know him and the power of his resurrection, and may share his sufferings, becoming like him in his death ...

Some Thoughts Drawn from Phil 3:8-11

Paul seeks a *deep personal* relationship with Christ, a relationship or righteousness not based on Law keeping, a relationship or righteousness that comes from God, a relationship or righteousness that depends on faith in Jesus Christ, a relationship with Jesus based on forgiveness and the power of Christ's resurrection.

Some Other Important Scriptures we intend to Visit in this Study

Phil 3:4-11, Rom 1:17, Rom 3:21-31, Rom 5:1, 2, Rom 4:1, Rom 9:30, and Rom 10:5-11.

Preliminary Comments

This is a complicated and loaded topic with several complex and loaded terms and concepts! Righteousness is often confused or poorly defined in our minds because of several factors or views on the subject which we have inherited from our various religious traditions and sort of homogenized or blended into our thinking!

In our Church of Christ tradition, we do not speak much of righteousness but focus more on salvation because of our special emphasis on Acts 2:38 and baptism. I do not know of a text that says we are baptized in order to be righteous, and in fact we react to that type of thinking because of a strong view that righteousness is by grace through faith and not by works. However, we do not work in baptism, God through his Holy Spirit does the work! In fact, we do not in our tradition connect baptism with righteousness! We have reacted to works salvation and so emphasized grace and faith that we overlook the fact that both grace and faith involve a requisite response in baptism! Cf. Gal 3:23-29:

> *Now before faith came, we were confined under the law, kept under restraint until faith should be revealed. ^{24} So that the law was our custodian until Christ came, that we might be justified by faith. ^{25} But now that faith has come, we are no longer under a custodian; ^{26} <u>for in Christ Jesus you are all sons of God, through faith. ^{27} For as many of you as were baptized into Christ have put on Christ.</u> ^{28} There is neither Jew nor Greek, there is neither slave nor free, there is neither male nor female; for you*

are all one in Christ Jesus. ²⁹ And if you are Christ's, then you are Abraham's offspring, heirs according to promise.

Furthermore, since we are keenly aware of our own weaknesses and sinful nature we have a hard time seeing ourselves as *righteous*. Our problem is that we have a misguided understanding of righteousness. Righteousness does not mean that we are right in the sight of God by our own efforts. We do not realize that being declared not guilty by God through our obedient faith in Jesus Christ, and therefore forgiven, we are in a right relationship with God as his children.

The Meaning of the Word Righteousness as Used in Greek

The Greek word for *righteousness* is surrounded by a word-group with several closely related meanings all related to the Greek root word, δίκη, *díkē*[2]. The word-group is:

First, justice, δίκη, *díkē*, "is a root word relating to the law court. It is found only three times, and always in the sense of "penal justice" or "punishment," with no distinctive features."[3]

Second, righteousness, δικαιοσύνη, *dikaiosúnē*, is "a noun from *díkē*, meaning just, righteous, justice, righteousness."[4] Kittel observes regarding righteousness:

> "*Righteousness*, represents the second stage of word construction in relation to *justice, díkē* ... We can also see a link between this construction and the development of *the Greek sense of law*. The very close connection between legal, ethical and religious terminology results from the central position occupied in early Greek thinking by justice, *díkē* as being right not merely in the legal, but also the political, the ethical and above all the religious sense."[5]

---

[2] *Dictionary of New Testament Theology*, ed., Colin Brown, Vol. 3, Zondervan, 1971.
[3] G. Kittel, G. W. Bromiley & G. Friedrich, Ed *Theological Dictionary of the New Testament, Vol. 2*: 1964, electronic ed., Grand Rapids, MI: Eerdmans.
[4] Spiros Zodhiates, *The Complete Word Study Dictionary: New Testament*, electronic ed., Chattanooga, TN: AMG Publishers, 2000.
[5] Kittel, *op. cit.*

Third, righteous, δίκαιος, *díkaios*, "that which is right, conformable to right, pertaining to right, that which is just. This is expected by the one who sets the rules and regulations whereby man must live, whether that be society or God."[6]

Fourth, to justify, δικαιόω, dikaióō, is a verb that derives from the noun *righteous*. It means "to make righteous," or "to establish as right," "to validate," to declare not guilty."[7] Kittel adds regarding δικαιόω, dikaióō:

> "In the NT it is seldom that one cannot detect *the legal connexion. To justify* is never used in the sense of "to regard as fair and right," as in Greek generally. The LXX, with its legal emphasis, has obviously had the greatest influence on NT usage."[8]

To justify, then means *to declare not guilty, forgiven*, regardless whether one was guilty or not. Once the judge declares *justified*, or *not guilty*, the person is *forgiven* and is *no longer guilty*, and is in a right relationship with the law.

Righteousness in the New Testament

The words righteous and righteousness can be used in both legal and ethical/moral contexts in The New Testament. Each use conveys a different meaning.

Ethical/Moral Righteousness, or Rectitude

In the religious sense, man is a sinner, not pure, not clean, not in a right relationship with God. This stresses that man is a sinner and will always remain a sinner; thus, never be righteous by his own rectitude. This leads to the view of *imputed righteousness*.

Only Christ has been found without sin, which is certainly true! Man is by nature a sinner, and has inherited that nature from their parents, or from Adam who fell from grace. Man is thus by nature corrupt and totally depraved.

This position is based on the recognition that man *remains a sinner* and is then by his own nature a sinner and not righteous.

---

[6] Zodhiates, *op. cit.*
[7] Kittel, *ibid.*
[8] Kittel, *op. cit.*

We refer to this as *imputed* righteousness in which repentant man has Christ's righteousness *imputed* to him by God's grace through faith in Jesus. Man, in his own person is not righteous but has Christ's righteousness imputed or granted to him because of his faith in Christ.

In Christ, we *receive* or *inherit* Christ's ethical/moral righteousness.

Atoning Relational Righteousness

Righteousness can also be seen in the sense of our being *forgiven* by God, thus *pronounced by God as not guilty*, hence, *legally right with God or righteous*.

This view of righteousness is built off the Greek, Roman, and Septuagint view of the law court and legal justification; that is being declared not guilty by a judge in a law court.

By God's grace through faith in Christ, repentant man is *declared not guilty of sin*. He is *forgiven* and is *then in a right standing or relationship with God*; he is therefore *legally righteous*.

This is the sense in which many Christian traditions understand righteousness.

Comment

How one determines or understands righteousness in the above two positions, ethical righteousness or atoning legal righteousness will determine how one defines righteousness.

We should note at this point that in this addendum we are discussing the *biblical view of personal righteousness* which is based on *atonement* in Jesus and *forgiveness* of sin *in Christ*. We are not discussing a view of salvation and forgiveness but rather the result of salvation and forgiveness.

A biblical view of salvation and forgiveness would involve hearing the message of Jesus' death, burial, and resurrection, believing in this, repenting of sin, being baptized in the name of Jesus and receiving the gift of the indwelling Holy Spirit (Cf. Acts 2:29-38).

Atoning Relational Righteousness versus Rectitudinal Righteousness

The doctrine of *atonement, forgiveness*, being *determined not guilty*, in and relational righteousness, based on the legal meaning of being declared not guilty in the law court, is not to be confused with *legal rectitude* which is understood as *being right in regard to some law;* as in *adhering to the terms of some legal system, either civil or religious*!

Legal moral *rectitude* carries the sense of being *morally honorable by acting in accordance with law in maintaining good conduct with others, or a legal system. We see this in the sense of acting in accordance with our laws, religious or civil.*

Legal Rectitude

We will argue that legal moral *rectitude* is what *Paul argued against* in both Romans and Galatians.

In contrast to this Paul argued for relational righteousness, *being declared not guilty by God,* our ultimate judge. This is the righteousness Paul argued for in Romans and Galatians.

The Jews thought they could be righteous by keeping laws, especially the law of Moses. Paul was opposed to the view that one can be righteous by keeping the Law. Simply put, the Jew thought that you could be put right, or be in a righteous relationship with God, by keeping the Law, which Paul vehemently denies in his Roman and Galatian Epistles.

Paul argued that righteousness cannot be earned by law keeping but is granted as a gift of God's grace through faith in Jesus and is based on forgiveness and being declared not guilty by God.

Righteousness, a *right relationship with God*, comes through God's grace, faith in the atoning death of Jesus, forgiveness, and being declared not guilty by God.

Atonement Relational Righteousness

Atoning relational righteousness results from the judge declaring one *innocent*, hence, *not guilty, forgiven*, and right with God.

In the Christian understanding, God forgives the sinner, declares the sinner not guilty, and justifies the sinner. This all takes place by God's grace, and through the sinner's faith in Christ's death on the cross.

God forgives the sinner and makes the sinner right with Him in and through Christ!

Because of Jesus' death, and through faith in Jesus, God thus declares the sinner to be *not guilty* and in a right relationship with God!

Righteousness in this legal theological sense does *not refer to moral or ethical rectitude*. We recognize that although we are forgiven we are still sinners! Luther was correct, "*Simul Justus et Peccator*," we are "*both righteous and a sinner.*"

Righteousness in this context is a *legal* and *relational* concept based in *atonement, being forgiven*, and *declared not guilty* by God!

Because of the faithfulness of Christ and our faith in him *we are forgiven, pronounced not guilty and right with God! In Christ, we are in a right relationship with God - hence righteous!*

This righteousness is not due to our being sinless, or our being right with some law. *Righteousness is based on being in a right relationship with God through Jesus Christ and not through the Law of Moses or any other law.*

A Look at Paul and Righteousness in Romans

The Theology of Romans:

Before we engage several texts in Paul's Epistle to the Romans we need to ask why Paul wrote Romans and what he hoped to achieve.

This is a hotly debated issue among scholars of this epistle. Cf. Karl P. Donfried, *The Romans Debate*. Hendriksen, 1991.

Paul had never visited Rome but knows several Christians in that city who are grouped in house churches.

Romans is a missionary epistle; Paul wanted the church in Rome to sponsor his mission trip to Spain. Paul reminded them that he was an apostle to the Gentiles but that he also wanted some fruit among the Jews. He explained that there is only one gospel for both Jews and Gentiles alike; Rom 1:16, 17:

> *For I am not ashamed of the gospel: it is the power of God for salvation to every one who has faith, to the Jew*

first and also to the Greek. ⁷¹ For in it the righteousness of God is revealed through faith for faith; as it is written, "He who through faith is righteous shall live."

The gospel good news that Paul preached was that God in Christ has provided salvation for all men, both Jews and Gentiles, and that this is good news, hence gospel!

The gospel is the power of God for salvation for all men. This gospel is accessed only by grace through faith in Jesus and not by law keeping. The Law of Moses had a purpose, to identify sin and its consequences, but not to save.

The theology of the gospel is not simply justification by grace through faith in Jesus, but justification by grace through the faithfulness of Jesus and faith in Jesus for all men, Jew and Gentile alike. This is great news based in the power of God and in the fact that God is a righteous God who justifies all men by the same principle.

The following themes will predominate in Romans: God is a righteous God, he justifies all men by the same principle, this principle involves God declaring all men innocent by faith in Jesus and not by legal rectitude of keeping the Law of Moses. This salvation, redemption, and reconciliation is according to God's covenant with Abraham brought forward by the faithfulness of Jesus in fulfilling God's covenant promise. It is available for all men, both Jew and Gentile, accessed in God's grace through faith in Jesus, and not by law keeping.

Rom 1:16, 17: The Righteousness of God

Thomas R. Schreiner, *Romans*: Baker Exegetical Commentary observes the following regarding Rom 1:17, "Defining *dikaiosunē theou*…righteousness of God…is crucial and intensely controversial. The secondary literature on this issue is so massive that only a full-length monograph could tackle the issue adequately."

Unpacking this text is indeed a challenge!

We should begin the discussion of righteousness with Rom 1:16, 17 since this is a text that we know so well yet might not know well enough!

First, we need to understand that it speaks primarily about God! God is a righteous God who declares all men righteous by the same means, by grace through faith in Jesus and not by Law keeping. Otherwise this would result in two different systems, one for the Gentiles who did not have the Law of Moses, and another for the Jews who did have the Law of Moses. The alternative would be that the Gentiles would have to conform to the Law of Moses which Paul vehemently opposes (cf. Galatians)!

If God treats the Jews differently from the Gentiles then he is not a righteous God!

So Paul lays down this foundational statement about God; a fundamental principle to the gospel of God – *he is a righteous God who treats all men on the same grounds.*

In our modern terminology, we have a meaningful statement, we all (Jew and Gentile) play on the same level playing field; we are all sinners and lost, justification for all is by God's grace through faith in Jesus Christ!

Note Paul's leading statement in Romans 1:16, 17:

> *"For I am not ashamed of the gospel: it is the power of God for salvation to everyone who has faith, to the Jew first and also to the Greek. ^{17} For in it <u>the righteousness of God</u> is revealed through faith for faith; as it is written, "He who through faith is righteous shall live."*

Joseph A. Fitzmyer, a noted NT scholar, observes regarding *the righteousness of God*; "for in it (*the gospel*) is revealed *the uprightness of God*, through faith and for faith ..."⁹

Some Views on the Righteousness of God, Δικαιοσύν Θεοῦ

Joseph A. Fitzmyer, *Romans.*

> The expression *"the righteousness of God* ... appears in 3:5, 21, 22, 25, 26, 10:3. Here *dikaiosunē theou* stands in contrast to *orgē theoú*, "the wrath of God" (1:18), an attribute, property, or quality of God... *theoú* is thus understood as a *possessive* or *subjective* genitive,

---

⁹ Joseph A. Fitzmyer, *Romans*: Anchor Bible Commentary, Anchor Bible, Doubleday, 1992, p. 257f.

descriptive of God's upright being and of his upright activity..."[10]

J. D. G. Dunn, *Romans 1-8*. Dunn finds a *relational* element in this expression *the righteousness of God*. Righteousness here relates to the relationship God has with his covenant to bless all nations (Gen 12; 17).

So too when it is predicated of God—in this case the relationship being the covenant which God entered into with his people ... *God is "righteous"* when he fulfills the obligations he took upon himself to be Israel's God, that is, to rescue Israel and punish Israel's enemies (e.g., Exod 9:27; 1 Sam 12:7; Dan 9:16; Mic 6:5) ... "righteousness" as "covenant faithfulness" (3:3-5, 25; 10:3; also 9:6 and 15:8).[11] ... *It is clearly this concept of God's righteousness which Paul takes over here...*[12]

Hence for Dunn *dikaiosunē theou* refers to a *relational* attribute of God relating to *his faithfulness to his covenant*.

Ernest Käsemann, *Commentary on Romans*, favors an eschatological interpretation which focuses on the *gospel and salvation representing the power of God* which builds on his nature as a saving God who has worked his salvation in history and which now converges on the eschatological fulfillment of his covenant to bless all nations. Käsemann emphasizes that biblical theology has shed an outdated view that set everything in a Greek understanding of the term *dikaiosunē* (righteousness) which saw it in an ethical context of meeting certain legal requirements.

At least in the last century we have freed ourselves from the Greek understanding of *dikaiosunē* as a norm of what is right for God and man...." "In biblical usage righteousness, which is essentially forensic, denotes a relation in which one is set, namely, the 'recognition' in which one, for example, is acknowledged to be innocent."[13] God is a saving god and the gospel represents

---

[10] Fitzmyer, *ibid.*
[11] J. D. G. Dunn, "Rom 1:17," *Romans 1-8*: Word Biblical Commentary, *Vol. 38A*, Dallas: Word, Incorporated, 1998. Italics mine for emphasis, IAF.
[12] J. D. G. Dunn, *ibid.*
[13] Ernst Käsemann, *Commentary on Romans*, p. 24.

"God's self-manifestation (which) is decisive for all history." The gospel "is an epiphany of God's eschatological power pure and simple."

The conclusion one draws from Käsemann's eschatological view is that *dikaiosunē theou* at Rom 1:17, at least, refers to *an attribute of God's eschatological saving power.*[14]

Leon Morris agrees with Käsemann and observes:

> With us it is an ethical virtue, as it was for the Greek generally. But among the Hebrews *righteousness was first and foremost a legal standing.* The righteous were those who secured the *verdict* when they stood before God. The terminology applied even in an earthly court, and the 'righteous' and the 'wicked' in the Old Testament often mean much what we mean when we speak of the 'innocent' and the 'guilty'...and *the man who is ultimately righteous is the one who is acquitted when tried at the bar of God's justice.*"[15]

John R. W. Stott observes that righteousness can be seen as a combination of several salient factors or attributes. It speaks of *a divine attribute or quality*, a divine activity, a divine achievement, and divine gift. He notes Fitzmyer's "strange expression" regarding the word meaning "the uprightness of God" and his comment that righteousness is "descriptive of God's upright being and his upright activity," and goes on to concede that it also expresses the "status of uprightness communicated to human beings by God's gracious gift." He concludes, "in other words, it is at one and the same time a quality, an activity, and a gift."[16]

R. H. Mounce takes an alternate view. Citing C. E. B. Cranfield, Mounce observes that Cranfield's "view

> ... is that the righteousness of God refers to humans' righteous status that results from God's justifying activity. He argues (1) that a number of occurrences of "righteousness" in Paul's letters support that view (e.g.,

---

[14] Ernest Käsemann, *ibid.*, Rom 1:17.
[15] Leon Morris, *The Epistle to the Romans*, William B. Eerdmans, 1988.
[16] John R. W. Stott, *The Message of Romans*, IVP, 1994.

Rom 5:17; 10:3; Phil 3:9; 1 Cor 1:30; 2 Cor 5:21), (2) the emphasis on faith in v. 17b favors the view that righteousness is a status conferred on persons rather than an activity of God, (3) the quotation from Habakkuk focuses attention on the one justified and not on God's justifying activity, and (4) the structure of the argument that lays heavy emphasis on the status of one who has received God's gift of justification."[17]

Mounce adds,

> By nature, we view righteousness as something we can achieve by our own meritorious action, the result of what we do. *The righteousness of God is totally different. It is a right standing before God that has nothing to do with human merit. ... But God's righteousness is a right standing he freely gives to those who trust in him.*[18]

R. D. G. Dunn draws on the gains theology has made by setting Paul's thought in a Hebrew context rather than in a Greek mindset. He observes regarding δικαιοσύνη γὰρ θεοῦ at Rom 1:17,

> "... for the righteousness of God." Δικαιοσύνη is a good example of the need to penetrate through Paul's Greek language in order to understand it in the light of his Jewish background and training. The concept which emerged from the Greco-Roman tradition to dominate Western thought was of righteousness/justice as *an ideal or absolute ethical norm against which particular claims and duties could be measured* ... <u>But</u> since the fundamental study of H. Cremer it has been recognized that in Hebrew thought (δικαιοσύνη, IAF) is essentially a concept of *relation*. Righteousness is not something which an individual has on his or her own, independently of anyone else; it is something which one has precisely in one's relationships as a social being. People are righteous when they meet the claims which others have on them by

---

[17] R. H. Mounce, R. H., *Romans*. The New American Commentary, Nashville: Broadman & Holman Publishers, 1995, pp. 72, 73.

[18] Mounce, R. H. *Romans*. The New American Commentary, Nashville: Broadman & Holman Publishers, 1995, p. 73.

virtue of their relationship... So too when it is predicated of God—*in this case the relationship being the covenant which God entered into with his people .... God is "righteous" when he fulfills the obligations he took upon himself to be Israel's God*, that is, to rescue Israel and punish Israel's enemies (e.g., Exod 9:27; 1 Sam 12:7; Dan 9:16; Mic 6:5— "righteousness" as "covenant faithfulness" (3:3-5, 25; 10:3; also 9:6 and 15:8)."[19]

Dunn adds:

What marks Paul's use of the concept off from that given to him in his Jewish heritage, however, is precisely his conviction that the covenantal framework of God's righteousness has to be understood afresh in terms of faith - "to all who believe, Jew first but also Gentile."[20]

Thus, the key to man's righteousness is faith in God's faithfulness and <u>uprightness to his covenant</u> to redeem both Jew and Gentile alike by faith and not by works.

Finally, we turn to Norman Tom Wright's significant focus on Paul's theology of righteousness or justification in his major work *Justification*.[21] Wright reacts to the once popular argument that Romans is all about justification by faith in Jesus. His point is that *Romans is, after all, primarily about God*.[22] Wright sets his argument for understanding δικαιοσύνη in the context of *the faithfulness of God in regard to his covenant promise to set the world right* into an overarching point that he believes defines what Romans is all about. He states, "the best argument for taking *dikaiosunē theoú* in Romans 1:17, 3:21 and 10:3 as *"God's faithfulness to the covenant with Abraham*, to the single-plan-through-Israel-for-the-world," is the massive sense it makes of passage after passage..."

---

[19] J. D. G. Dunn, *Romans 1-8*: Word Biblical Commentary, Dallas: Word, Incorporated, 1998.
[20] Dunn, J. D. G. *Romans 1-8*. Word Biblical Commentary, Dallas: Word, Incorporated, 1998, p. 42.
[21] N. T. Wright, *Justification*, IVP Academic, 2009, pp. 177ff.
[22] N. T. Wright, *Justification*, p. 40.

In the following long paragraph, I have condensed Wright's argument of righteousness/justification based on the *lawcourt not guilty justification view* which I believe is correct.

> Even a short reflection, therefore, suggests that the best argument for the "righteousness" in Romans 1:17 *being God's own, and referring to his (albeit strange and unexpected) faithfulness to the covenant*, is the argument of Romans itself. How then does the rest of the opening summary play out? ... We need to remind ourselves severely (because the point is so easily forgotten or allowed to slide sideways out of consciousness, making room for other competing notions) that "righteous" here does not mean "morally virtuous." *It means, quite simply, that the court has found in your favor.* Notice what has not happened within this lawcourt scene. The judge has not clothed the defendant with his own "righteousness." That doesn't come into it. Nor has he given the defendant something called the righteousness of the Messiah or, if he has, Paul has not even hinted at it. What the judge has done is to pass judicial sentence on sin, in the faithful death of the Messiah, so that those who belong to the Messiah, though in themselves "ungodly" and without virtue or merit, now find themselves hearing the lawcourt verdict, "in the right." And the point, putting covenant and lawcourt together, is that this is what the single plan-through-Israel for-the-world was designed to do! The covenant purpose is accomplished, being turned into the single-plan-through-Israel's faithful-representative-for-the-world. And "the world," therefore, must now include the rest of Israel as well as the Gentiles.[23]

Wright, therefore, sets *dikaiosunē theou* in the context of the lawcourt *and God's covenant faithfulness to set the world right through Jesus Christ* and more specifically also through *the faithfulness of Jesus to God's covenant plan.*

---

[23] Wright, *op. cit*, pp. 180-206.

Concluding Thought on Rom 1:16, 17 or More Specifically on Rom 1:17.

It is best in the context of Paul's theme in Romans in which he will argue that it was God's plan from the beginning to set his creation back in order through his covenant with Abraham that his point is that God justifies both Jew and Gentile alike through faith and not works of law as in the Law of Moses. God is a righteous God who treats all men alike according to his covenant with Abraham. The concept of righteousness must be kept in the legal context of the lawcourt and not in the Greco-Roman moral context of personal moral agreement with a set of legal principles. Righteousness in keeping with the Hebrew understanding must retain a relational meaning, that is, a relationship with God which can only be achieved through God's faithfulness to his covenant, his gracious forgiveness and not guilty verdict, and faith in the grace of God and not by personal effort.

Rom 3:20-31

Paul was beginning to develop the basis of the doctrine of the atonement he planned to preach in Rome, but also in Spain as he planned to move on in his mission outreach.

His plan was to demonstrate that all people, Jews and Gentiles, are justified by God by the same principle or system, faith in Jesus Christ.

Rom 3:22; 10:12 explained that God is not a respecter of persons; he treats all men alike, without ethnic distinction. He is a righteous God!

At Rom 3:23, 24 Paul argued that all men have fallen short of the glory of God and have sinned. All men will be justified alike through faith in Jesus, and not by works of the Law of Moses.

The text

For no human being will be justified in his sight by works of the law, since through the law comes knowledge of sin.
²¹ But now <u>the righteousness of God</u> has been manifested apart from law, although the law and the prophets bear

witness to it,²² <u>the righteousness of God through faith in Jesus Christ</u> for all who believe. <u>For there is no distinction;</u> ²³ since all have sinned and fall short of the glory of God, ²⁴ they are justified by his grace as a gift, through the redemption which is in Christ Jesus, ²⁵ whom God put forward as an expiation by his blood, to be received by faith. <u>This was to show God's righteousness</u>, because in his divine forbearance he had passed over former sins; ²⁶ it was to prove at the present time that <u>he himself is righteous</u> and that he justifies him who has faith in Jesus.

²⁷ Then what becomes of our boasting? It is excluded. On what principle? On the principle of works? No, but on the principle of faith. ²⁸ For we hold that a man is justified by faith apart from works of law. ²⁹ Or is God the God of Jews only? Is he not the God of Gentiles also? Yes, of Gentiles also, ³⁰ since God is one; and he will justify the circumcised on the ground of their faith and the uncircumcised through their faith. ³¹ Do we then overthrow the law by this faith? By no means! On the contrary, we uphold the law.

Fitzmyer Translation

But now, independently of the law, the uprightness of God has been disclosed, even though the law and the prophets bear witness to it, 22 the uprightness of God that has come through faith in Jesus Christ to all who believe, toward all without distinction. 23 For all alike have sinned and fall short of the glory of God; 24 yet all are justified freely by his grace through the redemption that cones in Christ Jesus. 25 Through his blood God has presented him as a means of expiating sin for all who have faith. This was to be a manifestation of God's uprightness for the pardon of past sins committed 26 in the time of his forbearance, a manifestation of his uprightness also at the present time to show that he is upright and justifies the one who puts faith in Jesus.[24]

---

[24] See Fitzmyer, *Romans*, *passim* the discussion of this text. See also Wright, *Justification*, *passim*; Dunn, *Romans 1-8*, *passim*. Pace C. E. B. Cranfield argues for this as an objective genitive or genitive of origin in which case this

Four Major Issues or Emphases Surface from this Text

All human righteousness is a result of the righteousness of God.

The faithfulness of Christ is the foundation of our faith and righteousness.

God is no respecter of persons; he maintains no distinction between Jews and Gentiles.

Righteousness is a gift of God's grace which He gives to all men according the same principle; through faith in Jesus Christ.

The righteousness of God

The expression *righteousness of God*, δικαιοσύνη θεοῦ, in one form or another appears four times in this pericope referring to *God's righteousness* or *God's uprightness*.[25]

The point being made is that God is the one, *a righteous God*, who justifies *all men in the same way*, through the redemptive work, *expiation, propitiation*, ἱλαστήριον, *hilastērion, atoning sacrifice* in Christ.

It is through faith in Jesus Christ that men are justified or put right with God, who by doing this equally for all men, is a righteous God.

The faithfulness of Christ

The expression *faith of Christ*, πίστεως Ἰησοῦ, being a *genitive* construction raises the issue whether Paul intended a *subjective* genitive, *faith of Christ*, the *faithfulness that is seen in Christ*, the faithfulness characteristic; or an *objective* genitive, *our faith in or toward Christ*.

Fitzmyer discusses this at length and cites those in favor of the subjective reading and those in favor of the objective reading.[26]

Fitzmyer himself prefers the *objective* genitive *faith in or toward Christ*.

---

would refer to the righteousness that God provides, *The Epistle to the Romans*: International Critical Commentary, T & T Clark, 1975, 1999, pp. 95ff.

[25] See note 24 above.

[26] Fitzmyer, *Romans*, Rom 3:21ff. Contrary to Wright, Hooker, Williams and others, Fitzmyer favors the objective genitive, *faith in Christ*. Dunn likewise favors the objective genitive, *Romans 1-8, passim*.

Some believe that in this case the genitive expression could refer to both a subjective and objective genitive, but this is a debatable solution. However, context should be the determining point in any interpretation.[27]

God is no respecter of persons

This point made so strikingly in Romans drives home the theme that God treats all men alike because he is a righteous God. This strengthens the argument that the righteousness of God is a subjective genitive speaking of God's uprightness.

Righteousness is a gift of grace given by God out of his righteousness which is based on faith in Jesus Christ

We never deserve righteousness! It is a gift from God by his grace based on our trusting him and what he has achieved in Jesus for us.

Righteousness based on faith and not works removes all boasting of personal righteousness based on our efforts.

Personal righteousness results from a proper relationship with God as a gift of God through faith in Jesus Christ.

Concluding Thoughts on Rom 3:21-31

Paul was building his argument introduced at Rom 1:17 that God is a righteous God who justifies all men, both Jew and Gentile in exactly the same way, by the redeeming work of Jesus Christ and the believer's faith in Jesus.

The Law of Moses plays no part in God's setting all men right again, that is, justifying all men, declaring them not guilty in Christ. Since all men have sinned and fallen short of the glory of God, and the glory in which God created them, all men are sinners. All men are set right with God, declared righteous, by faith in Jesus Christ, and not by the Law.

---

[27] Fitzmyer rejects this possibility, although admitting that context should determine the nature of the genitive. We should note that Paul should not be held to only one form of genitive construction and uses them both on occasion with a double meaning. E.g. 2 Cor 5:14, *"For the love of Christ controls us, because we are convinced that one has died for all; therefore all have died."* Paul speaks of the love of Christ for us and our consequential love for Christ.

The purpose of the Law was to clarify the nature of sin and not to justify anyone.

Both Jew and Gentile are justified in the same way through faith in God's redemptive work in Jesus' atoning death and resurrection.

God is a righteous God who justifies all men through faith in Jesus.

Rom 5:1, 2

The text

> *Therefore, <u>since we are justified by faith</u>, we have peace with God <u>through our Lord Jesus Christ</u>. ² Through him we have obtained access to this grace in which we stand, and we rejoice in our hope of sharing the glory of God.*

Three Things Stand Out from this Text

We are *justified* by *faith*. The verb *justified*, δικαιόω, *dikaióō*, is from the same root word as *righteousness*, δικαιοσύνη, *dikaiosúnē*. These words imply the same thing in the sense that the *righteous person* has been *justified* – *"righteoused"* and *declared righteous by God based on faith*.

Through Jesus Christ we obtain access to God's grace! That means through the faithfulness of Jesus dying on the cross we have access to God's grace. The death of Jesus on the cross is in turn a demonstration of the grace of God. Note Heb 4:14-16:

> *Since then we have a great high priest who has passed through the heavens, Jesus, the Son of God, let us hold fast our confession. ¹⁵ For we have not a high priest who is unable to sympathize with our weaknesses, but one who in every respect has been tempted as we are, yet without sin. ¹⁶ Let us then with confidence draw near to the throne of grace, that we may receive mercy and find grace to help in time of need.*

Through faith in what God was doing in Jesus' death, and in the grace of God we *stand* firmly *forgiven* and *justified*.

The Greek word stand, ἑστήκαμεν, is a perfect active verb ἵστημι, *hístēmi,* means *to stand firm* or be *confirmed*. We stand *confirmed* and *righteous*, not through our own ability or goodness, but through Jesus' faithfulness and God's gracious forgiveness.

Rom 4:1-8

The text

What then shall we say about Abraham, our forefather according to the flesh? ² *For if Abraham was justified by works, he has something to boast about, but not before God.* ³ *For what does the scripture say? "Abraham believed God, and it was reckoned to him as righteousness."* ⁴ *Now to one who works, his wages are not reckoned as a gift but as his due.* ⁵ *And to one who does not work but trusts him who justifies the ungodly, his faith is reckoned as righteousness."* ⁶ *So also David pronounces a blessing upon the man to whom God reckons righteousness apart from works:*

⁷ *"Blessed are those whose iniquities are forgiven, and whose sins are covered;*

⁸ *blessed is the man against whom the Lord will not reckon his sin.*

Several Things Stand Out from this Text

Abraham along with Moses was one of the heroes of faith in Israel and among the Jews.

For a Jew, you could not go higher than Abraham and Moses.

Abraham was not justified by works of law keeping, especially the Law of Moses!

Abraham was *justified, declared righteous by God*, by *believing* and *trusting* God, not by works of law keeping.

The word *reckoned* is interesting! *Reckoned* derives from the Greek λογίζομαι, *logizomai*, meaning *to reason...to account, to reckon, to impute, to number*.[28]

In Rom. 4:3 and later at vs. 6, the expression *reckoned* is used as a *technical term* applied to God's act of *justification* which is fully explained in vss. 6ff. It is that *reckoning* of

---

[28] Zodhiates, *op. cit.*, λογίζομαι *logizomai*.

righteousness whose correlative is *freedom from guilt*, and *forgiveness*.

Fitzmyer translates reckoned ἐλογίσθη as "*was credited*." He observes that this was a "bookkeeping term." Fitzmyer referenced the Hebrew history of the word as "the good and evil deeds of human beings were recorded in ledgers (Esth 6:1; Dan 7:10, et al) ... Thus, Abraham's faith was counted by God as uprightness."[29]

Notice this point from Rom 4:1-8 God *justifies* the *ungodly*, the sinners who have faith in Jesus Christ! That is not that he imputes to them some other form of righteousness! He declares them *righteous*, he *justifies* them based on their faith in Jesus Christ.

Rom 9:30-33

The text

> *What shall we say, then? That Gentiles who did not pursue righteousness have attained it, that is, <u>righteousness through faith</u>; ^{31} but that Israel who pursued the righteousness which is based on law did not succeed in fulfilling that law. ^{32} Why? Because they did not pursue it through faith, but as if it were based on works. They have stumbled over the stumbling stone, ^{33} as it is written,*
>
> *"Behold, I am laying in Zion a stone that will make men stumble, a rock that will make them fall; <u>and he who believes in him will not be put to shame</u>."*

Several Things Surface from this Text

We need to keep this text in the context of what Paul is discussing in Rom 9-11; God did not reject Israel but Israel rejected God.

Israel did not continue faithfully toward God, but relied on law keeping, which in any case they failed to fulfill.

But God will accept Israel back *through faith in Jesus*.

Again, *righteousness* comes *through faith* and not by works of law.

---

[29] Fitzmyer, *Romans*, p. 373.

The Gentiles received *righteousness*, were *justified*, through *faith*.

Israel stumbled over the stumbling stone, which for the Jew was faith *in Jesus Christ*.

Rom 10:5-12

The text

Moses writes that the man who practices the righteousness which is based on the law shall live by it. ⁶ *But the righteousness based on faith says*, Do not say in your heart, "Who will ascend into heaven?" (that is, to bring Christ down) ⁷ or "Who will descend into the abyss?" (that is, to bring Christ up from the dead). ⁸ *But what does it say? The word is near you, on your lips and in your heart (that is, the word of faith which we preach)*; ⁹ *because, if you confess with your lips that Jesus is Lord and believe in your heart that God raised him from the dead, you will be saved.* ¹⁰ *For man believes with his heart and so is justified, and he confesses with his lips and so is saved.* ¹¹ The scripture says, "*No one who believes in him will be put to shame.*" ¹² For *there is no distinction between Jew and Greek; the same Lord is Lord of all and bestows his riches upon all who call upon him.* ¹³ For, "*everyone who calls upon the name of the Lord will be saved.*

Several Things we Learn from these Texts in Romans

Romans is a magnificent text that summarizes Paul's "Romans gospel" theme!

It is dense or complicated in that Paul cites Lev 18:5 and Deut 30:14 in support of his argument but in regard to Deuteronomy he does a midrashic application with it to reinforce his argument![30]

Rom 10:5-12 begins by bringing Moses into his argument – no Jew would or should disagree with Moses!

---

[30] Cf. Fitzmyer *Romans, op. cit.*, and Dunn *Romans 9-16* for discussion on this.

Moses writes that the man who practices the righteousness which is based on the law shall live by it.

Shall live is an interesting construction! *Shall live* is a *future tense* which means "to live...to spend one's existence."[31] The future tense can function as either an *imperatival* or *gnomic future* in which case an action is stated as *a command or a statement of performance.*

In this case *shall live* becomes a *statement of necessity or command.* If you are going to live by the law then *you must live* by the law, which obviously, Paul argued the Jews had not, and had failed to keep the law as the law commanded.

But the *righteousness based on faith* says *you must confess your faith and believe that confession.*

In Paul's argument in Romans, *justification* comes through *trusting in the righteousness of God, the faithfulness of Jesus*, and *faith in Jesus* himself which the Jews refused to do.

One does not need to go up to heaven, nor to descend to the abyss (hell) to find the answer to righteousness, it is right there before you, *have faith in Jesus*!

If one believes *with all your heart in Jesus and confess their faith in Jesus* they will be *saved* and *justified*!

Notice *saved* and *justified* are parallel. *You are justified when you are saved*!

Justification and *righteousness* amount to being *declared forgiven* and *not guilty*!

There is no distinction between the Jew and the Gentile, both are *saved* and *justified* by the *same principle, faith in Jesus*!

Phil 3:4-11

Regarding Phil 3:9, N. T. Wright's expression "This is a dense text that we have to unpack carefully," has special meaning!

Karl Barth's expression likewise has significant meaning as we explore these texts; "God did not give us Scripture to master! That is an unforgivable sin! God gave us Scripture to be mastered by Scripture."

---

[31] Zodhiates, *op. cit.*, ζάω.

Thus, like all scripture, we must come to this text humbly, seeking to unpack its depth of meaning!

The Context of Phil 3:4-9

First: We Must Unpack the Theological Context of Philippians.

The church at Philippi was a church experiencing the spiritual "blahs"!

They needed encouragement.

They had some "false teachers" disturbing their faith.

They had some relational issues - two women and some members taking sides.

They were experiencing some issues with Jewish views of righteousness by law keeping.

Paul stressed that spiritual joy comes through being in Christ and being like Christ – a servant of others.

Second: The Secondary Context.

In Phil 2: Notice Jesus', Timothy's, & Ephraditus' humble service.

Real Christian joy comes through being like Christ, a servant of God!

Adopting a humility like Christ's is the key to this point!

Third: The Immediate Context.

Some false notions about righteousness and law keeping, the Law of Moses, were being taught.

Paul stressed that *righteousness through the faith of Jesus* was the only form of true righteousness.

On the grounds of his Jewishness Paul had much to boast about, but not in the presence of God, and in the context of genuine righteousness.

He emphasized that he would happily jettison all his Jewishness and *be found in Christ*, and *to know Christ* and the power of his resurrection.

The Text

> *Though I myself have reason for confidence in the flesh also. If any other man thinks he has reason for*

confidence in the flesh, I have more: ⁵ circumcised on the eighth day, of the people of Israel, of the tribe of Benjamin, a Hebrew born of Hebrews; as to the law a Pharisee, ⁶ as to zeal a persecutor of the church, as to righteousness under the law blameless. ⁷ But whatever gain I had, I counted as loss for the sake of Christ. ⁸ Indeed I count everything as loss because of <u>the surpassing worth of knowing Christ Jesus my Lord</u>. For his sake I have suffered the loss of all things, and count them as refuse, in order that I may gain Christ ⁹ and be found in him, <u>not having a righteousness of my own, based on law, but that which is through faith in Christ, the righteousness from God that depends on faith</u>; ¹⁰ that I may know him and the power of his resurrection, and may share his sufferings, becoming like him in his death, ¹¹ that if possible I may attain the resurrection from the dead.

In this text Paul explains that *according to law keeping under the Law of Moses he was righteous or guiltless*. However, he argued that *legal rectitude* did not bring one into, or sustain a right relationship with God. *Such a right relationship with God depends solely on faith*, which is a fundamental principle of Paul's theology and understanding of righteousness.

Two Scholarly Comments on this Text

First, I-Jin Loh with Eugene Nida is correct by observing that *righteousness* here should be understood as *legal rectitude*. He notes,

> The Greek noun rendered "righteousness" by most translators is a key term in Pauline thought. It is a difficult word with various shades of meaning. Depending on contexts, it can mean "religious duties," "the requirements of God," "that which is right," "righteousness," "uprightness," "justice," "right relationship with God," etc. In the present instance … "Legal rectitude" … is a good rendering, but it is too difficult for the average reader. Most translations retain the conventional rendering here. One can be more specific in rendering "so far as a man can

stand in a right relationship with God by obeying the commands of the Law ... *this was not possible.*[32]

Paul argued, however, that to boast in one's accomplishments amounted to nothing. One may boast before others in one's accomplishments, but not before God. At Rom 4:1, 2 he (Paul) drew an analogy from Abraham who dared not boast before God of any works! *What then shall we say about Abraham, our forefather according to the flesh? For if Abraham was justified by works, he has something to boast about, but not before God.* Paul could boast before his fellow Jews of his Jewish accomplishments and law keeping, *but before God they amounted to nothing more than refuse or rubbish*!

Second, Peter O'Brien observes regarding Paul's legal righteousness:

> But that was not all. As a measure of his great zeal for the law and the ancestral traditions, which he naturally understood as a true zeal for God, he persecuted the church. Finally, the culmination of his personal achievements lay in his scrupulous observance of the OT law, as interpreted along Pharisaic lines: *with regard to that righteousness rooted in the law Paul claims that he was without reproach.*[33]

O'Brien continues:

> "Finally, the *culmination* of these personal achievements is expressed in the third κατά-statement ... Lit. 'in relation to the righteousness that is in the law, having become blameless'. Each of the two previously mentioned achievements has focussed on a critical issue, namely νόμος ('law') and ζῆλος ('zeal'). This final ground of Paul's confidence in the flesh is tied in with δικαιοσύνη ('righteousness'), *and it is clear from v. 9, where two sharply contrasting kinds of righteousness are mentioned, that a major factor in the dramatic change in*

---

[32] I-Jin Loh and Eugene A. Nida, *A Handbook on Paul's Letter to the Philippians*, UBS Handbook Series, New York: United Bible Societies, 1977, Phil 3:6.
[33] Peter T. O'Brien, P. T., *The Epistle to the Philippians: A Commentary on the Greek Text*, New International Greek Testament Commentary, Grand Rapids: Eerdmans, 1991, Phil 3:6.

Paul's life had to do with this issue. Δικαιοσύνη is a key term in Pauline thought (see on v. 9) and can be rendered in English in a variety of ways. Depending on the contexts, it can mean 'that which is right', *'religious duties'*, 'the requirements of God', *'righteousness'*, *'uprightness'*, *'justice'*, or *'a right relationship with God'*."[34]

O'Brien obviously saw Paul making a distinction between two kinds of righteousness; the moral righteousness of keeping the law, and the legal relationship based on faith in Jesus, and being forgiven and declared not guilty by God.

Back to Paul at Phil 3:9

Having discarded all claims to "fame" according to his Jewish heritage, zeal, and law keeping, Paul stated unequivocally that his goal was to be found in Christ where righteousness or right relationship with God is to be found. He observed that he would rather *be found in him, not having a righteousness of my own that comes from the law, but that which comes through faith in Christ, the righteousness that comes from God that depends on faith ...*

Paul Makes Two Points in this Text

First, Legal rectitude according to the Law of Moses was not his goal. In fact, in the sight of God it is as rubbish!

Second, his goal was an intimate relationship with God which comes through God's initiative, the faithfulness of Christ, and the Christian's faith in Christ.

Most Scholars Understand the Two Kinds of Righteousness Encapsulated in this Text

First, a *legal rectitude based on law keeping* which Paul vehemently opposed, cf. Romans and Galatians.

Second, a *legal verdict of not guilty* in a *restored relationship* with God through the redemptive activity of God in Christ and the faithfulness of Christ to God's covenant purpose.

---

[34] Ibid.

> *Righteousness is thus not being right with the Law of Moses but being right with God through faith in the redemptive work of God in Christ and faith in Christ.*

The Expression *Faith in* or *Faith of* Christ Introduces a Challenging Dilemma!

The question arises in how we read the genitive case of διὰ πίστεως Χριστοῦ, *faith of Christ*.

Most translations translate this as *faith in Christ*, but the structure of the genitive form of *faith* (πίστεως) with a genitive Christ (Χριστοῦ) raises some interesting and challenging issues!

Several good scholars render this the *faithfulness of Christ* (a subjective genitive) while to the contrary several fine scholars prefer *faith in Christ* (an objective genitive).

Faith in Christ - Objective Genitive

Hawthorne favors the objective genitive form of *in Christ*, but note Hawthorne's comment,

> "Alternatively, the thrust of Paul's argument may be interpreted to be: restoring a right relationship is indeed God's doing (2 Cor 5:18); *the groundwork is laid in Christ's fidelity (πίστις) to his Father's will to save; and human faith is based on "Christ's faithfulness"* (Bockmuehl, 211-13). This seems eminently logical ..."[35]

Joseph Fitzmyer, on πίστεως Χριστοῦ at Rom 3:26, citing Käsemann, Moo, Wilkens, and Dunn, also prefers the *objective genitive*, faith in Christ, while recognizing the possibility of a subjective genitive, *faithfulness of Christ*.[36]

Leon Morris concurs with Fitzmyer that the expression is best understood as an objective genitive, *faith in Christ*.[37]

Schreiner, citing Dunn,[38] stresses that in his opinion the evidence in the New Testament of such constructions favors an *objective* genitive, *faith in Christ*.[39]

---

[35] Hawthorne, *Philippians,* Phil 3:9.
[36] Fitzmyer, *Romans*, p. 345.
[37] Leon Morris, *The Epistle to the Romans*, p. 184, fn. 149.
[38] J. G. D. Dunn, *Romans 1-8*, Word Bible Commentary, 1988, Rom 3:26.
[39] Thomas R. Schreiner, *Romans*, Baker, 1998, p. 185.

The Faithfulness of Christ – Subjective Genitive

Peter O'Brien takes the other position that Χριστοῦ is a *subjective* genitive referring to the *faithfulness of Christ*:

> "Χριστοῦ ... in our judgment the case for understanding πίστις Χριστοῦ as 'the faith[fulness] of Christ' is stronger. We note the following: (1) the genitive Χριστοῦ is best taken as subjective rather than objective. In the Pauline corpus πίστις followed by the genitive of a person (using either a noun or a personal pronoun) occurs twenty-four times, apart from those instances where πίστις Χριστοῦ or its equivalent turns up. Twenty of these refer to the faith of Christians (either individually or collectively), one to the πίστις of God (Rom. 3:3), two to the faith (fulness) of Abraham (Rom. 4:12, 16), and one to the person whose faith is reckoned for righteousness (Rom. 4:5). According to G. A. Howard, in every case reference is made to the faith *of* an individual, never to faith *in* an individual. Outside the Pauline corpus four instances in the NT occur where πίστις is followed by the genitive of the person of Christ or God: Mk. 11:22; Jas. 2:1; Rev. 2:13; 14:12. A difference of opinion exists as to the precise significance of these genitives, although Mk. 11:22, ἔχετε πίστιν θεοῦ, is probably the clearest example of an objective genitive. This construction after πίστις is possible, though rare, in the NT; significantly, there are no clear instances in the Pauline corpus. Most importantly, the expression ἐκ πίστεως Ἰησοῦ [Χριστοῦ] (Rom. 3:26; Gal. 3:22) has an exact parallel in Rom. 4:16, ἐκ πίστεως Ἀβραάμ, which is certainly subjective. Moreover, 'the use of *pistis* in Hellenistic Jewish literature as a whole supports the subjective genitive'. This noun followed by a personal genitive was quite rare; it was virtually always subjective...[40]

---

[40] O'Brien, *The Epistle to the Philippians: A Commentary on the Greek Text*, Phil 3:9.

N. T. Wright has the *subjective genitive* understanding of πίστεως Χριστοῦ which forms a major thesis in his theology of redemption. His point is that it was through the *faithfulness of Jesus* that God was able to fulfill his covenant promise to Abraham to bless all nations.[41]

Concluding Comments on Phil 3:8

Two Views

First, Paul's argument was that his *legal rectitude* with the Law of Moses might satisfy a sense of rightness in comparison with the efforts of other Jews, but *that was a righteousness based on his own effort in contrast to the covenant righteousness that God required which could only be achieved through faith in the faithfulness of Jesus and what God was doing in Jesus.*

Second, the sense of being *forgiven* and hence *not guilty* and *thus being in a right relationship with God* would be reflected in a covenant relationship with God that *depends on faith in Jesus and not law keeping.* Paul's desire was to have such a deep relationship with Jesus that he would really know Jesus and the power of his resurrection, and not depend on his own human efforts and legal rectitude rightness.

Paul desired to be *found in Christ*, not having a righteousness of his own, based on legal rectitude, but *one which comes through the faithfulness of Christ*, that is, *the righteousness granted by God that depends on faith in Jesus and not law*. He wanted to have *a deep relationship with Jesus and know the power of Jesus' resurrection*, not his own human effort which was only garbage in comparison with the righteousness granted by God.

Concluding Line of Reasoning in this Discussion of Righteousness

We have been discussing various views of righteousness. We have primarily discussed the difference between imputed righteousness and personal rightness. We have also discussed the difference between legal rectitude in regard to righteousness

---

[41] N. T. Wright, *Justification*, 117ff; 203; *passim*.

according to Law-keeping, commenting also on the difference between legal rectitude and personal righteousness based on God's grace and forgiveness.

In this study, we have focused primarily on Paul's epistle to the Romans and Phil 3:4-11.

Our leading purpose has been to examine the differing views of righteousness possible in the theological discussion of righteousness. We will comment below on imputed righteousness, legal rectitude, and personal righteousness based on faith in Jesus Christ.

Imputed Righteousness

We understand imputed righteousness to be a view that considers Christians not having personal righteousness due to their having a sinful nature of personal sin. Roman Catholic and Reformed theology hold to such a view.

This view is also common among Christians who are keenly aware of their humanness or sinfulness.

This righteousness is not the believer's own righteousness; rather it is Christ's righteousness 'imputed' to the believer.

We have demonstrated that the Pauline view of righteousness is not an ethical, moral righteousness in which the believer is required to live above certain legal standards or above sin, which they obviously on their own without the help of the Holy Spirit are not able to do.

1 John 1:5-10 obviously supports this view. The blood of Jesus constantly cleanses those who sin in weakness but who walk in the light.

Paul obviously understood the daily battle Christians have with doing right according to laws and rejoices that in Christ the Christian is no longer under condemnation having been declared not guilty in Christ by God, Rom 7:21-8:3.

Paul clearly held that no one is able to live a perfect life, and thus be justified morally by law keeping.

It is our understanding that contrary to a Pauline view of righteousness imputed righteousness holds that the Christian never will live completely above sin and therefore needs to receive Christ's righteous life imputed to the Christian by God's grace through faith in Jesus.

The Reformed view of imputed righteousness holds that Christians cannot earn righteousness by living moral lives, and so continuing as sinners must therefore have Christ's sinless life and righteousness *imputed* to them by God's grace through faith in Jesus.

Imputed righteousness holds that Christians "inherit" Christ's righteousness and have it counted in place of their own failure to be righteous.

Legal Rectitude According to the Law of Moses

Paul spoke of his righteousness according to the Law of Moses, intending legal rectitude in the sense of being morally righteous in regard to keeping the Law. However, he distinguished this from the personal righteousness which he maintained did not come through Law-keeping, but only came through God's grace, faith in Jesus Christ and his death and resurrection, and being forgiven by God and declared not guilty.

We explored Paul's views of a legal rectitude by keeping the Law of Moses, demonstrating that Paul never held to a person being declared righteous by Law keeping, and from as early as Abraham God had declared men righteous based on faith and not Law keeping.

Personal Righteousness

We understand this as being declared forgiven by God and declared not guilty; therefore, being in a right relationship with God as his children.

Personal righteousness does not represent a sinless life, but a life lived in close relationship with God through Jesus Christ.

This is a "law-court" type of righteousness; the judgment of *not declared guilty* by a merciful God as a gift of God's grace pronounced on those who have been redeemed and reconciled to God through faith in Jesus Christ.

We see this as an alternative to imputed righteousness in which the Christian *in their own right* is never righteous by receiving the righteousness of Christ imputed to them. In personal righteousness, the Christian is declared righteous in their own right, having been forgiven and pronounced not guilty by God.

We have proposed that the Pauline view of righteousness is one that believes personal righteousness, which is *relational*, results from the Christian being forgiven and declared not guilty by God through their faith in Jesus.

This righteousness is a "law-court" model of righteousness, based on a sinner being declared not guilty by a judge, but it is also biblical and hinges on Rom 3:21-27 and Paul's doctrine of atonement, redemption, and reconciliation.

God is a Righteous God who Forgives All Men by Grace Through Faith in Jesus, pronouncing them Forgiven and Not Guilty by the Same Gospel Message

Fundamental to Paul's view of personal righteousness is the belief that God is himself a righteous God who justifies and declares all men righteous, both Jew and Gentile, by the same principle of faith in Jesus Christ, and not by keeping any legal system as in the Law of Moses.

HCU Media LLC

Publishing in support of

Heritage Christian University – Ghana (HCU Ghana)

www.hcuc.edu.gh

HCU media has been established to support the publication of materials, both paper and electronic, created by faculty and friends of HCU Ghana. These materials will be offered initially in the USA & Ghana but may become available globally via other outlets.

www.ingramcontent.com/pod-product-compliance
Lightning Source LLC
Chambersburg PA
CBHW030108100526
44591CB00009B/332